Toyota Production System

Practical Approach to Production Management

Toyota Production System

Practical Approach to Production Management

Yasuhiro Monden
Professor, University of Tsukuba

Industrial Engineering and Management Press
Institute of Industrial Engineers

Industrial Engineering and Management Press, Norcross, Georgia

Published in 1983.
Printed in the United States of America
93 92 91 90 89   12 11 10 9 8

ISBN 0-89806-034-6

Additional copies may be obtained by contacting:
Publication Sales
Institute of Industrial Engineers
P.O. Box 6150
Norcross, Georgia 30091-6150

Quantity discounts available.

*To the faculty members, staff, and students
of the School of Management,
State University of New York at Buffalo*

Contents

Foreword

The technique we call the Toyota production system was born through our various efforts to catch up with the automotive industries of western advanced nations after the end of World War II, without the benefit of funds or splendid facilities.

Above all, one of our most important purposes was increased productivity and reduced costs. To achieve this purpose, we put our emphasis on the notion of eliminating all kinds of unnecessary functions in the factories. Our approach has been to investigate one by one the causes of various "unnecessaries" in manufacturing operations and to devise methods for their solution, often by trial and error.

The technique of Kanban as a means of Just-in-time production, the idea and method of production smoothing, and Autono.nation (Jidoka), etc., have all been created from such trial-and-error processes in the manufacturing sites.

Thus, since the Toyota production system has been created from actual practices in the factories of Toyota, it has a strong feature of emphasizing practical effects, and actual practice and implementation over theoretical analysis. As a result, it was our observation that even in Japan it was difficult for the people of outside companies to understand our system; still less was it possible for the foreign people to understand it.

This time, however, Professor Monden wrote this book by making good use of his research and teaching experiences in the United States. Therefore, we are very interested in how Professor Monden has "theorized" our practice from his academic standpoint and how he has explained it to the foreign people. At the same time, we wish to read and study this book for our own future progress.

At no other time in history has the problem of productivity received so much discussion. No longer is it solely an economic problem; now it presents a serious political problem in a form of trade frictions. At such a time it would be our great pleasure if the Toyota production system we invented could be of service to the problem of American productivity.

Although we have a slight doubt whether our Just-in-time system could be applied to the foreign countries where the business climates, industrial relations, and many other social systems are different from ours, we firmly believe there is no significant difference among the final purposes of the firms and people working in them.

Therefore, we hope and expect that another effective American production system will be created utilizing this book for reference.

Taiichi Ohno
Former Vice President,
Toyota Motor Corporation

President,
Japan Industrial
Management Association

Chairman,
Toyoda Spinning and
Weaving Co., Ltd.

Introduction

Japan attained dramatic economic growth in the last three decades through diligent work, application of new technologies, accelerated investment in new plants and equipment, and cooperation among business, government, and labor unions. This achievement was backed by a steady growth of productivity, particularly in the manufacturing sector. Until 1973 when the Arab oil embargo drastically reduced the economic activities of the world, Japan's industrial productivity had grown at the rate of about 10% per annum for two decades.

The entry into the slow growth era since then reduced the rate of increased productivity substantially as the long-practiced lifetime employment system forced management to retain an excessive labor force. Unable to reduce labor input commensurate with a decreasing demand in the market place, Japanese industries' performance suffered a faster decline in productivity as compared to many European countries where adjustment in labor input could be accomplished with relative ease. For four years following the oil shock, Japan struggled to revive its economy through accelerated investment in research and development and the creation of a new production and inventory control method that enabled corporations to reduce production costs.

Although the Toyota Motor Company, which developed the Toyota production system, has been practicing and refining the technique for ten years, it was in this period that the technique became popular in many manufacturing sectors outside the automotive industry. Small lot production, frequent delivery of parts and components, leveling of production volume, and reduction in set-up time of dies, practiced under this system through multiple-skill training of workers and concentrated efforts to improve quality of products enabled the Japanese to recover from the prolonged recessionary period through the drastic reduction in the cost of production. The application of the Toyota production system and the accelerated effort to institute flexible manufacturing systems with effective application of robots, manipulators, NC machine tools, and machining centers gave the Japanese a competitive edge in automobile and consumer electronics industries in recent years.

Although bits and pieces of information on the system have been introduced to the United States through seminars, workshops and articles, the concept and practical aspects were difficult for many American managers to understand due to the lack of structured writing on the subject.

In this book Professor Monden develops the theory and explains the step-by-step application of the system as it is being practiced in Japan. It is a good primer for the system and is highly recommended for reading by managers and engineers. *Toyota Production System: Practical Approach to Production Management* is well structured and easy to understand for it was written with an American readership in mind.

Joji Arai
Director, U.S. Office
Japan Productivity
Center

Preface

The Toyota production system is a technology of comprehensive production management the Japanese invented a hundred years after opening up to the modern world. More than likely, another gigantic advance in production methods will not appear for some time to come.

Mr. Taiichi Ohno, former vice-president of Toyota Motor Corp., who wrote the foreword to this book, is the inventor and promoter of the Toyota production system at Toyota. In developing the system, he has developed various unique ideas, implemented them, and corrected them. While machining department manager of the Honsha plant in 1949-50 up to vice-president in 1975 of Toyota, he gradually spread his original methods throughout the company, finally applying these methods to all the companies of the Toyota group.

Also, for the development and promotion of the Toyota system, the support of top executives, the strenuous efforts of Ohno's competent subordinates, and the various ideas of all Toyota's workers must be recognized. In a sense, Mr. Ohno has built and promoted the system as an excellent conductor for gathering together all the ideas developed by these people.

It was just after the first oil shock in late 1973 that the Toyota production system attracted the attention of Japanese industries. Facing unprecedented cost-push inflation, most of Japanese companies had run into the red, except Toyota, which had shown a huge profit. In order for these companies to overcome the oil shock, it became clear that the company constitution had to be made slim and tough. From this viewpoint it would not be too much to say that Japanese companies have conquered the depression of oil shock by introducing the Toyota production system partially or totally.

From this Japanese experience, the author firmly believes the Toyota production system can play a great role in the task for improving the constitutions of American and European companies as well as companies worldwide — especially those of the automotive industry. Thus, the author's chief purpose of publishing this book is to offer some support to the companies in the U.S. and elsewhere that are making efforts to improve productivity, thereby promoting friendship between Japan and many countries.

The basic idea of Toyota production system is to maintain a continuous flow of products in factories in order to flexibly adapt to demand changes. The realization of such production flow is called Just-in-time production at Toyota, which means producing only necessary items in a necessary quantity at a necessary time. As a result, the excess inventories and the excess work force will be naturally diminished, thereby achieving the purposes of increased productivity and cost reduction.

In 1980, the turnover ratio of inventory assets (= annual sales/average inventories) at Toyota Motor Company was 87; in other words, the inventory period (= average inventories/average monthly sales) was merely 0.138 months or 4 days. This means the Toyota Motor Company had inventories (including materials) for only four days of sales. Also, the inventory turnover ratio at Toyota Motor Sales Company was 40, while its inventory period was merely 9 days.

Moreover, the safety margin (= break-even point sales/sales plus other income) of Toyota Motor Corp. in 1980 was only 64%, which means Toyota can earn a profit even if the present sales might reduce to 64%. Such a remarkably low break-even point was created by decreasing the work force. It must be added that Toyota has consistently achieved these figures over the past several years, and in some cases even bettered them.

The basic principle of Just-in-time production is universally rational; that is, the Toyota production system has been developed by steadily pursuing the orthodox way of production management. Therefore, the author believes people in any country who evaluate the reasonableness can understand this system without any trouble. However, the problem for the author in writing the book was to find the reasonable framework of Toyota production methods.

As Mr. Taiichi Ohno mentioned in the foreword of this book, the Toyota production system "has a strong feature of emphasizing practical effects, and actual practice and implementation over theoretical analysis." The existing books on Toyota manufacturing methods have all been written by the practitioners of the system; they all contain proficient descriptions of individual topics of Toyota's methods, and my book is partially indebted to these books. However, as I see it, they do not incorporate the methods into a whole and present them in a theoretical, systematic manner. Certainly Toyota's unique manufacturing methods are linked by an underlying system; and certainly the benefits of these methods can be demonstrated; but it is very hard to explain the methods systematically and theoretically.

Mr. Ohno also said in his foreword, "We are very interested in how Professor Monden has *theorized* our practice from his academic standpoint and how he has explained it to the foreign people." Therefore, the central mission of this book is to develop a "theory" to the "practices" of Toyota manufacturing methods.

What is a theory or theorization? It is a process of building an ideal model of the real, empirical object by using the following procedures:

- Abstracting from the empirical world the important factors which seem most relevant to the research objective.
- Connecting the selected factors in a logical way.

Our research objective is to build a practically applicable model; that is, this model must be able to be utilized for each company to prepare and implement the actual system of production management. Further, since the Toyota production system is a kind of typical system which transforms various input factors to its outputs, this transformation mechanism, or the structure of goals-means relationships, must be described as a "theory" in this book.

Since this process of theorization seemed to me a very creative task, I approached it not as a mere commentator but as a "novelist," with the cooperation of many people of the Toyota group. Many times I visited not only the Toyota Motor Company, but also several companies of the Toyota group, observed their plants, and interviewed the managers of plants and staffs of production control departments. Moreover, the experiences I had in 1981 in visiting the plants of the General Motors Corporation and the Ford Motor Company were very useful when considering the uniqueness of the Japanese production systems.

As a result of these efforts, the simplest model of the Toyota production system was constructed as shown in Chapter 1, Fig. 1.1. Although this model excludes detailed relations, it describes the broad outline of relationships among various subsystems of the total system. The internal structure of each subsystem and its relations to various other subsystems are explained in detail in each chapter. Furthermore, the theoretical analysis of determining the number of Kanban (described in Appendix 1) is my original work. In this appendix I have proved the reasonableness of the "rules of thumb" of calculating the total number of Kanban by applying two alternative inventory control models; i.e. constant order-quantity system and constant order-cycle system.

However, the model of the Toyota production system is merely my model and will not necessarily coincide with the real manufacturing methods existing at Toyota. There are two reasons: first, there are many variations of Toyota production methods even among various plants of Toyota as well as among many cooperative companies of the Toyota group. Second, the Toyota production system itself is continually evolving, perfecting itself day by day in response to competition. As suggested in this book, the present and future development of the Toyota production system would be to adapt the system to the rapidly rising movement of factory automotion such as FMS, robotics, and CAD/CAM. Any errors which this edition might contain will hopefully be corrected with the aid of reader feedback.

Moreover, in this book I have also taken into account criticism of the Toyota system; I have especially considered criticisms made by the Japanese communist party and the Fair Trade Commission to check if some flaw in the system might exist. Also, the "contingency theoretic" approach was partially applied in various chapters concerning the topics such as the problem of geographical distance between suppliers and the paternal maker, the types of industries, the difference in industrial relations and wage payment methods, and the problem of financial ability to invest in multipurpose machines and autonomous defect-control systems. However, such critical considerations and the contingency approach are not the main subject of this edition. Such approaches will be taken more in the following editions. Also, there still remains several more topics to be discussed for this system. Such topics will also be included in the following editions.

Next, let us consider the productivity problem between different countries. The competitive power of Japanese automobiles lies in their low cost and high quality, which have been accepted by American consumers. This has caused the serious economic and political problems between two countries. The present situation between both countries resembles closely the evening before World War II. Now is the time both Japan and the U.S. should keep cool and not give themselves over to their emotions.

At this very time I would like to contend to American friends that the present success of the Japanese has been acquired by steady efforts of "self-help." One of the main purposes of this book is to offer evidence that the Japanese have been making efforts earnestly and independently to increase productivity and improve quality. This evidence may be merely a sample, but considering the heavy weight of the auto industry in Japan and U.S., it has an important meaning.

If Americans intentionally avoid recognizing the true problems behind the present situations of their industries and go to a policy of protectionism, it will not give any advantage to them in the long run because it cannot revive the vital power of the industries. Import restrictions would enable U.S. industries to perpetuate inefficient production methods and raise prices, thereby inflicting a loss on American consumers. Protectionism in the United States would also decrease the influence of U.S. foreign and defense policy because of counter-reactions around the world.

On the contrary, by observing the free trade system (and by accepting foreign challenges as good incentives), U.S. industries could improve their productivity and promote more innovation in new technologies. American people who respect freedom, friendship, and decorum will not resort to criticizing another nation to defend themselves. Expecting the rebirth of U.S. vitality, the author has written this book to support and encourage the movements of productivity improvement in the U.S. and many other countries.

Studying this book will be the first step to introduce the Toyota production system to each company. For this purpose, this book should be read not only by industrial engineers but by people in all levels of the company. The application of such a comprehensive production system as Toyota's will involve the entire revolution of the present system, which requires the understanding and strategic decisions of top executives. Also, the Toyota production system rests on a foundation of improvement activities by individual workers in the plant, so the book is hopefully read as a text for QC circle meetings, etc. At Toyota, the introductory manual of the Toyota manufacturing methods is given to all workers for their complete understanding of the methods.

Moreover, this book has advantages to Japanese companies, too. Without the prosperity of the U.S. and many other countries, Japan will not have a place to sell its products. If we Japanese could be of any help to reviving the world economy, our own survival itself could also be assured. In order for Japanese companies (including the automotive industry) to survive in the long run in this world market, we will have to cooperate with foreign companies so that Japanese companies can jointly produce products in foreign countries with foreign companies. Also, Japanese companies must go to foreign countries independently to manufacture products with foreign workers and managers. Therefore, the production system described in this book must also be used by the partner companies and foreign people. To advance Japanese technologies further in the future, we should recognize that "no human condition is ever permanent and we should not be overjoyed in good fortune."

In conclusion, even though different in race and nation, we are all children of mother earth. By encouraging each other to polish up each other's skills, people in all countries can survive and prosper at the same time.

Yasuhiro Monden
Tsukuba, Japan

Acknowledgements

I wish to acknowledge the many people who contributed greatly to the research for this book. There are two groups of contributors: contributors to the contents of the book and those who offered research opportunities to me.

Many businessmen in the Toyota group I contacted agreed to cooperate with me in this empirical study, even though it meant tying up some of their time. Without their enthusiastic cooperation, this research could not have been successful.

Among all, my sincere appreciation goes to Mr. Taiichi Ohno, ex-vice president of Toyota Motor Corporation and original developer of the Toyota production system, who gave me the opportunity to freely study and write about the system as well as learn the numerous subtle points of the system. I would like to thank the many people of the production control department at Toyota: Fujio Cho, Atsushi Masuyama, Mitsutoshi Sato, Hirosuke Terada, and Shigenori Kotani. My thanks also to Kozo Matsunaga at the Honsha plant and Zenzaburo Katayama of the quality assurance department of Toyota. Especially I wish to acknowledge the authors of the two articles for their permission to include them in this book as appendices 4 and 5: Y. Sugimori, K. Kusunoki, S. Uchikawa, and O. Kimura.

Cooperation from Yasushi Tsuboi, Michikazu Tanaka, Yoshiteru Noboru, Masa-aki Yutani, and Teruhiko Yoshioka at Daihatsu Motor Co., Ltd., a partner of Toyota, was most helpful. My research on the supplier's systems owes much to the many people at Aishin Seiki Co., Ltd: Mitsukane Matsushita, Katsuetsu Tsukada, Tasuku Aoyama, Akira Takada, Junichi Okamoto, and Mitsuhiko Kamiya. Concerning the Aishin Seiki's computer system for Kanban, my thanks go to Tsutomu Kawakatsu, Shuhei Fujii, and Masatake Goto. Also, I thank the people of Nippon Denso Co., Ltd. for showing me their FMS and QC techniques: Katsuo Aoki, Akio Ito, and Masayuki Hattori. Further, Yoshiki Iwata of Toyoda Gosei Co., Ltd.; Hideto Okajima of Toyota Auto Body Co., Ltd.; and Toshitatsu Iwasaki, Takamasa Yoshida, Itsumitsu Shibata, and Hiroshi Suzuki of Toyoda Automatic Loom Works, Ltd. were also very helpful.

Next, I would like to note how the book was published in the United States. During the 1980-81 academic year, I was a Visiting Associate Professor of Accounting at State University of New York at Buffalo. During my stay at SUNY, I published four articles in *Industrial Engineering* (January, May, August, and September 1981 issues). The first article in *IE* entitled "What Makes The Toyota Production System Really Tick?" attracted considerable attention, and subsequently I was invited to speak on the Toyota system at ten professional meetings throughout the country. I am very grateful to the many American industrial engineers, executives, and professors I met at these meetings for enlightening me to the various problems facing the U.S. concerning the question if Japanese systems were introduced to U.S. industries. A list of such people and meetings follow: (1) Norman Bodek, publisher of the *Productivity* newsletter; Dennis Butt, plant manager at Kawasaki Motors Corp., U.S.A. and currently general manager of A. Timpte Industries Company; and Professor Robert W. Hall of Indiana University at the Productivity Seminar held by Productivity Inc., February 23, 1981, Chicago. (2) Mike Kasprzyk and Thomas R. Evans at the Chevrolet Motor Division of General Motors Corporation, Buffalo plant, February 24, 1981. (3) Joji Arai at a one-day seminar held by the U.S. Office of the Japan Productivity Center and the Society of Manufacturing Engineers, Rochester Chapter 16, March 2, 1981, Rochester, New York. (4) Professors Robert W. Hall of Indiana University and H.L. Verma of Wayne State University at the American Institute for Decision Sciences, Midwest

Chapter, April 16, 1981, Detroit. (5) Professor Vernon M. Buehler at the Sixth Annual Productivity Seminar held at Utah State University, April 23, 1981, Logan, Utah. (6) Professor John A. White of Georgia Institute of Technology and President-elect of IIE at the First Executive Forum for the Electronics Industry sponsored by Material Management Foundation and coordinated by Texas Instruments, Inc., May 3-6, 1981, Dallas. (7) Dr. David L. Belden and Jim F. Wolbrink at the 1981 Spring Annual Conference of the Institute of Industrial Engineers, May 17-20, 1981, Detroit. (8) Irvin Otis, IE manager of American Motors Corp. and Vice-president of IIE; A.M. Paiva, IE department manager at Ford; and Mr. Shultz at the Automotive Assembly Division of Ford Motor Company, May 20, 1981, Dearborn, Michigan. (9) Professor C. Carl Pegels at the Affiliate Key Executive Session held by the School of Management at SUNY/Buffalo, June 22, 1981. (10) Professor Takako Michi at the Summer Institute of Japanese Language, Culture, and Thought at SUNY/Buffalo, July 24, 1981.

Further, I wish to express my thanks to Mary Ann Sadlo, Mark Renne, and K.S. Ravindran of SUNY/Buffalo for their helpful comments in refining the original papers of this book. My sincere appreciation also goes to Professors Kazuo Mizoguchi and Tetsuo Kobayashi of Kobe University for their valuable comments at the seminar in Kobe, Japan. Professor Tatsuo Ohara also presented comment and materials of the Toyota system.

I would like to thank those who offered research opportunities to me. Three professors of the School of Management at SUNY/Buffalo: Ronald J. Huefner, chairman of the Operations Analysis Department; Joseph A. Alutto, Dean; and Stephen C. Dunnett, Director of the Intensive English Language Institute; Mr. Joji Arai, manager of the U.S. Office of the Japan Productivity Center; and Dr. David L. Belden, Executive Director of the Institute of Industrial Engineers. Among all, Dr. Huefner is most appreciated for arranging my visiting professorship at SUNY/Buffalo.

Also I am very grateful to my colleagues, the staff, and students at SUNY for their cordial acceptance and encouragements during my stay: Lawrence D. Brown, Robert Chatov, Sanford C. Gunn, Robert Hagerman, Susan Hamlen, Frank C. Jen, Francis Kearns, John Lee, Wendy Lin, C. Carl Pegels, Charles Trzinka, Edward Wallece, Stanley Zionts, and Mark E. Zmijewski. Fran Kearns greatly helped the daily lives of my family as our neighbor. Thanks to my secretary Janet C. Ansell for some of the typed manuscripts and trip arrangements for my speaking engagements, and particularly for the time she spent to enrich my family's American lives. It was by the Kearns family and Jan Ansell that eased the transition from Japan to the U.S. for my family. My assistants Kumaraswamy S. Ravindran and Sreenivas Kamma; my students Gary Damon and Kevin Buhse; and my friends Hans Sprohge, Toshio Matsutami, and Professor Ki Myung Kim of Inha University, Korea gave me special encouragements.

Moreover, I wish to acknowledge Professors Rintaro Muramatsu of Waseda University, Japan and Hidetoshi Kawai of Aichi University, Japan for their encouragements to write on the Toyota system. My acknowledgements must also go to the former deans Dr. Hideyo Ichihashi and Dr. Sadao Wada, and all of my colleagues at the University of Oasaka Prefecture in Japan for granting a sabbatical to me. Some of the materials on the Toyota system were collected by Professor Yutaka Kato, Mr. Noboru Izeki, and Masatoshi Yamashita of Nikkan Kogyo Shinbun Co., Ltd. Miss Takako Yamauchi and Mrs. Michie Kaneme neatly typed some of the manuscripts of this book.

Also I wish to thank the people of the Institute of Industrial Engineers: Al'n Novak, John C. DeVore, Shirley Kii, Greg Balestrero, and Janet Folk for their editing and revising the original manuscripts. Greg Balestrero reviewed the drafts and made valuable contributions to make the book readable and understandable. His revisions were rather laborious because of the difference in ways of thinking between Japanese and Americans, the great distance that separated us, and manuscript development on a chapter-by-chapter basis. Certainly he played a critical role in transplanting the technology from one country to another country.

Finally, forgive me to thank my late father Masanori Monden who encouraged me when I was young by saying: "Live on behalf of other people" and "The process is more significant than the effect." I am indebted to my wife's father Shintaro Kitakaze. I am also grateful to my children, Akito, Yasuto, and Hanako. Further, I owe the greatest debt to my wife Kimiko for her constant cooperation in completing this book.

1

Total Framework of the Toyota Production System— Its Goals-Means Relationship

The Toyota production system was developed and promoted by Toyota Motor Corporation and is being adopted by many Japanese companies in the aftermath of the 1973 oil shock. Though the main purpose of the system is to reduce costs, the system also helps increase the turnover ratio of capital (i.e., total sales/total assets) and improves the total productivity of a company as a whole.

Even during periods of slow growth, the Toyota production system could make a profit by decreasing costs in a unique manner—that is, by completely eliminating excessive inventory or workforce. It would probably not be overstating our case to say that this is another revolutionary production management system. It follows the Taylor system (scientific management) and the Ford system (mass-assembly line). This chapter examines the basic idea behind this production system, how it makes products, and especially in what areas Japanese innovation can be seen.

Furthermore, the framework of this production system is examined as a unit by connecting its basic ideas or goals with the various tools and methods used for achieving these goals.

Basic idea and framework

The Toyota production system is a reasonable method of making products since it completely eliminates unnecessary elements in production for the purpose of cost reduction. The basic idea in such a production system is to produce the kind of units needed, at the time needed, and in the quantities needed. With the realization of this concept, unnecessary intermediate and finished product inventories would be eliminated.

However, although cost-reduction is the system's most important goal, it must achieve three other subgoals in order to achieve its primary objective. They include:

1. Quantity control, which enables the system to adapt to daily and monthly fluctuations in demand in terms of quantities and variety;
2. Quality assurance, which assures that each process will supply only good units to subsequent processes;
3. Respect-for-humanity, which must be cultivated while the system utilizes the human resource to attain its cost objectives.

It should be emphasized here that these three goals cannot exist independently or be achieved independently without influencing each other or the primary goal of cost reduction. It is a special feature of the Toyota production system that the primary goal cannot be achieved without realization of the subgoals and vice versa. All goals are outputs of the same system; with productivity as the ultimate purpose and guiding concept, the Toyota production system strives to realize each of the goals for which it has been designed.

Before discussing the contents of the Toyota production system in detail, an overview of this system is in order (Fig. 1.1). The outputs or results side (costs, quality, and humanity) as well as the inputs or constituents side of the Toyota production system are depicted.

A continuous flow of production, or adapting to demand changes in quantities and variety, is created by achieving two key concepts: Just-in-time and Autonomation. These two concepts are the pillars of the Toyota production system. *Just-in-time* basically means to produce the necessary units in the necessary quantities at the necessary time. *Autonomation* ("Jidoka" in Japanese) may be loosely interpreted as autonomous defects control. It supports Just-in-time by never allowing defective units from a preceding process to flow into and disrupt a subsequent process (Fig. 1.1).

Two concepts also key to the Toyota production system include *Flexible Workforce* ("Shojinka" in Japanese) which means varying the number of workers to demand changes, and *Creative thinking or inventive ideas* ("Soikufu"), or capitalizing on worker suggestions.

To realize these four concepts, Toyota has established the following systems and methods:

1. Kanban system to maintain Just-in-time production (Chapters 2 and 3).
2. Production smoothing method to adapt to demand changes (Chapter 4).
3. Shortening of the setup time for reducing the production lead time (Chapter 6).
4. Standardization of operations to attain line balancing (Chapter 7).

2

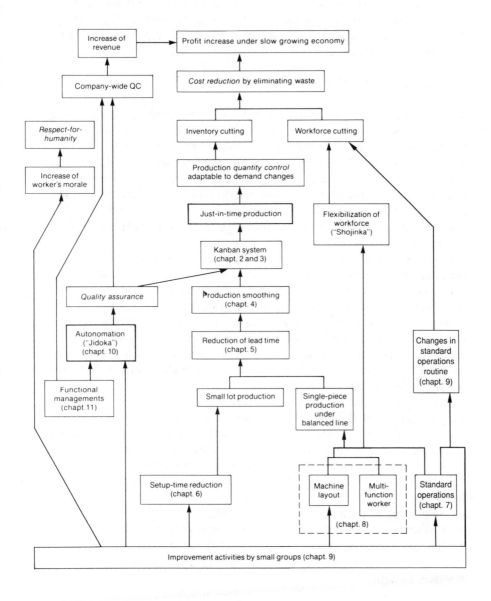

Fig. 1.1   How costs, quantity, quality and humanity are improved by the Toyota production system.

5. Machine layout and the multi-function worker for the flexible workforce concept (Chapter 8).
6. Improvement activities by small groups and the suggestion system to reduce the workforce and increase the worker's morale (Chapter 9).
7. Visual control system to achieve the Autonomation concept (Chapter 10).
8. "Functional Managements" system to promote company-wide quality control, etc. (Chapter 11).

Just-in-time production

The idea of producing the necessary units in the necessary quantities at the necessary time is described by the short term Just-in-time. Just-in-time means, for example, that in the process of assembling the parts to build a car, the necessary kinds of subassemblies of the preceding processes should arrive at the product line at the time needed in the necessary quantities. If Just-in-time is realized in the entire firm, then unnecessary inventories in the factory will be completely eliminated, making stores or warehouses unnecessary. The inventory carrying costs will be diminished, and the ratio of capital turnover will be increased.

However, to rely solely on the central planning approach which instructs the production schedules to all processes simultaneously, it is very difficult to realize Just-in-time in all the processes for a product like an automobile, which consists of thousands of parts. Therefore, in the Toyota system, it is necessary to look at the production flow conversely; in other words, the people of a certain process go to the preceding process to withdraw the necessary units in the necessary quantities at the necessary time. Then what the preceding process has to do is produce only enough quantities of units to replace those that have been withdrawn.

In this system what kind of units and how many units needed are written on a taglike card called *Kanban*. The Kanban is sent to the people of a preceding process from the subsequent process. As a result, many processes in a plant are connected with each other. This connecting of processes in a factory allows for better control of necessary quantities for various products.

In the Toyota production system, the Kanban system is supported by the following:

- Smoothing of production
- Reduction of setup time
- Design of machine layout
- Standardization of jobs
- Improvement activities
- Autonomation

Kanban system

Many people call the Toyota production system a Kanban system: this is incorrect. The Toyota production system is the way to make products, whereas the Kanban system is the way to manage the Just-in-time production method. In short, the Kanban system is an information system to harmoniously control the production quantities in every process. Unless the various prerequisites of this system are implemented perfectly (i.e., design of processes, standardization of operations and smoothing of production, etc.), then Just-in-time will be difficult to realize, even though the Kanban system is introduced.

A Kanban is usually a card put in a rectangular vinyl envelope. Two kinds are mainly used: withdrawal Kanban and production-ordering Kanban. A *withdrawal* Kanban details the quantity which the subsequent process should withdraw, while a *production-ordering* Kanban shows the quantity which the preceding process must produce. These cards circulate within Toyota factories, between Toyota and its many cooperative companies, and within the factories of cooperative companies. In this manner, the Kanbans can contribute information on withdrawal and production quantities in order to achieve Just-in-time production.

Suppose we are making products A, B, and C in an assembly line. The parts necessary to produce these products are a and b which are produced by the preceding machining line (Fig. 1.2). Parts a and b produced by the machining line are stored behind this line, and the production-ordering Kanbans of the line are attached to these parts. The carrier from the assembly line making product A will go to the machining line to withdraw the necessary part a with a withdrawal Kanban. Then, at store a, he picks up as many boxes of this part as his withdrawal Kanbans and he detaches the production-ordering Kanban attached to these boxes. He then brings these boxes back to his assembly line, again with withdrawal Kanbans.

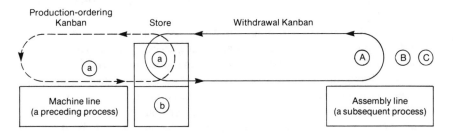

Fig. 1.2　The flow of two Kanbans.

At this time, the production-ordering Kanbans are left at store a of the machining line showing the number of units withdrawn. These Kanbans will be the dispatching information to the machining line. Part a is then produced in the quantity directed by that number of Kanbans. In this machining line, actually, parts a and b are both withdrawn, but these parts are produced according to the detached order of the production-ordering Kanbans.

Fine-tuning production

Let's consider the fine-tuning of production by using a Kanban. Assume that an engine manufacturing process must produce 100 engines per day. The subsequent process requests five engines per one-time lot by the withdrawal Kanban. These lots are then picked up 20 times per day, which amounts to exactly 100 engines produced daily.

Under such a production plan, if the need occurs to decrease all processes by 10% as a fine-tuning procedure of production planning, the final process in this example has to withdraw engines 18 times per day. Then, since the engine process produces only 90 units in a day, the remaining hours for 10 units of production will be rested by stopping this process. On the other hand, if there is a need to increase production quantities by 10%, the final process must withdraw the engines 22 times per day with the Kanban. Then the preceding process has to produce 110 units, and the additional 10 units would be covered by overtime.

Although the Toyota production system has the production management philosophy that units could be produced without any slack or unnecessary stock by regarding all of the human resources, machines, and materials as perfect, the risk of variations in production needs still exists. This risk is handled by the use of overtime and improvement activities at each process.

Smoothing of production

The smoothing of production is the most important condition for production by Kanban and for minimizing slack time in regards to manpower, equipment, and works in process; it is the cornerstone of the Toyota production system.

As described previously, the subsequent processes go to the preceding processes to withdraw the necessary goods at a necessary time in the necessary quantities. Under such a production rule, if the subsequent process withdraws parts in a fluctuating manner in regards to time or quantity, then the preceding processes should prepare as much inventory, equipment, and manpower as needed to adapt to the peak in the variance of quantities demanded. Also, where there are many sequenced processes, the variance of the quantities withdrawn by each subsequent process may become larger further back to preceding processes. In order to prevent such large variances in all production lines, including the external subcontracted companies, an effort must be made to minimize the fluctuation of production in the final assembly line. Therefore, the assembly line of finished cars, as the final process in the Toyota factory, will convey each type of automobile in its minimum lot size, realizing the ideal of "one-piece" production and conveyance. The line will also receive the necessary parts, in their small lot sizes, from the preceding processes.

In short, production smoothing minimizes the variation in the withdrawn quantity of each part produced at each subassembly, thereby allowing the subassemblies to produce each part at constant speed or at a fixed quantity per hour. Such a smoothing of production can be illustrated by the following example: Suppose there is a production line which is required to produce 10,000 Coronas with 20 eight-hour operating days in a month. The 10,000 Coronas consist of 5,000 sedans, 2,500 hardtops and 2,500 wagons. Dividing these numbers by 20 operating days results in 250 sedans, 125 hardtops and 125 wagons per day; this is the smoothing of production in terms of the average daily number of each kind of car.

During an eight-hour shift of operation (480 min.), all 500 units must be produced. Therefore, the *unit cycle time*, or the average time required to produce one vehicle of any type, is .96 minutes (480/500) or approximately 57.5 seconds.

The proper mix or production sequence can be determined by comparing the actual cycle time to produce one vehicle of any type with the maximum permitted time to produce a specific model of Corona. For example, the maximum time to produce one Corona sedan is determined by dividing the shift time (480 min.) by the number of sedans to be produced in the shift (250); in this case, the maximum time is 1 min., 55 sec. This means that a sedan must and will be generated every 1 min., 55 sec.

Comparing this time interval with the cycle time of 57.5 seconds, it is obvious that another car of any type could be produced between the time one sedan is completed and time when another sedan must be produced. So, the basic sequence is sedan, other, sedan, other, etc.

The maximum time to produce a wagon or a hardtop is 3 min., 50 sec. (480/125). Comparing this figure with the cycle time of 57.5 seconds, it is obvious that three cars of any type can be produced between each wagon or hardtop. If a wagon follows the first sedan in production, then the production sequence would be sedan, wagon, sedan, hardtop, sedan, wagon, sedan, hardtop, etc. This is an example of the smoothing of production in terms of the varieties of products.

Considering the actual manufacturing machines or equipment, a conflict arises between product variety and production smoothing. If a great variety of products are not produced, having specific equipment for mass production will usually be a powerful weapon for cost reduction. In Toyota, however, there are various kinds of cars differentiated in various combinations by types, tires, options, colors, etc. As one example, three or four thousand kinds of Coronas are actually being produced. To promote smoothed production corresponding to such a variety of products, it is necessary to have general-purpose or "flexible" machines. By putting minimum instruments and tools on these machines, Toyota has specified production processes to accommodate the general usefulness of these machines.

An advantage of smoothed production responding to product variety is that the system can adapt smoothly to the variations in customer demand by gradually changing the frequency (times) of lots without altering the lot size in each process, or fine-tuning of production by Kanban. In order to realize the smoothed production, the reduction of production lead time will be necessary to promptly and timely produce various kinds of products. Then the reduction in lead time will require the shortening of setup time for minimizing the lot size.

Setup problems

The most difficult point in promoting smoothed production is the setup problem. In a pressing process, for example, common sense dictates that cost reduction can be obtained through continuously using one type of die, thereby allowing for the biggest lot size and reducing setup costs. However, under the situation where the final process has average its production and reduced the stocks between the punchpress and its subsequent body line, the pressing department as a preceding process must make frequent and speedy setups, which means altering the types of dies for the pressing corresponding to a great variety of products, each frequently withdrawn by the subsequent process.

At Toyota, the setup time of the pressing department had been about 2 or 3 hrs. from 1945 to 1954. It was reduced to a quarter hour in the years 1955–64, and after 1970, it dropped to only 3 min.

In order to shorten the setup time, it is important to neatly prepare in advance the necessary jigs, tools, the next die and materials, and remove the detached die and jigs after the new die is settled and the machine begins to operate. This phase of setup actions is called the *external* setup. Also, the worker should concentrate on such actions needed while the machine is stopping. This phase of setup actions is called the *internal* setup. The most important point is to convert as much as possible of the internal setup to the external setup.

Design of processes

Consider the design or layout of processes in a plant. Previously in this factory, each of five stands of lathes, milling machines, and drilling machines were laid out side by side, and one machine was handled by one worker, e.g., a turner handled only a lathe. According to the Toyota production system, the layout of machines would be rearranged to smooth the production flow. Therefore, each worker would handle three types of machines; for example, a worker might handle a lathe, a milling machine, and a drilling machine at the same time. This system is called *multi-process holding*. In other words, the single-function worker, a concept which previously prevailed in Toyota factories, has become a *multi-function worker*.

In a multi-process holding line, a worker handles several machines of

8

various processes one by one, and work at each process will proceed only when the worker completes his given jobs within a cycle time. As a result, the introduction of each unit to the line is balanced by the completion of another unit of finished product, as ordered by the operations of a cycle time. Such production is called *one-piece* production and conveyance. The rearrangement leads to the following benefits:

- Unnecessary inventory between each process can be eliminated.
- The multi-process worker concept can decrease the number of workers needed, and thereby increase productivity.
- As workers become multi-functional workers, they can participate in the total system of a factory and thereby feel better about their jobs.
- By becoming a multi-functional worker, each worker can engage in teamwork, or workers can help each other.

Such a multi-process worker or multi-functional worker concept is a very Japanese-like method. In American and European companies there are many sorts of craft unions in one plant; a turner, for example, handles only a lathe and will not usually work on any other kind of machine, whereas in Japan there exists only an enterprise-union in each company, which makes the mobility of a laborer or the multi-process holding by a laborer very easy. Obviously, this difference may pose one of the major obstacles for American and European companies that might wish to adopt the Toyota production system.

Standardization of jobs

The standard operation at Toyota is a bit different from the usual operation in that it shows mainly the sequential routine of various operations taken by a worker who handles multiple kinds of machines as a multi-functional worker.

Two kinds of sheets show standard operations: the *standard operations routine sheet,* which looks like a usual man-machine chart, and the *standard operations sheet,* which is tacked up in the factory for all workers to see. The latter sheet specifies the cycle time, standard operations routine, and standard quantity of the work in process.

A cycle time, or tact time, is the standard specified number of minutes and seconds that each line must produce one product or one part. This time is computed by the following two formulas. Initially, the necessary output per month is predetermined from the demand side. Then:

$$\text{Necessary output per day} = \frac{\text{necessary output per month}}{\text{operating days per month}}$$

$$\text{Cycle time} = \frac{\text{operating hours per day}}{\text{necessary output per day}}$$

Each production department will be informed of this necessary quantity per day and the cycle time from the central planning office once in each previous month. In turn, the manager of each process will determine how many workers are necessary for this process to produce one unit of output in a cycle time. The workers of the entire factory then must be repositioned in order that each process will be operated by a minimum number of workers.

The Kanban is not the only information to be given to each process. A Kanban is a type of production dispatching information during the month in question, whereas the daily quantity and cycle time information are given in advance to prepare the master production schedule throughout the factory.

The standard operations routine indicates the sequence of operations that should be taken by a worker in multiple processes of the department. This is the order for a worker to pick up the material, put it on his machine, and detach it after processing by this machine. This order of operations continues for various machines he handles. The line balancing can be achieved among workers in this department since each worker will finish all of his operations within the cycle time.

The standard quantity of work-in-process is the minimum quantity of work-in-process within a production line, which includes the work attached to machines. Without this quantity of work, the predetermined sequence of various kinds of machines in this whole line cannot operate simultaneously. Theoretically, however, if the invisible conveyor belt is realized in this line, there is no need to have any inventory among the successive process.

Autonomation

As noted previously, the two pillars which support the Toyota production system are Just-in-time and Autonomation. In order to realize Just-in-time perfectly, 100% good units must flow to the subsequent process, and this flow must be rhythmic without interruption. Therefore, quality control is so important that it must coexist with the Just-in-time operation throughout the Kanban system. Autonomation means to build in a mechanism a means to prevent mass-production of defective work in machines or product lines. The word Autonomation (in Japanese, "Ninben-no-aru Jidoka," which often abbreviates to "Jidoka") is not automation, but the autonomous check of abnormals in a process.

The autonomous machine is a machine to which an automatic stopping device is attached. In Toyota factories, almost all machines are autonomous, so that mass-production of defects can be prevented and machine breakdowns are automatically checked. The so-called *Foolproof* ("Bakayoke" or "Pokayoke") is one such mechanism to prevent defective work by putting various checking devices on the implements and instruments.

The idea of Autonomation is also expanded to the product lines of manual work. If something abnormal happens in a product line, the worker pushes his stop button, thereby stopping his whole line. The Andon in the Toyota system has an important role in helping this autonomous check, and is a typical example of Toyota's "Visual Control System." For the purpose of detecting troubles in each process, an electric light board, called *Andon*, indicating a line stop, is hung so high in a factory that it can easily be seen by everyone. When some worker calls for help to adjust his delay of a job, he turns on the yellow light on the Andon. If he needs the line stopped to adjust some problem with his machines, he turns on the red light. In summary, Autonomation is a mechanism that autonomously checks something unusual in a process.

Improvement activities

The Toyota production system integrates and attains different goals (i.e., quantity control, quality assurance, and respect-for-humanity) while pursuing its ultimate goal of cost reduction. The process by which all these goals are realized is improvement activities, a fundamental element of the Toyota system. This is what makes the Toyota production system really tick. Each worker has the chance to make suggestions and propose improvements via a small group called a *QC circle*. Such a suggestion-making process allows for improvement in quantity control by adapting standard operations routine to changes in cycle time; in quality assurance, by preventing recurrence of defective works and machines; and, lastly, in respect-for-humanity, by allowing each worker to participate in the production process.

Summary

The basic purpose of the Toyota production system is to increase profits by reducing costs—that is, by completely eliminating waste such as excessive stocks or workforce. The concept of *costs* in this context is very broad. It is essentially cash outlay in the past, present, or future deductible from sales revenue to attain a profit. Therefore, *costs* include not only manufacturing costs (reduced by cutting the workforce), but also administrative costs and capital costs (reduced by inventory cutting) and sales costs. To achieve cost reduction, production must promptly and flexibly adapt to changes in market demand without having wasteful slacks. Such an ideal is accomplished by the concept of Just-in-time, producing the necessary items in the necessary quantities at the necessary time. At Toyota, the Kanban system has been developed as a means of dispatching production during a month and managing Just-in-time. In turn, in order to implement the Kanban system, production must be smoothed to level the quantities and variety in the withdrawals of parts by the final assembly line. Such smoothing will require the reduction of the production lead time, since various parts must be produced promptly each day. This can be attained by a small lot production or one piece production and conveyance. The small lot production can be achieved by shortening the setup time, and the one piece production will be realized by the multi-process worker who works in the multi-process holding

11

line. Standard operations routine will assure the completion of all jobs to process one unit of a product in a cycle time. The support of Just-in-time production by 100% "good" products will be assured by Autonomation (autonomous defects-control systems). Finally, improvement activities will contribute to the overall process by modifying standard operations, remedying certain defects, and finally, by increasing the worker's morale.

Where have these basic ideas come from? What need evoked them?

They are believed to have come from the market constraints which characterized the Japanese automobile industry in post-war days: great variety within small quantities of production. Toyota thought consistently from about 1950 that it would be dangerous to blindly imitate the Ford system (one which could minimize the average unit cost by producing in large quantities). American techniques of mass production have been good enough in the age of high-grade growth, which lasted until 1973. In the age of the low-level growth after the oil shock, however, the Toyota production system was given more attention and adopted by many industries in Japan in order to increase profit by decreasing costs or cutting waste.

The Toyota production system is a unique, revolutionary system; however, there is no problem for foreign companies in adopting this system except for the possibility of union problems (i.e., the multi-function worker). In its simplest terms, the Toyota production system might be interpreted as a special case of material requirements planning.

American and European companies could adopt this system, but might encounter some difficulties if they used it partially. Many Japanese companies are already using it in its imperfect form as well as its perfect form. The Kanban system and the smoothing of production could be particularly important to American and European companies. To implement the Toyota system perfectly, however, top management must proceed through the bargaining process with their union people. Such a process has often been experienced by many Japanese companies, too.

2

Adaptable Kanban System
Maintains Just-In-Time Production

The Kanban system is an information system that harmoniously controls the production of the necessary products in the necessary quantities at the necessary time in every process of a factory and also among companies. This is known as *Just-in-time* production. At Toyota, the Kanban system is regarded as a subsystem of the whole Toyota production system. In other words, the Kanban system is not equivalent to the Toyota production system, although many people erroneously call the latter the Kanban system. In this chapter, the various types of Kanbans, their usages, and rules are described. How Kanbans are connected with many supporting routines in production lines is also discussed.

Pulling system for Just-in-time production

Toyota's Just-in-time production is a method of adapting to changes due to troubles and demand changes by having all processes produce the necessary goods at the necessary time in the necessary quantities. The first requirement for Just-in-time production is to enable all processes to know accurate timing and required quantity.

In the ordinary production control system, this requirement is met by issuing various production schedules to all of the processes: parts-making processes as well as the final assembly line. These parts processes produce the parts in accordance with their schedules, employing the method of the preceding process supplying the parts to its following process, or, the *push system*. However, this method will make it difficult to promptly adapt to changes caused by trouble at some process or by demand fluctuations. For adapting to these changes during a month under the ordinary system, the company must change each production schedule for each process simultaneously, and this approach makes it difficult to change the schedules frequently. As a result, the company must hold inventory among all processes in order to absorb troubles and demand changes. Thus, such a system often creates an inbalance of stock between processes, which often leads to dead stock, excessive equipment, and surplus workers when model changes take place.

By contrast, the Toyota system is revolutional in a sense that the subsequent process will withdraw the parts from the preceding process, a method known as the *pull system*. Since only the final assembly line can accurately know the necessary timing and quantity of parts required, the final assembly line goes to the preceding process to obtain the necessary parts in the necessary quantity at the necessary time for vehicle assembly. The preceding process then produces the parts withdrawn by the subsequent process. Further, each part-producing process withdraws the necessary parts or materials from preceding processes further down the line.

Thus, it is not required during a month to issue simultaneous production schedules to all the processes. Instead, only the final assembly line can be informed of its changed production schedule when assembling each vehicle one by one. In order to inform all processes about necessary timing and quantity of parts production, Toyota uses the Kanban.

What is a Kanban?

A *Kanban* is a tool to achieve Just-in-time production. A Kanban is a card usually put in a rectangular vinyl envelope. Two kinds of Kanbans are mainly used: a withdrawal Kanban and a production-ordering Kanban. A *withdrawal* Kanban specifies the kind and quantity of product which the subsequent process should withdraw from the preceding process, while a *production-ordering* Kanban specifies the kind and quantity of product which the preceding process must produce (Figs. 2.1 and 2.2). The production-ordering Kanban is often called an in-process Kanban or simply a production Kanban.

The Kanban in Fig. 2.1 shows that the preceding process which makes this part is forging, and the carrier of the subsequent process must go to position B–2 of the forging department to withdraw drive pinions. The subsequent process is machining. Each box contains 20 units and the shape of the box is B. This Kanban is the fourth of eight sheets issued. The item back number is an

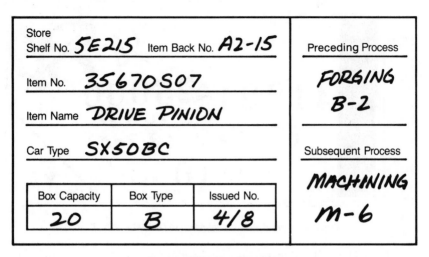

Fig. 2.1 Withdrawal Kanban.

Store Shelf No. **5E215**	Item Back No. **A2-15**		Preceding Process
Item No. **35670S07**			**FORGING B-2**
Item Name **DRIVE PINION**			
Car Type **SX50BC**			Subsequent Process
Box Capacity	Box Type	Issued No.	**MACHINING M-6**
20	**B**	**4/8**	

Fig. 2.2 Production-ordering Kanban.

Store Shelf No. **F26-18**	Item Back No. **A5-34**	Process
Item No. **56790-321**		**MACHINING SB-8**
Item Name **CRANK SHAFT**		
Car Type **SX50BC-150**		

abbreviation of the item. The Kanban in Fig. 2.2 shows that the machining process SB-8 must produce the crank shaft for the car type SX50BC–150. The crank shaft produced should be placed at store F26-18. See Fig. 2.3 for a photograph of a withdrawal Kanban.

Several other kinds of Kanbans exist. For making withdrawals from a vendor (a part or materials supplier, also called a subcontractor), a *supplier* Kanban (also called a subcontractor Kanban) is used. The supplier Kanban contains instructions which request the subcontracted supplier to deliver the parts. In the case of Toyota, in principle, the company withdraws parts from the subcontracted factories. However, since the shipping costs are included in the unit price of the part based on the contract, the supplier generally delivers the parts to Toyota. If Toyota actually withdraws the parts, the shipping cost

Fig. 2.3   Actual withdrawal Kanban (actual size 4x8″).

must be deducted from the part price. Therefore, the supplier Kanban is, in its real sense, another type of withdrawal Kanban.

The Kanban in Fig. 2.4 is used for delivery from Sumitomo Denko (a supplier) to Toyota's Tsutsumi plant. Although Kanbans used within the Toyota plant are not bar coded, all supplier Kanbans of Toyota are bar coded. The number 36 refers to the receiving station at the plant. The rear-door wire delivered to station 36 will be conveyed to store 3S (8-3-213). The back number of this part is 389.

Since the Toyota production system engages in small lot-size production, frequent transport and delivery each day is necessary. Therefore, delivery times must be written explicitly on this Kanban.

Also, Toyota has no special warehouse; therefore, the receiving place must be written clearly on this Kanban. Sometimes in the space under the supplier's name, a notation is written such as "1•6•2," which means that this item must be

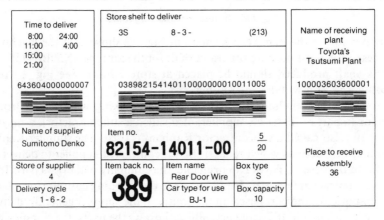

Fig. 2.4   Detail of supplier Kanban.

delivered six times a day and the parts must be conveyed *two delivery times later* after the Kanban in question is brought to the supplier. Fig. 2.4 is based on the actual supplier Kanban pictured in Fig. 2.5.

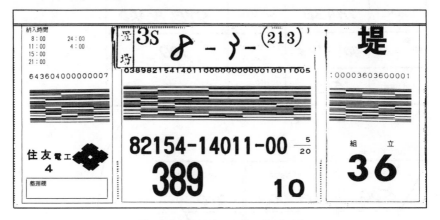

Fig. 2.5   Actual supplier Kanban.

Next, to specify lot production in the diecasting, punchpress, or forging processes, a *signal* Kanban is used. As seen in Fig. 2.6, a signal Kanban is tagged to a box within the lot. If withdrawals are made down to the tagged position of this Kanban, the production order must be set in motion.

Of the two types of signal Kanbans, the first one is a *triangular* Kanban. In Fig. 2.6, the triangular-shaped Kanban orders punchpress process #10 to produce 500 units of a left door when the containing boxes are withdrawn down to the last two boxes; that is, the reorder point is two boxes or 200 units of a left door. Fig. 2.7 shows a triangular Kanban for a blacket cab mounting. A triangular Kanban is made from a metal sheet and is fairly heavy.

The second type of the signal Kanban is rectangular-shaped and called a *material-requisition* Kanban. In Fig. 2.6, press process #10 must go to store 25 to withdraw 500 units of a steel board when the left doors were brought to the assembly line by two boxes. In this example, the reorder point for material requirements is three boxes of a left door. See Fig. 2.8 for a classification of the main types of Kanbans.

How to use various Kanbans

Fig. 2.9 shows how the withdrawal Kanban and the production-ordering Kanban are used. Starting from the subsequent process, the various steps utilizing the Kanban are:
1. The carrier of the subsequent process goes to the store of the preceding process with the necessary number of withdrawal Kanbans and the empty pallets (containers) on a forklift or jeep. He does this when a certain

Material-Requisition Kanban

Preceding Process	STORE 25 ⟶ PRESS #10		Subsequent Process
Back No.	MA 36	Item Name	STEEL BOARD
Material Size	40×3'×5'	Container Capacity	100
Lot Size	500	No. of Container	5

Triangular Kanban

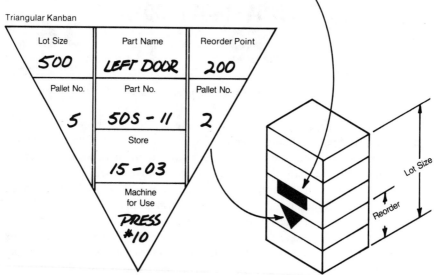

Lot Size	Part Name	Reorder Point
500	LEFT DOOR	200
Pallet No.	Part No.	Pallet No.
5	50S - 11	2
	Store	
	15 - 03	
	Machine for Use	
	PRESS #10	

Fig. 2.6 Signal Kanbans.

predetermined number of detached withdrawal Kanbans have accumulated in his withdrawal Kanban post (i.e., receiving box or file) or at regular predetermined times.

2. When the subsequent process carrier withdraws the parts at store A, he detaches the production-ordering Kanbans which were attached to the physical units in the pallets (note that each pallet has one sheet of Kanban) and places these Kanbans in the Kanban receiving post. He also leaves the empty pallets at the place designated by the preceding process people.

3. For each production-ordering Kanban that he detached, he attaches in its place one of his withdrawal Kanbans. When exchanging the two types of Kanbans, he carefully compares the withdrawal Kanban with the

Fig. 2.7   Triangular Kanban for a blacket cab mounting.

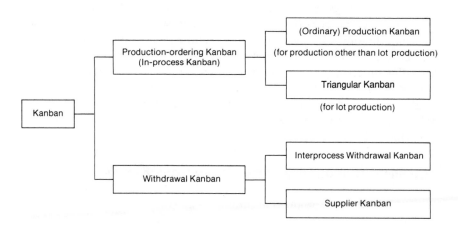

Fig. 2.8   Framework of the main types of Kanbans.

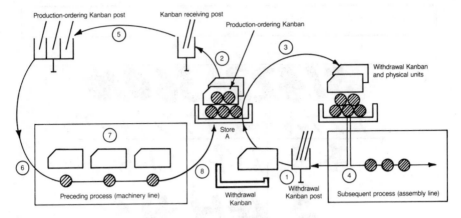

Fig. 2.9   Steps involved in using the two Kanbans.

production-ordering Kanban for consistency.

4.   When work begins in the subsequent process, the withdrawal Kanban must be put in the withdrawal Kanban post.

5.   In the preceding process, the production-ordering Kanban should be collected from the Kanban receiving post at a certain point in time or when a certain number of units have been produced and must be placed in the production-ordering Kanban post in the same sequence in which it had been detached at store A.

6.   Produce the parts according to the ordinal sequence of the production-ordering Kanbans in the post.

7.   The physical units and the Kanban must move as a pair when processed.

8.   When the physical units are completed in this process, they and the production-ordering Kanban are placed in store A, so that the carrier from the subsequent process can withdraw them at any time.

Such a chain of two Kanbans must exist continuously in many of the preceding processes. As a result, every process will receive the necessary kinds of units at a necessary time in the necessary quantities, so that the Just-in-time ideal is realized in every process. The chain of Kanbans will help realize line balancing for each process to produce its output in accordance with the cycle time (Fig. 2.10).

Two methods of utilizing production-ordering Kanbans

One method for using production-ordering Kanbans is shown in Fig. 2.11; it is used to issue many sheets of production-ordering Kanbans. Each sheet of the Kanban corresponds to container capacity. Production is undertaken according to the ordinal sequence in which the Kanbans were detached from the containers. Where many different kinds of parts exist, Kanbans are circulated in a manner depicted in Fig. 2.11. The classified frames in the Kanban post and the classified labels at the store of finished goods is also shown.

The second method uses the single sheet of a signal Kanban (Fig. 2.6). In the pressing department, for example, the production quantity is so large and the production velocity so rapid that the signal Kanban is used.

The signal Kanban can be tagged onto the edge of a pallet. At the store, it should be tagged at the position of the reorder point. When the goods at the store are withdrawn and the pallets are picked up, the signal Kanban should be moved to the reorder point instructions post. When it is moved to the dispatching post, operations will begin.

According to the ordering point system, when the reorder point and lot size are determined, there is no need to worry about daily production planning and followup. Simply keep watch on the timing of orders. This timing is automatically explicit when using the triangular Kanban, which orders production, and the rectangular Kanban, which instructs material-requistions.

If several kinds of parts are produced at a certain process, these triangular Kanbans can instruct automatically what kind of part should be processed first.

At some suppliers and also at some processes of Toyota, the triangular Kanban is used as a support for the ordinary production-ordering Kanbans. In this case, each individual part box contains its own production-ordering Kanban, and at the same time the triangular Kanban is tagged and positioned at the reorder point of the piled boxes.

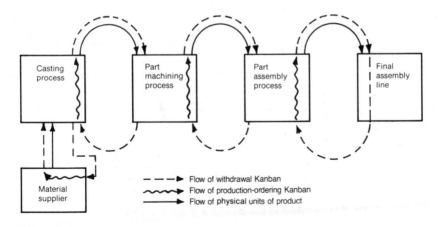

Fig. 2.10   Chain of Kanbans and physical units.

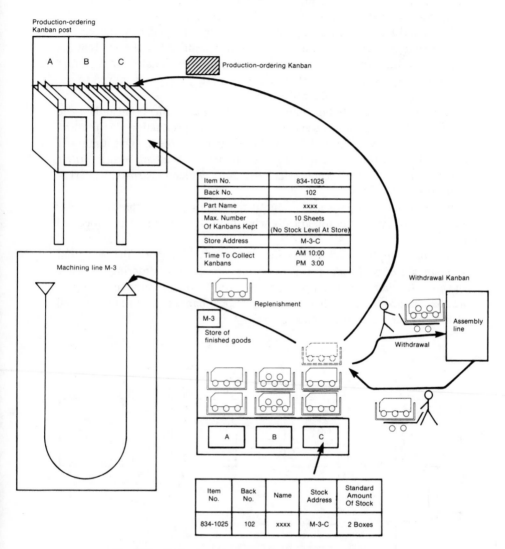

Production-ordering
Kanban post

A   B   C

Production-ordering Kanban

Item No.	834-1025
Back No.	102
Part Name	xxxx
Max. Number Of Kanbans Kept	10 Sheets (No Stock Level At Store)
Store Address	M-3-C
Time To Collect Kanbans	AM 10:00 PM 3:00

Machining line M-3

Replenishment

Withdrawal Kanban

M-3
Store of finished goods

Assembly line

Withdrawal

A   B   C

Item No.	Back No.	Name	Stock Address	Standard Amount Of Stock
834-1025	102	xxxx	M-3-C	2 Boxes

Fig. 2.11   Ordinal sequence of many kinds of Kanbans.

22

Kanban rules

In order to realize the Just-in-time purpose of Kanban, the following rules must be followed:

Rule 1. The subsequent process should withdraw the necessary products from the preceding process in the necessary quantities at the necessary point in time.

If the production manager alone wished to introduce the Kanban system into the factory, his position would be so weak that he could not implement this first Kanban rule. To implement this rule, the top management of the company must win over all workers and should also make a critical decision to upset the previous flow of production, transport, and delivery. This decision will probably be met with much resistance because Rule 1 requires a complete change of the existing production system.

The following subrules will also accompany this rule:
- Any withdrawal without a Kanban should be prohibited.
- Any withdrawal which is greater than the number of Kanbans should be prohibited.
- A Kanban should always be attached to the physical product.

It should be noted that as prerequisites of the Kanban system, the following conditions should be incorporated into the production system: smoothing of production, layout of processes, and standardization of jobs.

The smoothing of production, or leveled daily production, is a necessary condition for a small-lot withdrawal and a small-lot production of subsequent processes, and is most important for implementing Rule 1. For example, if only the Kanban system is applied to withdrawing the parts from outside subcontracted companies without any smoothed production in the production line of the manufacturer, then the Kanban will be a very dangerous weapon and its original purpose will be lost. Subcontractors need a large amount of inventory, equipment, and manpower to respond to fluctuating demands from the manufacturer.

To use an example from Chapter 1, in the Corona assembly line, sedans are assembled and conveyed every one unit interval, while hardtops and wagons are assembled and conveyed in three unit intervals. The final output is then: sedan, hardtop, sedan, wagon, sedan, hardtop, etc.

However, even if Rule 1 was applied, Just-in-time production could not easily be attained because Kanban itself is merely a dispatching means for actual production actions during each day at each process. Before entering the phase of dispatching the jobs by Kanban, overall planning throughout the plant must be made in advance. For this purpose, Toyota will inform each process and each supplier each month of a predetermined monthly production quantity for the next month's production so each process and each supplier in turn can prepare in advance its cycle time, necessary workforce, necessary number of materials, and required improvement point, etc. Based on such overall plans, all processes in the plant can start to apply the Rule 1 simultaneously from the first day of each month.

Concerning withdrawal methods by Kanban, two additional features should be mentioned. At Toyota, there are two kinds of withdrawal systems: the *constant quantity, but inconstant cycle* withdrawal system, and the *constant cycle, but inconstant quantity* withdrawal system. Details of these systems are discussed in Appendix 1; here, two examples will be explained: the method for conveying a set of various parts in constant quantities and the method for conveying parts at a regular time with a round-tour mixed-loading system.

Whirligig. A whirligig beetle is an insect that whirls on the surface of water very swiftly. The carrier in the Toyota factory is also called the whirligig ("Mizusumashi"), because he travels between preceding processes and subsequent processes again and again. For example, when the parts necessary for assembling a small lot of accelerators (five units is a lot size) need to be withdrawn, the carrier will go around various stores at the various machining processes and withdraw the parts necessary to make a set of five accelerators. The whirligig conveyance is a representative example of withdrawing the parts in constant quantities as a set.

Constant Cycle and Round-Tour Mixed-Loading System. The round-tour mixed-loading system is used by the subcontractor. As far as withdrawals from subcontracted companies are concerned, it is the subcontractor who usually delivers its product to the company. Consequently, the carrying hours become important because of the frequent deliveries due to small-lot production.

For example, four subcontracted companies, A, B, C and D, are located in one area and must bring their products to Toyota four times a day in small lot sizes. Although such frequent delivery can decrease the level of inventory remarkably, it is unfeasible for each of the subcontractors because of high distribution costs.

So, the first delivery at 9 a.m. could be made by subcontractor A, also picking up on the way products from companies B, C, and D on A's truck. The second delivery at 11 p.m. could be made by company B similarly picking up the products of A, C, and D on the way. The third delivery at 2 p.m. would be made by C company. This is called the constant cycle, round-tour mixed-loading system.

In the United States, however, this system may be hard to apply in some cases. Since America is so wide in a geographical sense, sometimes subcontracted company A might be very far from other subcontractors B, C or D. In order to implement the Kanban system in such a situation, some additional strategies must be developed, such as exploring the possibilities of hiring subcontractors closer to the manufacturer, decreasing the rate of dependence on subcontractors, or withdrawing parts with a fairly large lot size. Also, in order for the suppliers to respond to frequent withdrawals by the main company, they should adopt the Toyota production system and shorten their production lead time.

Rule 2.   The preceding process should produce its products in the quantities withdrawn by the subsequent process.

When Kanban Rules 1 and 2 are observed, all production processes are combined so they become a kind of conveyor line. The balancing of the production timing among all processes will be maintained by strictly observing these two rules. If problems occur in any of the processes, the whole process might stop, but the balance among processes is still maintained. Therefore, the Toyota production system is a structure which realizes such an ideal conveyor line system, and Kanban is a means of connecting all the processes. As a result, the inventory kept by each preceding process will be minimized.

The subrules for the second rule follow:

- Production greater than the number of sheets of Kanbans must be prohibited.
- When various kinds of parts are to be produced in the preceding process, their production should follow the original sequence in which each kind of Kanban has been delivered.

Since the subsequent process will require in a single unit or in a small lot size to attain smoothed production, the preceding process must make frequent setups according to the frequent requisitions by the subsequent process. Therefore, the preceding process should make each setup very quick.

Rule 3.   Defective products should never be conveyed to the subsequent process.

The Kanban system itself will be destroyed unless this third rule is followed. If some defective items were discovered by the subsequent process, then the subsequent process itself makes its line stop because it does not have any extra units of inventory, and it sends those defective items back to the preceding process. Such line stoppage of the subsequent process is very obvious and visible to everyone. The system is based on the idea of Autonomation described in Chapter 1. Its purpose is simply to prevent recurrence of such defects.

The meaning of defective is expanded to include defective operations. A defective operation is a job for which standardization is not fully attained and inefficiencies then exist in manual operations, routines, and labor hours. Such inefficiencies would likely cause the production of defective items as well. Therefore, these defective operations must be eliminated to assure rhythmic withdrawals from the preceding process. The standardization of jobs is, therefore, one of the prerequisites of a Kanban system.

Rule 4.   The number of Kanbans should be minimized.

Since the number of Kanbans expresses the maximum inventory of a part, it should be kept as small as possible. Toyota recognizes the inventory level increase as the origin of all kinds of wastes.

The final authority to change the number of Kanbans is delegated to the supervisor of each process. If he improves his process by decreasing the lot size and shortening the lead time, then his necessary number of Kanbans can be decreased. Such improvements in his process will contribute to the observance of Rule 4. If it is desired to inspire improved managerial ability, authority to determine the number of Kanban must first be delegated.

The total number of each Kanban is kept constant. Therefore, when the daily average demand has increased, the lead time should be reduced. This requires the reduction of the "cycle time" of a standard operations routine by changing the allocation of workers in the line. However, because the number of Kanbans is fixed, a workshop incapable of such improvements will suffer line-stops or force the use of overtime. At Toyota, it is virtually impossible for workers to hide production problems in their workshop, for the Kanban system actually visualizes trouble in the form of line-stops or overtime, and will swiftly generate improvement activities to solve the problem. Shops might increase the safety stock or the total number of Kanban to adapt to demand increase. As a result, the size of safety inventory can be an indicator of the shop's ability.

In case of a demand decrease, the cycle time of the standard operations routine will be increased. However, the probable idle time of workers must be avoided by reducing the number of workers from the line. Details of how to determine the number of Kanban is discussed in Appendix 1.

Rule 5.   Kanban should be used to adapt to small fluctuations in demand (fine-tuning of production by Kanban).

Fine-tuning of production by Kanban refers to the Kanban system's most remarkable feature: its adaptability to sudden demand changes or exigencies of production.

To illustrate what is meant by adaptability, we will first examine the problems faced by companies using ordinary control systems: i.e., companies not using Kanban. These companies lack the means to deal smoothly with sudden, unexpected demand changes. The ordinary control system centrally determines production schedules and issues them simultaneously to production processes; therefore, sudden demand changes will require at least a seven- to ten-day interval before schedules can be revised and reissued to the factory—the time interval for the computer to compile and calculate updated data. As a result, the various production processes will be faced from time to time with abrupt, jolting changes in production requirements; these problems will be compounded by the processes' lack of smoothed production.

Companies using the Kanban system, on the other hand, do not issue detailed production schedules simultaneously to the preceding processes during a month; each process can only know what to produce when the production-ordering Kanban is detached from the container at its store. Only the final assembly line receives a sequence schedule for a day's production, and this schedule is displayed on a computer which specifies each next unit to be assembled. As a result, even though the predetermined monthly plan demanded manufacture of six units of A and four units of B in a day, this proportion may be reversed at day's end. No one has instructed the plan changes to all processes; instead, each change has arisen naturally from market demand and exigencies of production, according to the number of Kanbans detached.

Here we see the meaning of *fine-tuned production*. Where Kanban is used, and production is leveled, it becomes easy to react to changes in the market by producing a few more units than the number predetermined by schedule. For example, 100 units a day must be produced as part of the predetermined plan for January, but on January 10th we find that 120 units per day would be necessary for February. According to Toyota's approach, we will adapt to the change by producing 105 or 107 units daily from January 11th on, instead of keeping at the 100 unit rate for a week or ten-day interval required for the production schedule to be revised—as is the case in ordinary production control systems. Moreover, we will not feel the changed plan, since production at each process is always subject to instruction by Kanban.

Such fine-tuning of production by Kanban can only adapt to small fluctuations in demand. According to Toyota, demand variations of around 10% can be handled by changing only the frequency of Kanban transfers without revising the total number of Kanban.

In the case of fairly large seasonal changes in demand, or the case of an increase or decrease in actual monthly demand over the predetermined load or the preceding month's load, all of the production lines must be rearranged. That is, the cycle time of each workshop must be recomputed and correspondingly the number of workers in each process must be changed. Otherwise, the total number of each Kanban must be increased or decreased.

In order to cope with the bottom and the peak in variation of demand during the year, top management has to make a decision either to level the sales volume for the whole year, or construct a flexible plan for rearranging all the production lines corresponding to seasonal changes during the year.

Lastly, concerning the adaptability of Kanban, it should be noted that the Kanban can be used also for parts in unstable use, although the safety stock will be somewhat greater in this case. For example, small iron pieces called balance weights must be attached to the drive shaft of a car by a worker to prevent any irregularity in its gyration. There are five kinds of balance weights, and they must be selected according to the grade of irregularity in the rotation of a shaft. If the rotation is even, no balance weight is necessary. If the rotation is irregular, one or more weights must be attached. Therefore, the demand for these five kinds of balance weights is entirely unstable and cannot be leveled at all.

In Toyota, however, a Kanban is attached to these balance weights, too. Since the inventory levels of the five kinds of balance weights will not increase

27

more than the total number of each Kanban, the inventory levels and the order quantities become measurable, and the safety inventory also can be reasonably controlled.

Although the Kanban transfer is made at a regular point in time, the number of Kanban for each kind of balance weights will somewhat fluctuate depending on the demand change. However, if we wish to minimize such fluctuations of Kanban, we have to improve the manufacturing process itself in some way.

Other types of Kanbans

Express Kanban.   An express Kanban is issued when there is a shortage of a part. Although both the withdrawal Kanban and the production-ordering Kanban exist for this type of problem, the express Kanban is issued only in extraordinary situations and should be collected just after its use (Fig. 2.12).

As an example, imagine a situation where the carrier for a subsequent process (assembly line) goes to the store of a preceding process (machining line) and finds that part B has not been sufficiently replenished and is in dire shortage (Fig. 2.13). In such a case, the following steps will be taken:
1. The carrier issues the express Kanban for the part B and puts it in the express Kanban post (often called the *red post*) beside the production-ordering Kanban post at the machining process.
2. At the same time, the carrier pushes a button for the machining line making the part B. The button used to call various machining lines is installed on a board beside the production-ordering Kanban post.
3. On an electric light board called *Andon*, a light corresponding to part B will be activated, indicating a spur in part B's production.

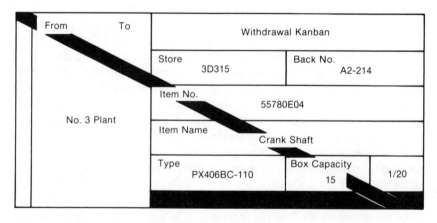

Fig. 2.12   Express Kanban.

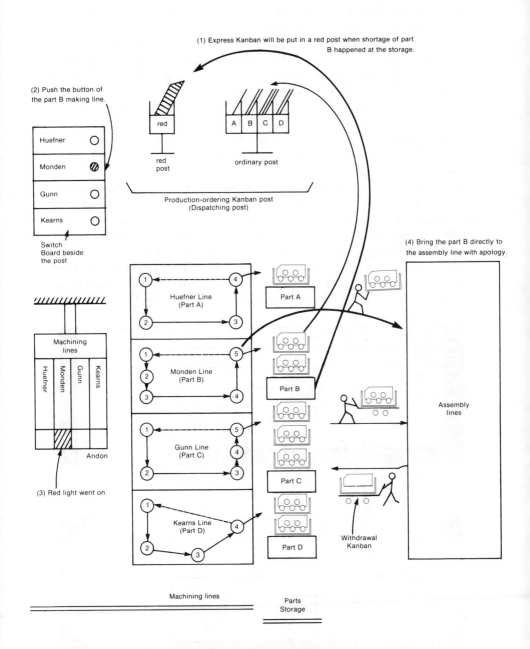

(1) Express Kanban will be put in a red post when shortage of part B happened at the storage.

(2) Push the button of the part B making line.

red

A | B | C | D

red post

ordinary post

Huefner ○
Monden ⊘
Gunn ○
Kearns ○

Switch Board beside the post

Production-ordering Kanban post (Dispatching post)

(4) Bring the part B directly to the assembly line with apology.

Machining lines

Huefner | Monden | Gunn | Kearns

Andon

(3) Red light went on.

Huefner Line (Part A)

Part A

Monden Line (Part B)

Part B

Assembly lines

Gunn Line (Part C)

Part C

Kearns Line (Part D)

Part D

Withdrawal Kanban

Machining lines

Parts Storage

Fig. 2.13   How express Kanban is used.

4. At that point of the line where the light has come on, the worker must produce the part B immediately, and bring it to the subsequent process (assembly line) himself with apology for its shortage. If the red lamp disappears immediately, the worker will be praised.

Emergency Kanban. An emergency Kanban will be issued temporarily when some inventory is required to make up for defective units, machine troubles, extra insertions, or a spurt in a weekend operation. This Kanban also takes a form of either a withdrawal Kanban or a production Kanban, and must be collected just after its use (Fig. 2.14).

Job-Order Kanban. While all the aforementioned Kanbans will be applied to the line of recurrently produced products, a *job-order* Kanban is prepared for a job-order production line and is issued for each job order (Fig. 2.15).

Through Kanban. If two or more processes are so closely connected with each other that they can be seen as a single process, there is no need to exchange Kanbans between these adjacent processes. In such a case, a common sheet of Kanban is used by these plural processes. Such Kanban is called a *through* Kanban (or *tunnel* Kanban), and is similar to the "through ticket" used between two adjacent railways. This Kanban can be used in those machining lines where each piece of a product produced at a line can be conveyed immediately to the next line by chute one at a time. Or, this Kanban

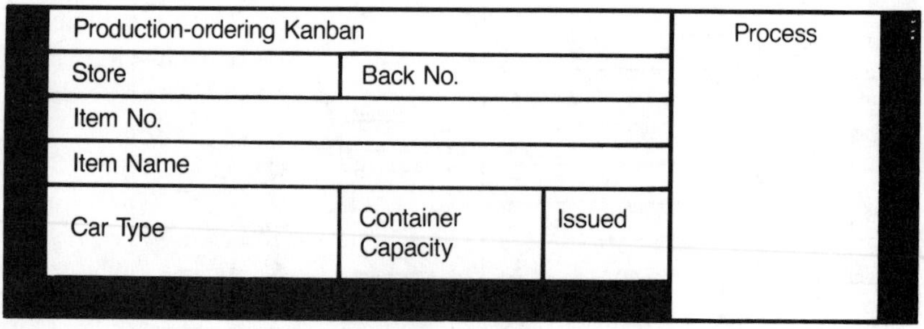

Production-ordering Kanban			Process
Store	Back No.		
Item No.			
Item Name			
Car Type	Container Capacity	Issued	

Fig. 2.14   Emergency Kanban.

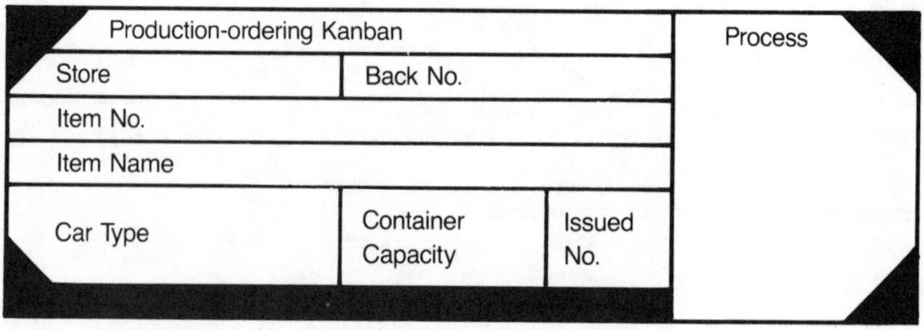

Production-ordering Kanban			Process
Store	Back No.		
Item No.			
Item Name			
Car Type	Container Capacity	Issued No.	

Fig. 2.15   Job-order Kanban.

can be used in process plants such as heat treatment, electroplating, scouring, or painting.

Common Kanban. A withdrawal Kanban can also be used as a production-ordering Kanban if the distance between two processes is very short and one supervisor is supervising both processes.

The carrier of the subsequent process will bring the empty boxes and the *common* Kanbans to the store of the preceding process. Then, he will bring the Kanbans to the Kanban receiving post (Fig. 2.9), and withdraw as many boxes as the number of Kanbans brought. However, he need not exchange Kanbans at the store.

Cart or Truck as a Kanban. Kanban is often very effective when used in combination with a cart. In the Honsha plant of Toyota, in order for the final assembly line to withdraw large unit parts such as engines or transmissions, a cart is used which can load only a limited quantity.

In this case, the cart itself also plays a role as a Kanban. In other words, when the number of transmissions at the side of the final assembly line is decreased to a certain reorder point (say three or five pieces), then immediately the people engaged in putting transmissions into cars will bring the empty cart to the preceding process, i.e., to the transmission assembly process and withdraw a cart loaded with the necessary transmissions in exchange for the empty cart.

Although a Kanban must be attached to the parts as a rule, the number of carts in this case has the same meaning as the number of Kanbans. The subassembly line (transmission department) cannot continue to make its product unless an empty cart remains, thereby preventing excessive production.

As another example, at the Obu plant of the Toyoda Automatic Loom Works, Ltd. (a supplier of Toyota), the foundry equipment casts the cylinder blocks, crankshafts, and motor cases, etc. In this plant, raw materials such as pig iron and scrap iron are conveyed by a truck from the suppliers to input them into the cupola (furnace). No container or boxes exist to count and load these materials. In this case, the truck is regarded as a sheet of Kanban.

Label. A chain conveyor is often used to convey the parts to the assembly line by hanging the parts on hangers. A label specifying which parts, how many and when the parts will be hung is attached to each hanger with a smoothed interval. In this case, a label is used as a kind of Kanban, though not actually called Kanban, to instruct the worker putting various parts on the hanger from the parts store or the worker assembling various parts at the subassembly line. As a result, the subassembly process can produce only the parts required. A hanger with a label is called *reserved seat* at Toyota.

A label is also applied to the final assembly line to instruct the sequence schedule of mixed models to be assembled (Figs. 2.16 and 2.17).

Full-Work System. Among automated machining processes where there are no workers, how is it possible for the preceding machine to produce units only in the quantity withdrawn? Differences exist in the capacity and speed of production among various machines, and the preceding machine might continue its processing without considering any problems which might occur in the subsequent machining process.

The *full-work system* is employed with automated machining processes. For example, preceding machine A and subsequent machine B are connected to each other and the standard inventory level of work in process on machine B is six units. If machine B has only four units in process, machine A automatically begins to operate and produce its output until six units are placed in machine B. When machine B is full with the predetermined quantity (six units), a limit switch automatically stops the operation of machine A.

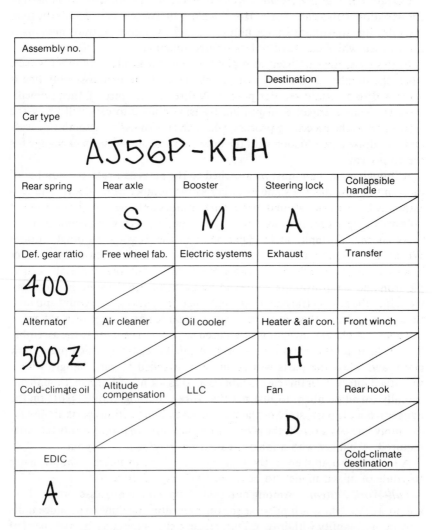

Assembly no.					
			Destination		
Car type					
AJ56P-KFH					
Rear spring	Rear axle	Booster	Steering lock	Collapsible handle	
	S	M	A	/	
Def. gear ratio	Free wheel fab.	Electric systems	Exhaust	Transfer	
400	/				
Alternator	Air cleaner	Oil cooler	Heater & air con.	Front winch	
500 Z	/	/	H	/	
Cold-climate oil	Altitude compensation	LLC	Fan	Rear hook	
	/		D	/	
EDIC				Cold-climate destination	
A					

Fig. 2.16   Sample of a label used at the final assembly line.

Fig. 2.17 Samples of labels.

Thereby, the standard quantity of work is always placed in each process, thus preventing unnecessary processing in the preceding process (Fig. 2.18). Because such electric control by a limit switch has come from the idea of a Kanban in a workplace where there are laborers and processes situated far from each other, the full-work system is also called an *electric* Kanban.

As another example, suppose the blanking machine (the machine which punches the sheet metal) produces 90 units per minute, whereas the pressing

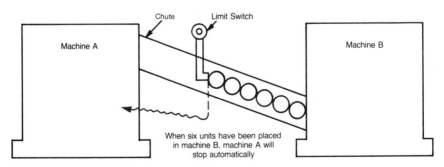

Fig. 2.18 Full-work system.

machine in the punching and bending process produces only 60 units per minute. Due to its high capacity, usually the blanking machine operates only during the first two-thirds of the month and is idle the last third. But this method may produce unnecessary inventory in the blanking machine.

Suppose then, that the blanking machine was directly connected to the pressing machine and the magazine was set between the two. If the magazine becomes full with punched metals, the blanking machine stops automatically. If only a few units remain in the magazine, the blanking machine automatically starts to operate again. In other words, the blanking machine operates for about two minutes, then rests for about a minute.

At Toyota, in order to attain line balancing with regard to production quantities, intermittent operation by the full-work system is adopted in all the production lines. The system leads to the following advantages:

- Elimination of unnecessary inventory of work-in-progress.
- Grasping the overall capacity of production lines and disclosing the bottle-neck process.
- Shortening of the lead time.
- Minimization of the final product inventory.
- Prompt adaptability to changes in demand.

3
Supplier Kanban and the Sequence Schedule for Use by Suppliers

Sometimes a very powerful manufacturer may instruct his suppliers to bring their parts Just-in-time. In this case, if this user manufacturer applied Kanban to his vendors without changing his own production systems, the Kanban system will be a demon to the vendors. Although the Kanban system is a very effective means to realize the Just-in-time concept, it should not be applied to the supplier without corresponding changes in the overall production system of the user company. The Kanban system is merely a subsystem of the Toyota production system; and the Toyota production system requires an overall rearrangement of existing production systems.

If the subsequent process withdraws parts with large variance in terms of quantity or timing, the preceding process must necessarily prepare slack capacities of manpower, facility, and inventory. In the same way, since the paternal manufacturer is connecting to the supplier through the Kanban system, the supplier would suffer if the manufacturer ordered parts in a fluctuating manner. Thus, an effort must be made to minimize the fluctuation of production in the final assembly line of the paternal manufacturer.

In 1950, the Honsha plant of Toyota began to install a line-balancing scheme between the final assembly line and machining lines. Then, the Kanban system was developed and gradually spread into further preceding processes. As a result, since 1962 the Kanban system has been applied to *all* of Toyota's plants. Thus, it was in 1962 that Toyota began to apply Kanban to its suppliers. By 1970, Toyota had applied Kanban to 60% of its vendors. As of

1982, Toyota has applied its *supplier* Kanban to 98% of its vendors, although still only 50% of the vendors are using *in-process* Kanban (or, *production-ordering* Kanban) in their own plants.

This chapter will cover the following topics:

- Monthly information and daily information provided to the supplier.
- Later replenishment system by Kanban.
- Sequenced withdrawal system by the sequence schedule table.
- Problems and countermeasures in applying Kanban to the subcontractors.
- How supplier Kanban should be circulated within the paternal manufacturer.

The author collected data for this chapter by interviewing and observing Aisin Seiki Co., Ltd., one of the largest suppliers to Toyota.

Monthly information and daily information

Toyota provides two kinds of information to its suppliers: The first is a predetermined monthly production plan which is communicated to the supplier in the middle of the preceding month. Using this predetermined monthly production plan, the supplier will determine the following planning dates:

1. Cycle time of each process.
2. Standard operations routine which rearranges the allocation of workers appropriate to the cycle time at each process.
3. Quantities of parts and materials to be ordered to subsuppliers.
4. Number of each Kanban for subsuppliers.

The second type of information is daily information, which specifies the actual number of units to be supplied to the customer company (i.e., Toyota). This daily information takes on two different forms: a Kanban or a sequence schedule table (often called a unit order table). These two forms of information are applied alternatively, depending on the withdrawal methods of Toyota.

Toyota uses two types of withdrawal methods: a *later replenishment* system, and a *sequenced withdrawal* system.

The later replenishment system, ("Ato-Hoju"), is a method of using a supplier Kanban. Alongside the assembly line at Toyota, there are many boxes which contain parts and supplier Kanban. While the parts are used by the assembly line these boxes will empty, and then at a regular time the empty boxes and their supplier Kanbans will be conveyed to each respective supplier by a truck. From the supplier's store of finished parts, other boxes filled with parts will be withdrawn by the truck.

Let's consider the sequenced withdrawal system. In some cases Toyota may provide a supplier with the sequence schedule for many varieties of finished parts, enabling Toyota to withdraw various parts in a sequence conforming to its sequence schedule for mixed model assembly line. Such a system is called the sequenced withdrawal system ("Junjo-Biki"). For example, if the sequence schedule of various automobiles at Toyota's final assembly line is

$$[A - B - A - C - A - B - A - C - \ldots]$$

then the sequence schedule of various transmissions to be subassembled by the supplier must be

$$[Ta - Tb - Ta - Tc - Ta - Tb - Ta - Tc - \ldots]$$

where Ta means the transmission for car A.

Later replenishment system by Kanban

How the supplier Kanban should be applied to the supplier

As depicted in Fig. 3.1, the flow of a supplier Kanban consists of two steps:
1. At 8 a.m. the driver of a truck conveys the supplier Kanban to the supplier. This truck also conveys the empty boxes to the supplier.
2. When the truck arrives at the store of the supplier, the driver hands out the supplier Kanban to the storeworkers. Then, the driver immediately mans another truck already bearing the part and its Kanbans, and drives back to Toyota. In this situation, two matters should be noted:
   a. *The supplier Kanban and the supplier's production lead time.* The number of the supplier Kanban brought to the supplier's store at 8 a.m. does not necessarily correspond to the boxes which the driver brings back to Toyota at 8 a.m. For example, if the parts are conveyed twice a day (8 a.m. and 10 p.m.), we can assume that the supplier Kanban contained in the filled boxes at 8 a.m. this morning is the same Kanban brought at 10 p.m. last night. (See the remarks on the supplier Kanban in Fig. 3.1. The time needed for loading the parts on the truck has been omitted to simplify the figure.)
   b. *How to use trucks for Kanban system: the three trucks system.* The diagrammed situation must involve three trucks. One truck is being driven by the driver, while the other trucks are stationed at Toyota's store for unloading the delivered parts and at the supplier's store for loading the parts. Three people participate: the truck driver and two workers engaged in simultaneous loading and unloading.

Advantages of this conveyance system include:
- Shortened conveyance time between the supplier and the paternal maker, for the driver has no waiting time, loading time, or unloading time at each store. As a result, the total lead time will be shortened. In other words, the system can eliminate the driver's idle time, since other people load and unload while another truck is on the road.
- While this system's required three trucks have three times the depreciation

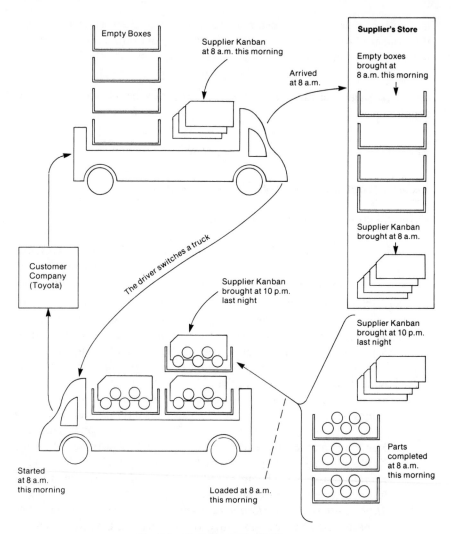

Fig. 3.1 Flow of supplier Kanban.

costs of one truck, the actual duration period is three times one truck. In the long run the system will not increase production costs. On the other hand, if parts are conveyed by only one truck, more than two persons are needed for loading and unloading to reduce total conveyance time as much as possible. These additional workers will increase production costs.

- Although the Kanban system requires frequent conveyances, the merits of reducing inventory are immeasurably greater than the increased conveyance costs. Further, the reader should consider the benefits of the mixed loading, traveling conveyance system that Toyota applies to plural suppliers, as explained in Chapter 2.

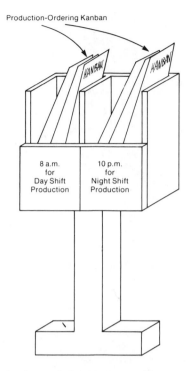

Production-Ordering Kanban

8 a.m.
for
Day Shift
Production

10 p.m.
for
Night Shift
Production

Fig. 3.2   Production-ordering Kanban post *(Dispatching Post).*

How the in-process Kanban will circulate in the supplier's plant

Suppose again that parts will be withdrawn by the automaker twice a day: 8 a.m. and 10 p.m. To correspond to this time schedule, the production ordering post for a manufacturing process is divided into two frames as depicted in Fig. 3.2.

The 8 a.m. file contains as many production Kanbans as equal to the number of customer Kanbans brought at 8 a.m., and will instruct production during the day shift. The production of parts will be completed at the latest by 10 p.m. that night, and the parts will be loaded on the truck at 10 p.m. to convey them to Toyota.

The 10 p.m. file contains as many production Kanbans as equal to the number of customer Kanbans brought at 10 p.m., and will instruct the production for the night shift.

The required parts will be finished at the latest by 8 a.m. the next morning, and again will be loaded on the truck at 8 a.m. for delivery to Toyota. (Note that for simplicity loading time allowances are not included.) These operations are seen in Fig. 3.3.

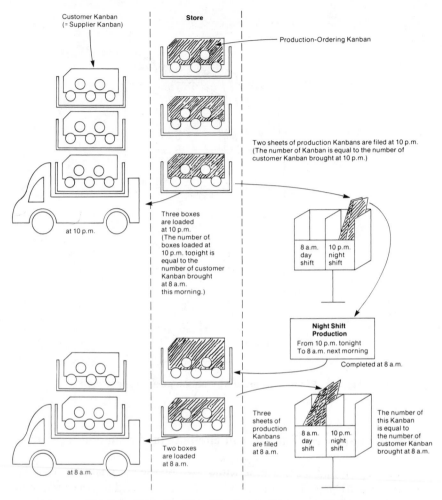

Fig. 3.3 Flow of customer Kanban and in-process Kanban.

How the paternal company determines the total number of supplier Kanbans is detailed in Appendix 1. The number of supplier Kanbans which a supplier dispatches to the second step subsupplier is determined by applying the same formula. These formulas are calculated by computer. Also, the formula determining the total number of an in-process Kanban is explained in the Appendix 1.

Sequenced withdrawal system by the sequence schedule table

Once a day, Toyota communicates the sequence schedule for various parts to the computer office of the vendor's plant. In some cases this sequence information will be memorized in a supplier's diskette and then, by using this diskette, the computer will print out labels which specify details of the parts to be assembled one by one on the supplier's assembly line. (The details of this EDP system used by a supplier are described in Appendix 3.)

The Shiroyama plant of Aisin Seiki Co., Ltd. (a Toyota supplier), for example, now relies on a magnetic tape delivered by Toyota, which specifies the sequence schedule for the day's production of transmissions. (In the future, however, an on-line computer system between the Shiroyama plant and Toyota will communicate the sequence schedule in a real time manner.) This sequence schedule table is called the *unit order table*, and is communicated to the assembly line on every hour (16 times a day), four hours before the delivery to Toyota. Notice how short lead time is! Such information flow is depicted in Fig. 3.4.

Both the later replenishment system and the sequenced withdrawal system are applied not only to the parts of a supplier, but also to the parts produced internally within Toyota Motor Corp. For example, when Toyota's Honsha

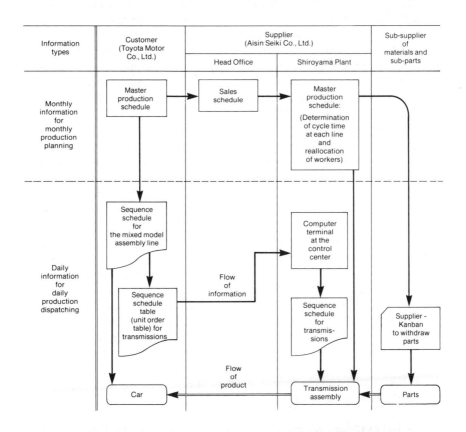

Fig. 3.4 Information system under the sequenced withdrawal system.

plant withdraws engines produced at Toyota's Kamigo plant, the sequenced withdrawal system is applied to the Kamigo plant.

In order to transmit the sequence schedule within Toyota's plants, a computer terminal has been installed in most of the plants. Formerly, however, Toyota used an interwriter, and the paper tape had been electrically transmitted to the subassemblies.

Store-space and a variety of products

In order to reduce the inventory level of a store, it is also necessary to minimize the store's space size. However, the present state of the Just-in-time production system by Kanban necessarily assumes that some amount of inventory exists at the store of parts completed by the previous process. The reasons follow:

- When the *constant quantity and inconstant cycle withdrawal system* is used, the preceding process must have some inventory of finished parts to adapt to any irregular timing of withdrawals. The timing of withdrawals must necessarily be irregular under this system because of fluctuating demands in the outside market.

- When the *constant cycle and inconstant quantity withdrawal system* is used, the preceding process must again have some inventory to adapt to inconstant quantities of withdrawals by the subsequent process. Again, under this system, the withdrawn quantity must fluctuate because of the vagaries of customer demand.

Therefore, the ideal of nonstock productions has not yet been realized under the present state of the Just-in-time approach at Toyota, although inventory level has been very well controlled by the Kanban itself. Of course, if the ideal of invisible conveyor belt lines is realized throughout the plant, it follows that the nonstock production or Just-*on-time* production is attained. Still production at Toyota is far from this ultimate ideal, and the term Just-*in-time* is more appropriate for the present situation than the term Just-*on-time*.

At Toyota's Kamigo plant, for example, the store of finished products (engines) is classified for delivery to its various client plants and companies. On the other hand, if the store is classified for a broad variety of finished parts, the total quantities of parts will increase. Therefore, if the size of the part is quite large (for example, transmissions or engines), and its varieties are many, the sequenced withdrawal system must be applied to minimize the store space. However, if the part size is small, the later replenishment system will be applied.

How the sequence schedule is used in the assembly lines of a supplier

Let us first examine the production situation at the Shiroyama plant of Aisin Seiki Co., Ltd. Its major products and their monthly production volumes (as

Products	Volume	Customers
Manual transmission (T/M)	20,000	Toyota Motor Co., Ltd. Daihatsu Kogyo Co., Ltd.
Semi-automatic transmission (for the automobile) (ATM)	3,000	Suzuki Motor Co., Ltd.
Semi-automatic transmission (for the industrial vehicle) (T/C)	1,000	Toyota Automatic Loom Works Co., Ltd. International Harvester Co.
Power steering (P/S)	2,500	Toyota Motor Co., Ltd. Hino Motors Co., Ltd.

Table 3.5.   Major products and their monthly production volume.

of 1981) can be seen on Table 3.5. The production character of these products—large variety and short runs—is depicted in Fig. 3.6.

Now we will consider how the Shiroyama plant is coping with such productions of large variety and short runs. Considering the design process, it is possible to expand a basic model transmission to adapt to the large variety of cars in which they will be used (Fig. 3.7).

This design process is incorporated into the various assembly lines as seen in Fig. 3.8. The assembly line is divided into two parts (main and sub) and the storages for half-finished and finished transmissions are installed. This divided assembly line responds to the many varieties of customer's orders. The lead time from the half-finished parts store to the finished parts store is only fifteen minutes, and the conveyance to Toyota takes one hour. As a result, these assembly lines can respond to the large variety of orders demanded by Toyota—orders whose sequence information is introduced only four hours before the delivery.

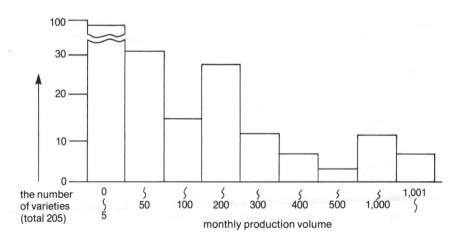

Fig. 3.6   Production character of a large variety and short runs.

43

Model	basic	4 speeds 5 speeds	engine gasoline diesel	frame truck bus	steering right left	final model
Variety	1	2	8	■ ■ ■	■ ■ ■	■ ▶ 74

Fig. 3.7 Design process from a basic model to the final models.

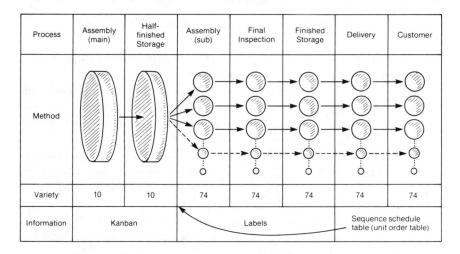

Process	Assembly (main)	Half-finished Storage	Assembly (sub)	Final Inspection	Finished Storage	Delivery	Customer
Variety	10	10	74	74	74	74	74
Information	Kanban		Labels		Sequence schedule table (unit order table)		

Fig. 3.8 Information and production method on the assembly lines.

At the head of the subassembly line, a label will be fastened to each transmission one by one, and these labels will sequence the 74 varieties of transmissions completed by the subassembly line. Meanwhile, each semi-finished transmission at the main assembly line will receive its own Kanban, and successive production of the ten basic transmission types will be ordered by these Kanbans.

It must be emphasized here that the transmission is a unique example; while in most cases one Kanban will dispatch several—perhaps five—units, in the case of the transmission, each unit receives its own Kanban. The reason for this is that although each transmission is a large unit in itself, production must be able to respond to the large variety of demand.

Problems and countermeasures in applying the Kanban system to the subcontractors

There must be some discrepancy between the quantities of parts the paternal company specifies in its monthly predetermined production plan and the quantities it actually orders during the month (based on Kanban or the sequence schedule table). This discrepancy is usually about 10%. However, there is no concept of plan revision in the operating processes of the plants because only production information in the form of Kanban or labels is given in a real time manner.

Concerned by the discrepancy and other related problems which might occur in the transactions between a paternal manufacturer and its subcontractors, the Japanese Communist Party, along with the Japanese Government's Fair Trade Commission, has strongly criticized the Toyota system. The following sections will address their criticism and guidance as well as Toyota's countermeasures, together with the author's opinion on this problem.

Criticism by the Communist Party against the Toyota production system

The Taylor System was once opposed by American labor unions contending that the scientific management neglected humanity and regarded man as a machine. Indeed, so intense did the dispute become that the United States found it necessary to investigate the subject through a special committee.

Now, just as scientific management once became an issue of the U.S. House of Representatives, the Toyota production system has come under the scrutiny of the Japanese House.

In 1977, just four years after the first oil shock hit Japan in late 1973, and when most Japanese companies were still suffering from its effects and the consequent inflation of yen currency, Michiko Tanaka, a member of the House of Representatives and also a member of Japan Communist Party questioned Premier Fukuda about the Toyota production system as follows:

> The management situation of medium and small enterprises is so severe that it can hardly be compared with big companies. However, the supplementary budget at this time restricts the amount of loans and cannot offer a promising future to the minor companies.
>
> Especially severe are the problems faced by subcontractors, who supply 60% of manufacturers. For example, the Toyota Motor Co., Ltd. has earned the current profit of 210 billion yen (about $1 billion). Behind this huge profit how many subcontractors have dropped tears? Toyota's completely rationalized production system strictly instructs its subcontractors to deliver the required parts within today or by tomorrow. Therefore, there is no excessive parts inventory at Toyota, and thus there is no warehouse and no sleeping funds invested in the inventory.
>
> However, subcontractors are in a precarious situation if they occupy positions as low as the third, fourth or fifth steps in the vertical line among manufacturers. The reason is if they cannot deliver their parts just in time for the needs of the paternal company, the contracts will be cancelled. Thus, they must engage in estimated production, and if their estimates were mistaken, they have to undertake all the loss themselves. Though

payment remains unchanged or is actually decreased, the subcontractors must put up with severe conditions to get their contracts.

Moreover, a serious matter which cannot go unnoticed is that this Toyota system is now prevailing among many industries and a vast number of subcontractors are likely to fall victims to this system. If this practice of bullying the subcontractors is left unrestricted, the Japanese economy will be thrown into chaos.

You have said that you will initiate a compassionate policy in behalf of medium and small enterprises, but how do you cope with these very wicked methods which take a superior position? I would like to hear your belief. (Proceedings at the Japanese House of Representatives, No. 4: October 7, 1977, p. 63.)

Fukuda responded as follows:

Now, concerning your opinion on Toyota's rationalized production system, I hear that the Fair Trade Commission is now guiding the company. The government will also give assurance that the paternal manufacturer will not force its rationalization at the sacrifice of the subcontractor's interests. This is my conviction. (Proceedings, op. cit. p. 65.)

Guidance by the Fair Trade Commission based on the Subcontractors Law and the Anti-Monopoly Law

Thus, the Fair Trade Commission and the Small and Medium Enterprises agency of the government in Japan have guided the paternal manufacturers not to violate the Subcontractor's Law and the Anti-Monopoly Law. The Subcontractor's Law is an abbreviation of the "Anti-Deferment-of-Payment-to-the-Subcontractor's Law." This law was established in 1956 to maintain a fair subcontracting trade and to guard the subcontractors' interests.

The problematic points of the Kanban system which concerned the Fair Trade Commission were as follows:

1. *When production is managed by the Kanban system, the ordering time is obscure.* According to the Toyota production system, it is only during the last eleven days of a previous month that a supplier will be notified of the predetermined monthly production plan concerning specific items, quantities, dates and times, etc. On the other hand, the Kanban system and the sequence schedule specify similar information. Therefore, the ordering time is not obvious: is it the time when the predetermined monthly production plan was offered or the Kanban and the sequence schedule were offered.

    However, according to the Subcontractor's Law (Article IV), even though the ordering action by a paternal maker is an informal notification, the point in time when the instruction is concretely made is regarded as the ordering time.

2. *According to the Kanban system, there must be some discrepancy between the monthly quantity that is informally ordered and the quantity actually delivered by Kanban dispatchings.* In other words, the essence of Kanban system lies in fine tuning production or making minor

adaptations to demand changes.

When the quantity of goods dispatched by the Kanbans turns out to be smaller than the quantity originally ordered by the monthly informally-communicated master production schedule, the difference must be regarded as the rejection of acceptance, because Article I states that the actual order occurs when the supplier receives instructions from the informal production table.

In addition, the Subcontractor's Law (Article IV - 1 - 1), prohibits the paternal manufacturer from rejecting all or part of the delivered goods it has ordered.

3. *The Kanban delivery system should not be forced on the supplier.* According to the Japanese Anti-Monopoly Law (Article 19): "A business company must not use unfair trading methods." In 1953, as an example of unfair trading methods, the following action was cited: "Realizing its superior position in regard to a dependent company, a business company must not trade with conditions exceptionally unfavorable to the other company in the light of normal business conventions."

Therefore, when applying the Kanban system to its supplier, a paternal company must secure an agreement with the subcontractor, and should never force implementation in a one-sided manner. In the trading contract, it should be noted that without such agreement the Kanban system will not be applied. Also, even if the subcontractor agrees to the application of Kanban, it must receive an adequate preparation period in order for it to adjust to the new system. Further, the paternal company should not urge the introduction of Kanban on vendors without adjusting the technical prerequisites of its own plant and without having full knowledge about the whole Toyota production system.

The other possible detrimental effects that Kanban may have on the subcontractor follows (referring to the paper of Mr. Hyogo Kikuchi, subcontract section manager of the Fair Trade Commission):

Most of the first-step subcontractors that adopted Kanban system are enjoying the same advantages as Toyota. However, the second, third or fourth preceding step subcontractors may suffer from certain detrimental effects for which, essentially, the paternal companies are responsible. These detriments are:

• The subcontractors may have to increase their inventory to achieve the expected production, since they have to deliver parts as quickly as possible in response to withdrawal by Kanban. They may also have to utilize overtime to cope with the unexpected.

Such increase of inventory in the stores of subcontractors is a consequence similar to situation effected by the Cock System (or, "On-the-Premises Warehouse System") which was popular in Japan after World War II. In the Cock System, a subcontractor will hold a certain amount of its finished parts inventory and bear the risk himself by borrowing a part of the paternal maker's factory. Thus, the paternal maker could use the necessary items in the necessary quantities at the necessary time (Just-in-time), and could issue the order sheet at the time of withdrawal. This system was criticized as a violation of the Subcontractor's Law, and the paternal manufacturers were dissuaded from its use.

- Notwithstanding standard increases in the quantity of monthly delivery, application of the Kanban system will increase overall conveyance times. The resulting increases in conveyance expenses will obviously increase the subcontractor's overall costs.
- The most important prerequisite of Just-in-time production is production smoothing, or small lot production. When implemented by a large, paternal manufacturer, this process requires the installment of multi-purpose machines and speedy setup actions. However, this brings up the subcontractor's obligation to install the same multi-purpose machines and improved setup actions in order to supply the part at the price which the user company has calculated based on its own smoothed, well-equipped production.

How Toyota is coping with criticism

The main problem pointed out by the Fair Trade Commission was the discrepancy between quantities ordered by the predetermined monthly production plan and the daily Kanban or sequence schedule instructions. Toyota's countered this problem as follows:

- Toyota is trying to hold the aforementioned discrepancies down to less than 10% of the monthly plan, and is requesting that suppliers allow this much difference.
- Since a model of an automobile will usually be produced for about four years, the supplier will not suffer seriously from monthly fluctuations, for these fluctuations are averaged out over many months.
- Toyota is promising its suppliers that it will give advance notice when it is about to stop production of a certain model. At that time it will establish a compensation structure.
- Toyota is telling its suppliers not to start production until instructed by the Kanban. Therefore, over production is not likely to occur.
- In order for the supplier to adjust to order-oriented production, it must shorten production lead time. Toyota is teaching how to achieve such reductions.

As a result of these steps, there is almost no confusion among Toyota's suppliers caused by plan revisions ordered by Kanban.

The author especially supports Toyota's countermeasure No. 2. When a dealer's demands are declining, the actual quantity of goods withdrawn by Kanban is likely to be less than the monthly predetermined quantity.

If Toyota was to withdraw this difference in quantity at the end of the month in question, the informally instructed quantity for the next month would be correspondingly smaller than the quantity previously forecasted, and as a result the subcontractor would be surprised to see a sudden, steep drop in his orders. This would never happen at Toyota. According to its production system, Toyota withdraws only the quantity which corresponds closely as possible to actual demand during the month. To achieve this approach, the quantities ordered both by Kanban and by the monthly predetermined instruction must be smoothed in daily production levels. As a result, the supplier would not be confused by the sudden fall in the actual ordered units. The supplier could adapt to the demand change smoothly by fine-tuning each month. The most remarkable advantage of the Kanban system, the adaptation to demand change by smoothing the changes of a plan, will begin to function at this point.

In regard to the various problems cited by the subcontract section of the Fair Trade Commission, the author holds the following opinions:

- Concerning the supplier's risk of holding of a large inventory, most of this problem will be resolved if the paternal manufacturer completes the various prerequisites of the Kanban system, especially the smoothing of production. Therefore, if this problem does arise, the Kanban system is guiltless and the paternal company must be blamed.

  On the other hand, suppose a supplier is supplying parts to several manufacturers and only some of the manufacturers are applying Kanban to the supplier. This supplier might have problems even if the manufacturers using Kanban are completing the prerequisite conditions. However, since so many Japanese industries have adopted Kanban, this problem is diminishing. The use of Kanban is especially widespread throughout the auto industry.

- As for the problem of increased conveyance costs due to more frequent withdrawals, it can be solved by the round-tour mixed loading system and the three truck system explained earlier in this chapter.

  If large geographic distances prevents the effective use of such systems, as in the case of the United States, the following approaches can be considered:

  a. Instead of relying on subcontractors, the paternal manufacturer should incorporate parts producing processes in its own factory. In the United States, automobile makers do not rely on subcontractors as much as Japanese automakers.

  b. Instead of making frequent orders to suppliers in small lot sizes, the user company should order in fairly large lot sizes. This practice can be seen in the case of Japanese automakers sending parts to foreign countries for overseas production. Kawasaki Motors U.S.A. is a good example of a company that has adopted the Toyota production system in the United States (1979).

49

- As for the difficulty the subcontractor may face in offering a part at the instructed price, such a problem can be resolved if the subcontractor itself adopts the Toyota production system. This problem also relates to the first problem. Even if the paternal maker has smoothed its production, the subcontractor might not be able to decrease his inventory and at the same time handle frequent withdrawals unless he can change his dies quickly.

Although Toyota is making an effort to keep monthly discrepancies down below 10%, some of the suppliers have reported that differences may run to plus-or-minus 20% of the initial monthly plan. However, if they are able to adapt to such demand changes in their own processes, this discrepancy does not pose serious problems. For example, as of 1981, the Kariya plant of Aisin Seiki Co., Ltd. has 0.7 days of safety stock ready for delivery to the customer. This means that it delivers parts three times a day to its customer, while holding safety inventory equivalent to two deliveries per day (i.e. $2/3 = 0.7$). The level of safety stock indicates the supplier's ability to adapt.

Therefore, subcontractors must also rationalize their production systems. They should not succumb to the easy attitude that rationalization must only be carried out by paternal manufacturers, for rationalization decreases costs, and cost reduction is a shared obligation of both manufacturers and subcontractors.

Fig. 3.9 shows that most of the big suppliers of Toyota were once part of the Toyota Motor Corp. Since each of them can be seen as simply another production process of the Toyota plant, the aforementioned problems do not exist among these companies.

Mr. Taiichi Ohno, original developer of Toyota production system, says: "In order to make the Toyota production system truly effective, we should recognize its limitations. Only if Toyota shares its destiny with surrounding cooperative manufacturers as a single community can it approach the perfect realization of this system. Therefore, the Toyota Motor Co. is improving the physical capabilities of our cooperative manufacturers by sending our I.E. staffs to them."

In short, paternal manufacturers must teach suppliers to implement the Toyota system, and at the same time the supplier must also frankly accept such guidance in order to make real improvements. With the existence of such a give-and-take relationship, warehouses are actually disappearing from the yards of Toyota's cooperative companies, including the second and third steps vendors.

It must be added, however, that it is somewhat difficult for a supplier to introduce a Kanban system independently unless its paternal company dispatches the supplier Kanban with smoothed order quantities.

Finally, another problem must be mentioned briefly: although there is no obvious resistance against the Toyota production system among Toyota's laborers, some people feel that this system will force the intensification of labor. At the present time it is difficult to justify such an argument with

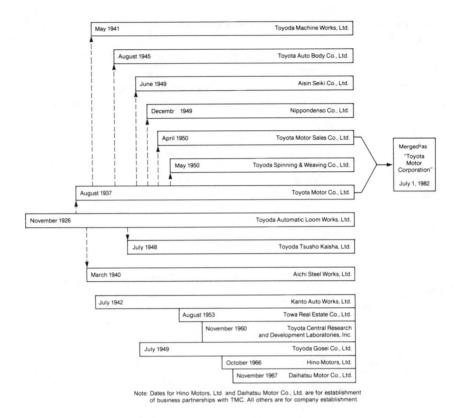

Fig. 3.9   Formation of the Toyota Group.

objective data. If we take into account the increasing number of suggestions per workers per year, we see that the humanity of laborers is well respected in this system. How Toyota has resolved the conflict between productivity and humanity will be discussed in Chapter 9. (Also see Muramatsu and Tanaka, 1980, 1981.) It is quite obvious that the Toyota production system cannot be implemented in a company or organization where a labor union opposes productivity increase itself. This point may be the critical condition which will restrict the application of the Toyota production system. Unless there is opposition from a labor union, this system can be applied to any company in any country.

How the supplier Kanban should be circulated within the paternal manufacturer

The production line is usually situated at a little distance from material or parts storage, and in such situations the following steps will be taken to request supplier's materials (each step number corresponds to the number in Fig. 3.9):

1. When a worker at the production line sees a material box empty out, he will push the switch beside the line.
2. The material-calling Andon located beside the material store will activate a lamp just under the metal plate indicating the material in question.

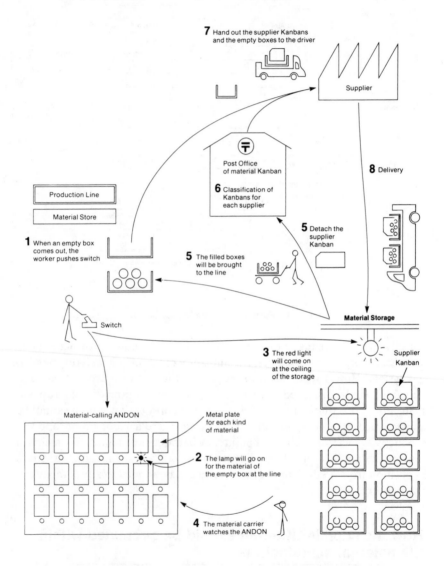

Fig. 3.10 Material-calling ANDON for the later-replenishment system.

3. At the same time, a large red light will come on at the material storage.
4. The material carrier at the store will watch the material-calling Andon to see which metal plate is lit.
5. Then, the carrier brings the box containing the material in question to the line. This box also contains the supplier Kanban, but the carrier must detach it before he brings the box to the production line.
6. The supplier Kanbans will be brought to a post office for supplier Kanbans, where these Kanbans will be classified for each supplier in the same way as a post office will classify letters for each address.
7. The processed and classified supplier Kanban will be given to the truck driver for subsequent delivery to the supplier. The empty boxes have already been loaded on the driver's truck.

The metal plate for each kind of material, which is part of the material-calling Andon, is essentially a kind of *withdrawal* Kanban. At the Aisin Seiki Co., Ltd., this metal plate is called Kanban, and there is no Kanban in the material boxes beside the production line. However, although the author saw the similar metal plate board at the Honsha plant of Toyota, Toyota does not call this metal plate a Kanban and each material box beside the line contains a standard supplier Kanban.

The Honsha plant of Daihatsu Motor Co., Ltd., which has a business partnership with Toyota is using also a plate-sliding file as depicted in Fig. 3.10. In this plant, the metal plate, which a lamp has highlighted, will be placed in a plate-sliding file according to the order of its lamp's activation. Then, the

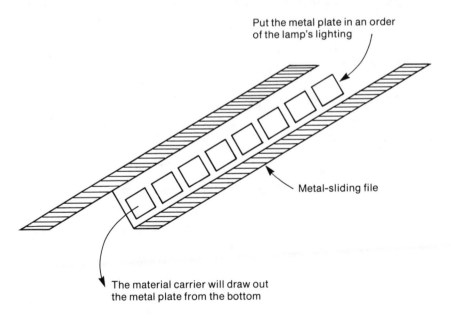

Put the metal plate in an order of the lamp's lighting

Metal-sliding file

The material carrier will draw out the metal plate from the bottom

Fig. 3.11 Metal plate sliding file.

carrier will withdraw the plate from the bottom of this sliding file, collect the materials designated by the plates from various stores in the plant, and bring them to the line. The material-calling Andon or the metal-plate board has various forms in different companies. Each company devises its own forms.

The inside of the post office for supplier Kanbans is shown in Fig. 3.11. The post office is located beside or inside the material storage. Recently, however, companies are sorting the supplier Kanbans by computer.

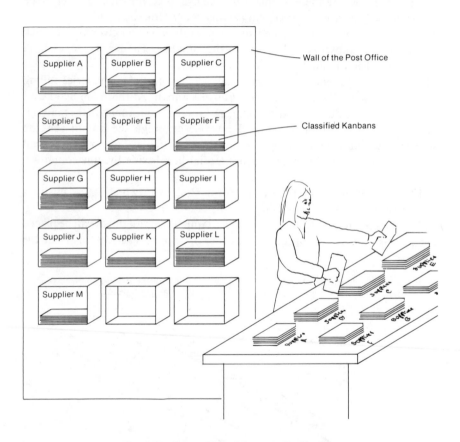

Fig. 3.12   Post office of the supplier Kanbans.

4

Smoothed Production Helps Toyota Adapt to Demand Changes and Reduce Inventory

The ultimate purpose of the Toyota production system is to increase profit by reducing costs. Cost reduction is made possible by eliminating waste, especially by doing away with unnecessary inventories. This purpose is achieved by Just-in-time production. In sales, the Just-in-time concept will be realized by supplying the salable products only in the salable quantities. This situation is characterized as production promptly adaptable to demand changes. As a result, excess inventories of finished products can be eliminated.

At Toyota, the means for adapting production to variable demand is called *production smoothing*. Through production smoothing, a production line is no longer committed to the manufacture of a single type of product in vast lot sizes; instead, a single line must produce many varieties each day in response to variegated customer demand. Therefore, production is kept up-to-date and inventory is cut.

Fig. 4.1 analyzes the two phases of production smoothing. The first phase shows the adaptation to monthly demand changes during a year (monthly adaptation), in the second phase, adaptation to daily demand changes during a month (daily adaptation). Monthly adaptation will be achieved by monthly production planning: the preparation of a master production schedule instructing the averaged daily production level of each process in the plant. This master production schedule is based on a three-month demand forecast and a monthly demand forecast.

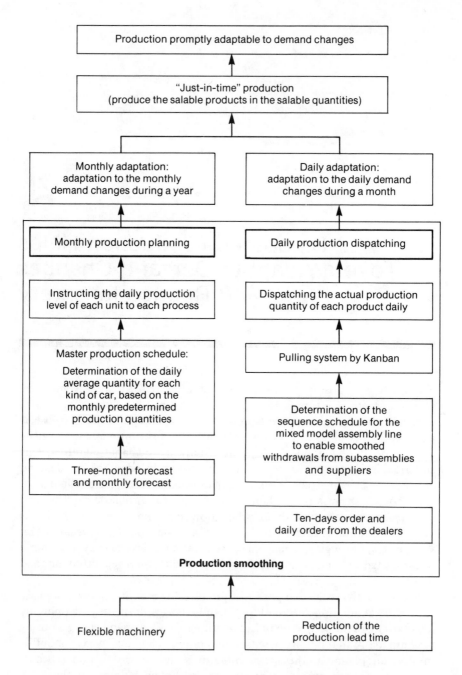

Fig. 4.1 Framework of Toyota's production smoothing.

The next phase, daily adaptation, is made possible by daily production dispatching. Here is the role of the Kanban system in production smoothing, for daily production dispatching can only be achieved through the use of a pulling system: Kanban and a sequence schedule. Only when a sequence schedule is prepared for the mixed-model assembly line can Toyota make smoothed withdrawals from its suppliers and subassemblies.

Though production cannot be smoothed without a reduction of lead time, we will discuss lead time in Chapter 5 and reserve this chapter for a discussion of the two aforementioned aspects of production smoothing, along with a comparison of the Kanban system and another production information system called MRP in terms of adaptability.

Monthly production planning

The Toyota Motor Corp. has a yearly production plan which shows how many cars to make and sell in the current year. It also has a two-step monthly production plan. First, car types and quantities are suggested two months before, and then the detailed plan is determined one month before the particular month in question. Such suggested and determined information is also communicated to the subcontracted companies at the same time. From this monthly production plan, the daily production schedule is set. For the Toyota production system, this daily production schedule is particularly important because the concept of smoothed production is incorporated into this schedule.

Smoothed production must extend into two areas: the averaged total production of a product per day and the averaged quantity of each variety of product within the greater total. For example, in Toyota's factory, there are many final assembly lines—the Corona line, the Crown line, the Celica line, etc. Suppose the Corona line has to produce 20,000 units in a month of 20 operating days. This means that 1,000 Coronas must be produced per day. This is a smoothing of production in terms of the daily production quantity, i.e., averaging the total quantity to be produced per day.

But at the same time, the Corona line has to be averaged in terms of the various Coronas available. The Corona line assembles about 3,000 or 4,000 kinds of Coronas, which are differentiated by the different combinations of engines, transmissions, accelerators, number of doors, outside and inside colors, tires, and various options. Each of these different types of Coronas must also be averaged for daily production. Suppose there are four major types of automobiles in the Corona line and the number of monthly operating days is 20. The daily average quantity of each type can be seen in Table 4.2.

In the latter part of the previous month, each line will be informed of each variety's daily average quantity. Such information, along with various other planning data, is calculated by computer at a central production control department. (For details on the use of the EDP system in determination of a monthly production plan, see Appendix 3.)

Once a production process receives its monthly schedule for averaged daily production, it must adapt its operations to the new information. For example, the load on a machine ordinarily is set at about 90% of its full capacity and each worker, operating as a multi-function worker, might handle as many as ten machines. When demand increases, temporary workers will be hired and each worker will handle less than ten machines, thereby enabling 100% utilization of machine capacity. It is, however, necessary to have machines that even a newly hired, unskilled laborer will be able to become fully proficient on within three days. On assembly lines, for example, if a single worker has handled the job with one minute cycle time, he will be able to handle the same job in 30 seconds cycle time by increasing the number of temporary workers. As a result, the production quantity can be doubled. This approach will also be applied to long-range plans for additional man and machine capacities.

Table 4.2   Smoothed quantity of each product to be produced each day.

Types	Monthly demands	Daily average output	Cycle time	Units per 9 min 36 sec
A	8,000 units	400 units	480 min x 2 shifts	4 units
B	6,000	300	1,000 units	3
C	4,000	200		2
D	2,000	100	= 0.96 min/unit	1
	20,000 units	1,000 units/day		10 units

Toyota can adapt to a relatively short-term increase in demand by introducing early attendance and overtime, which can fill up blank hours between the first shift (8 a.m.–5 p.m.) and the second shift (9 p.m.–6 a.m.), thereby enabling an increase in capacity of up to 37.5%. Moreover, various improvements within each process can cause slack that can be used during a period of increased demand.

On the other hand, if demand decreases, adaptation is considerably more difficult, but steps could be taken. In the parts manufacturing processes, the number of machines handled by each single worker will increase because temporary workers will be dismissed. On the assembly line, cycle time will increase due to the reduced demand quantity. How then should redundant manpower be utilized? Toyota believes that it is better to let extra workers take a rest than to produce unnecessary stock. The following are examples of activities that may be organized during a slack period:

• Transfer of workers to other lines.
• Decrease in overtime.
• Quality control circle meetings.
• Practicing set-up actions.

- Maintenance and repair of machines.
- Manufacturing improved tools and instruments.
- Repairing water leaks in the plant.
- Manufacturing parts which had been previously purchased from suppliers.

The most important goal is improving the process to meet demands with a minimum number of workers. However, although the concept of a minimum number of workers is important, Toyota does not consider it necessary to meet the demand with a minimum number of machines. Instead the company usually has too much machine capacity. Therefore, when demand increases, only temporary workers are needed so that effective production capacity can easily be expanded. As of 1982, Toyota has no temporary workers, although some of the companies which belong to the Toyota group employ some. Instead of hiring and dismissing temporary workers, Toyota is utilizing overtime and the transfer of workers to different lines to adapt to demand changes.

Daily production dispatching

Sequence schedule and Kanban as dispatching tools during the month

After the calculation of a monthly production plan, the next step in the smoothing of production is the preparation of each day's sequence schedule. This sequence schedule specifies the assembly order of various cars coming through the final assembly lines: for example, A – B – A – C and so on. The sequence is timed so that the cycle time expires and one car is completed before another car on the schedule is introduced to the line.

The sequence schedule is communicated only to the starting point on the final assembly line and not to any other process. This is the most characteristic aspect of Toyota's information system. In other systems, every production process must be informed of its particular production schedule from the central information office as is done in MRP (Material Requirement Planning). At Toyota, however, the processes which precede the final assembly line, such as machining, casting or pressing, are given only rough monthly estimates of the quantities that will be required of them. From such monthly predetermined figures, the supervisor of each process can arrange the necessary workforce for the month in question.

Therefore, when the final assembly line is assembling a car by using the parts stored beside the line, the withdrawal Kanban for these parts is detached. A worker then goes to withdraw the parts from the preceding processes which, in turn, will produce the parts in the exact quantities withdrawn. Therefore, any preceding process will not need its own particular sequence schedule in advance; in other words, Kanban functions so that production instructions go backward to the preceding processes step by step.

Sequencing method for smoothed production

How is the sequence schedule determined? In the case of Table 4.2—production in nine-minute and 36 second intervals for types A, B, C and D—the sequence would be: AAAA, BBB, CC and D. Or it could be more complicated: D, A, B, A, C, A, B, A, C, B, etc.

Attaining the optimal sequence schedule of mixed production is somewhat difficult, but Toyota is trying to determine such a schedule by applying a heuristic computer program. Perfection in sequencing would entail using each part while keeping the speed and quantity of withdrawal constant. Under the pulling system of Kanban, the variation of consumed quantity of each part at the final assembly line must be minimized. Therefore, the consumed quantity per hour or consumption speed of each part at the assembly line must be kept as constant as possible. The details of Toyota's sequencing method (called "The Goal-Chasing Method") are in Appendix 2.

How the sequence schedule will be transmitted
to the assembly lines

On the assembly line, workers need to know only what type of car they must assemble next. To receive such information, the final assembly line uses a printer or a display apparatus of a computer terminal. In accordance with the sequence schedule determined by the central computer, the information of what kind of car next to be assembled will be transmitted to the printer or display at the head of the assembly line in an on-line real-time manner.

Along with other information, the terminal provides a label for each car. By following these label specifications, the workers on the assembly line can put together a specific car. Although the label or the sequence schedule is used only on the assembly line, the overwhelming number of processes in the automobile factory such as casting, forging, and machining through parts assembly use Kanbans to control the production quantities.

However, the label or sequence schedule is in many cases applied not only to the *final* assembly line (body chassis), but also to the other parts assembly lines or suppliers which make big-size units such as transmissions or engines etc. This is based on the idea of the *sequenced withdrawal system*. The sequence schedule of many varieties of finished parts to be produced in the subassembly lines may sometimes be offered to these subassembly lines or to the supplier so that the final assembly line can withdraw these parts in sequence conforming to the sequence schedule of its various body assembly. All other part-producing processes and suppliers are given Kanban as a dispatching information or, the *later replenishment system.*

The assembly line of Toyota is now using a printer or display to know the sequence schedule in a real time manner. The printer is mainly used because some records of the sequence schedule must be kept at the assembly line. In case there is no need to keep the record, the display is utilized. Toyota once has used an interwriter for this purpose. At that time, in accordance with the sequence schedule printed by the central computer at the central office, the staff of this office wrote the specifications on the paper tape by hand of each individual car, such as the type, transmissions, tires, etc. Then, this tape would be electrically transmitted to the beginning points of the assembly lines, such as the body chassis, engine, transmission, etc.

A supplier of the Nissan group (Nissan is also adopting Kanban system by naming it as "Action Plate Method" or APM) is using a telex to receive orders from Nissan to the assembly line of this company. Another example is to use a magnetic tape, which is conveyed by the truck driver. As seen by these varieties of information media, the communication systems in the Toyota production system are still being developed.

Relations among ten-days order, daily order and sequence schedule

A dealer's order finds its place on the final assembly line's sequence schedule in the following manner:
1. The ten-days order arrives from a dealer to the Toyota Motor Sales Co., Ltd.
2. A daily order (or daily alteration) goes from a dealer to the Toyota Motor Sales Co.
3. Daily order from the Toyota Motor Sales Co. goes to the Toyota Motor Co., Ltd.
4. The daily sequence schedule is released to Toyota's plants and suppliers.
    Now we will examine these individual steps:
1. A month is divided into three ten-day periods, and the ten-day order will arrive about seven days before the start of one of these periods, as seen in Fig. 4.3.

    In the ten-days order, the dealer must anticipate his need for a stock of automobiles with standard specifications, i.e., those automobiles which are being sold in large quantities. The Toyota Motor Co., Ltd. then uses this ten-days order to revise the smoothed production plan for the daily schedule. In other words, although the monthly predetermined production plan is based on a monthly sales forecast, the ten-days order is based on the dealer's most up-to-date forecast of his monthly sales. Thus,

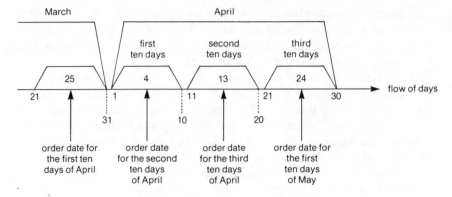

Fig. 4.3 Ten-day order from the dealer.

Toyota can revise its average quantities to prepare the daily sequence schedule.

2. Each day, the main office of Toyota Motor Sales Co. receives daily orders from all dealerships throughout the country. As seen in Fig. 4.4, such daily orders are received four days before the line-off of the car at the body-chassis assembly line of Toyota Motor Corp. The lead time is very short for this order. A dealer actually bases this order (often called the daily alteration) on actual customer demand, so all orders are up-to-the-minute.

The daily order differs from the ten-day order in that it is written according to the whims of the individual customer; that is, it specifies and

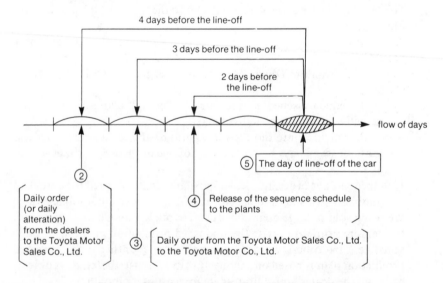

Fig. 4.4 Steps from dealer's order to the line-off of cars.

details certain options and preferences which the dealer could not possibly include in his stock. Toyota uses the daily order to revise its ten-days order and will base its production and deliveries on such a revised order.

3. The computer at Toyota Motor Sales Co. classifies the dealer's orders according to the variety of cars, body types, engines, grades, transmissions, and colors specified. This classified information will be supplied to Toyota Motor Co. three days before the line off of cars. The importance of this information cannot be overstated, for it informs the plant of actual necessary production quantities.

4. Just after Toyota Motor Co. receives the daily order from its sales associates it will prepare the sequence schedule for its mixed-model assembly line. The sequence schedule is released, at the earliest, just two days before the automobile rolls off the assembly line. Again note that a sequence schedule is prepared and released each day. Fig. 4.4 depicts this ordering process from step 2 to step 4.

As a result of this four-step ordering process, a car will roll off the assembly line only four days after the dealer has given his order for it to the Toyota Motor Sales Co.; the actual production lead time is limited to only one day. However, actual conveyance lead-time and shipping will differ from dealer to dealer because of varying geographies. These steps have not changed even after the Toyota Motor Sales Co. merged with the Toyota Motor Co. on July 1, 1982 because the two companies are merely sales and production divisions of the same entity (Toyota Motor Corp.).

The daily adaptation to the actual demand for various kinds of automobiles during a month is the ideal of Just-in-time production, which in turn requires the daily smoothed withdrawals of each part from the subassembly lines and suppliers.

Flexible machinery can support smoothed production

Since production smoothing requires production of many varieties of products on the same line each day, it necessarily gets more complicated and difficult to achieve as variety is promoted in the marketplace. Fortunately, Toyota has developed facilities to resolve the conflict between market variety and the ideal of production smoothing: i.e., multi-function machines in the line. The exclusive purpose machine is a powerful means of reducing mass-production costs, but it is not suitable for varied short-run productions. Thus, it is necessary to add minimum apparatus and tools to such exclusive machines, turning them into the type of multi-purpose machines required in Toyota plants.

Another mechanical means for supporting the smoothing of production is the FMS (Flexible Manufacturing System). Narrowly defined, the FMS is an automatic production system consisting of an automatic processing instrument, an automatic conveyance instrument, a material handling instrument, and a microcomputer system which controls these instruments. The FMS functions to automatically control alterations in specifications, processing time, and lot size, etc. by using the production schedule program memorized in the microcomputer.

Introduction of FMS enables a factory to respond to many variety and short-run production by means of hardware. Though Toyota has not made the same advances in this aspect as it has in other areas of production—the FMS has not yet been applied to the Toyota group as a whole—it has made great progress in its use of multi-purpose machines and Autonomation. However, such progress can sometimes be achieved by significant investment for the purpose of gaining proper facilities to support production. In such a case, the Toyota production system may create some problems for medium and small-sized manufacturers.

Comparison of Kanban system with MRP

From the viewpoint of adapting production to demand changes during a month, MRP and the Kanban system both aim to realize Just-in-time production. For the MRP technique, the concept of a *time bucket* is very important. A time bucket is a specifically-allotted period of time in which a certain quantity of units must be produced. In a sense, such a time bucket concept can be seen in the Kanban system in one day; yet whereas a day is of short duration, a typical MRP bucket will entail at least a week. Further, MRP necessitates the *time-phasing* concept which requires making up *inter-buckets* schedule that dispatches parts to a product by using lead time data.

The Kanban system does not essentially require the time-phasing concept, since it is based on smoothed production. However, the delivery cycle must often be considered in determining the number of Kanban based on the lead time of the production process (see Fig. 2.4 and Appendix 1). In cases where certain conditions—for example, job-order production on very short production runs—make smoothing production very difficult, MRP may be more appropriate. To smooth production, there must be a certain quantity of goods scheduled to be produced daily.

The Kanban system requires that an overall production schedule be circulated throughout the plant before actual production begins. Such an overall plan is called a *master schedule* in MRP. This master schedule is very important for MRP, because it is a target to be rigorously maintained. In the Kanban system, the overall plan does not strictly target production, but merely sets up a loose framework that prepares the plant-wide arrangement of materials and workers at each process.

Consequently, in the MRP system there must be a review at the end of every planned production interval—or bucket—that compares planned production with actual performance. If the review discovers a discrepancy between planned and actual performance, then remedial action must be taken. Since these are bucket sizes of at least a week, the master schedule must be revised weekly.

The Kanban system does not require any comparisons between planned and actual performance at the end of a production interval—i.e., one day—because such comparisons must necessarily evolve out of the daily actual production process and the daily dispatching of production by Kanban. If the daily production plan—the sequence schedule—requires revision, such revision will be based on the dealer's daily orders and will reflect daily market conditions.

Further, since the Kanbans actually flow backward through the plant from the final assembly line to the preceding processes, only the final assembly line needs to be notified of any changes in sequence for the entire plant's production to be modified accordingly. Hence, the Kanban system is characterized as a "pull system" while other means of dispatching production information, such as MRP, are characterized as "push systems," where the push comes from a central planning office.

However, the Kanban system can be compatible with MRP. After MRP made the master schedule, the Kanban system could be applied as a dispatching tool of production within each bucket. Yamaha Motor Co., Ltd. is employing this system as "Synchro MRP." (See Mori and Harmon [1980] and Hall [1981]).

5

How Toyota Shortened
Production Lead Time

The daily adaptation to the actual demand for various kinds of automobiles is the purpose of Just-in-time production. Just-in-time production will require the daily smoothed withdrawal of each part from the subassembly lines and suppliers in order to minimize the variation of withdrawals. As a result, in order to produce many varieties of parts each day simultaneously, the production lead time of each must be reduced remarkably. Earlier chapters also explained how Toyota's ideal of adapting production to daily demand changes has a necessary consequence at the end of each month: a 10% discrepancy between production quantities ordered by the predetermined monthly plan and the quantities dispatched daily by Kanban and the sequence schedule. In order to prevent this discrepancy from causing problems such as excessive inventory or work force, Toyota must be ready to start production immediately after it receives a dealer's order. Suppliers especially must command rapid means of production, for they stand to suffer from a 10% surfeit in inventory if they do not wait until Toyota dispatches its order by Kanban; therefore, when an order arrives, they must be prepared to produce immediately. Of course, production on such short notice requires a remarkable shortening of lead time so that an engine cast of 8 a.m., for example, will be ready for installation in a finished car rolling off the assembly line at 5 p.m.

The following advantages can be attributed to this shortening of the production lead time:

- Toyota can achieve job-order oriented production that requires only a short period to deliver a particular car to the customer.

- The company can adapt very quickly to changes in demand in the middle of the month, so the inventory of finished products maintained by Toyota's sales division can be minimized.
- Work-in-progress inventory can be significantly decreased by minimizing unbalanced production timing among the various processes and also by reducing the lot size.
- When a model change is introduced, the amount of "dead" stock on hand is minimal.

The production lead time of any product—assuming production takes place in a multi-process factory and consists of three components: processing time for supply lot for each process, waiting time between processes, and conveyance time between processes. How Toyota minimizes the time required by each of these components is explained in Fig. 5.1.

Single-unit production and conveyance: Concept of invisible conveyor systems

As a first step in reducing lead time, Toyota has refined the moving assembly concept on the conveyor system which characterizes the Ford System. This conveyor system, in its standard form, operates in accordance with a certain time interval in which one unit of a finished automobile will roll off at the terminal point of the final assembly line. The operation time plus conveyance time of every process in this line must be equalized. Therefore, the assembly line must be divided to make the operation time of each work place the same so the operations of every work place can start and end at precisely the same time. The conveyance times between the work places in the line must be equalized. In other words, conveyance time between work places must start and end at the same time. In the Ford System, the belt conveyor is used to equalize the conveyance times between processes.

The basic idea of the Toyota production system is based on a similar conveyor system concept. According to the conveyor system, a unit of a finished automobile can be produced in every cycle time, and simultaneously each unit of the output of any process in this line will be sent on to the next process. The cycle time or tact time is the total time which consists of the equalized operation time and conveyance time. In Toyota, such a production flow is called *single-unit production and conveyance* ("Ikko Nagare").

Although this single-unit flow of production concept is now quite prevalent in most companies' assembly line systems, processes making parts to be supplied to the assembly line are usually based on lot production. Moreover, their lot size is still fairly large.

Toyota, however, has extended the idea of single-unit flow to processes such as machining, welding, pressing, etc. Even if a process doesn't involve single-unit production, the operation is still limited to small lot production. In

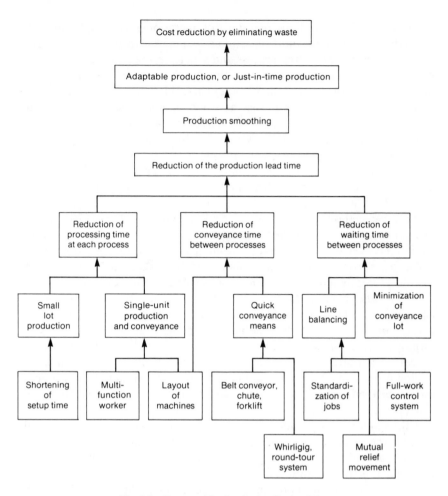

Fig. 5.1 Framework of reducing the lead time.

this manner, Toyota's plants are realizing firm-wide integrated single-unit flows of production, which all connect to the assembly line. In this sense the Toyota production system is an extension of the idea behind the Ford System.

Multi-function workers

To achieve this goal of single-unit production, Toyota had prepared new work place layouts that allowed for multi-process holding by multi-function workers. The machine layout was changed so that each worker could handle several different types of machines at the same time.

In the gear manufacturing process, for example, each worker attends to 16 machines. Unlike many typical production situations where a worker would interface with only one type of machine, the Toyota set-up involves 16 machines which perform different types of operations: grinding, cutting, etc. The laborer as a multi-function worker first picks up one unit of a gear brought from the preceding process and sets it on the first machine. At the same time, he detaches another gear already processed by this machine and puts it on a chute to roll in front of the next machine. Then, while he is walking to the second machine, he pushes a switch between the first and second machines to start the first machine. He performs a similar operation on the second machine, and then he moves to the third machine pushing a button again to start the second machine and so on, until he has worked on all 16 machines and finally returns to his initial process. This is done in exactly the cycle time necessary, perhaps five minutes, so one unit of a finished gear will be completed in five minutes.

With this method, only one item of stock is involved in the work in process in each machine, and the goal of single-unit production and conveyance is realized between different types of machines. The inventory level is minimized and also the production lead time is shortened. Such shortened lead time helps Toyota promptly adapt to demand changes or customer orders.

On the other hand, in the typical machining plant, a turner handles only a lathe and a welder handles only the welding. The layout of machinery often consists of 50 or 100 stands of lathes that are laid out as a block. After the turning process is finished, the output must be sent as a large lot to the drilling process. Then after drilling operations, the output must be brought to the milling process in a large lot quantity, and so on. Even though each process uses a belt conveyor, the output doesn't flow as single-unit production conveyance.

Although large-lot production can minimize the average unit cost, it will increase the inventory level of each department and also increase the total production lead time. This makes prompt adaptations to customer orders in the middle of the month infeasible.

Under the requirements of smoothed production, all processes in Toyota must ideally produce and convey only one piece corresponding to each single unit that is coming off the final assembly line. In addition, each process must ideally have only one piece in stock both between machines and between processes. In short, all workshops must ideally avoid all lot production and lot conveyance. Although Toyota has succeeded in reducing lot size, some processes still remain which are operated with lot production and lot conveyance. Fig. 5.2 shows an overall outline of Toyota's production processes.

Outline of Toyota's plants

The processes can be roughly classified into five categories:
1. *Casting and pressing.* Includes the casting process, which is mainly the foundry for engines, the sintering process for parts, the forging process

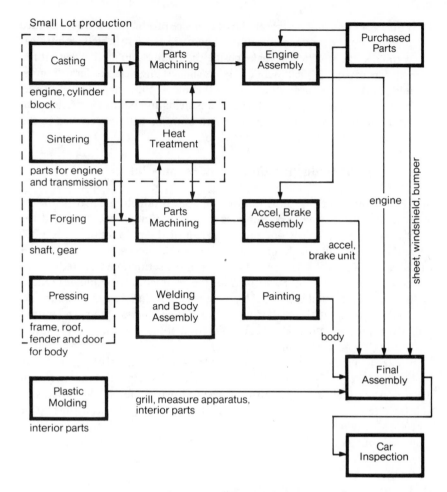

Small Lot production

Fig. 5.2 Toyota's production processes.

for shafts and gears, and the pressing process for bodies. These processes involve lot production because they have large-scale automated plants. Some of them, however, have fairly small lot sizes (mostly for two shifts' use) because of speedy setup actions.

2. *Parts machining.* Engaged mainly in small-lot production or single-unit production and conveyance.

3. *Machine (parts) assembling.* Workshops to assemble engines or accelerators and brake units. These processes are engaged in single-unit production and conveyance.

4. *Body-making.* Workshops that weld pressed parts, assemble them for a car body, grind, sand, and finally paint these parts. One-piece production/conveyance is the method used in these processes.

71

5. *Final assembly line.*   Operated by one-piece production and conveyance directed by the sequence schedule. There are parts to which withdrawal Kanbans are attached in racks beside the final assembly line so that the workers can easily pick them up. Parts such as engines, accelerator units, and brake units are attached to the auto body here, and various measurement apparatuses, sheets, windshields and bumpers, etc., are also attached here. After inspection, the automobile will be conveyed to the holding yard of Toyota's sales division.

Shortening the production time for the supply lot

In order to shorten the production time in a lot production department, the setup time must be reduced. Suppose the setup time is one hour and the processing time per unit is one minute. Then, if the production lot is 3,000 units, the total production hours = setup time + total processing time = 1 hour + 1 minute × 3,000 units = 51 hours. However, if the setup time were reduced to six minutes, or, to $1/10$ of the initial time, the production lot could be reduced to 300 units, or $1/10$ of the initial lot. The reason is that if production by 300 unit lots is repeated 10 times, the total number of production hours and output will be the same as before. Or, total production hours = (6 minutes + [1 minute × 300 units]) × 10 = 51 hours.

In general, if the setup time were reduced to $1/n$ of its initial time, the lot size could be reduced to $1/n$ of its initial size without changing the loading rate of the process in question. This also has the following effects: The processing time of one time lot will be reduced by $1/n$, enabling the lead time to be shortened so that the company can adapt to customers' orders very quickly. Also, the number of Kanban will be reduced by $1/n$, and therefore the inventory level itself will be markedly reduced.

Reduction of waiting time

The waiting time is the time spent at each process stage waiting for products completed in the preceding process; it excludes the conveyance time. Of the two kinds of waiting time, one is caused by unbalanced production time between processes, and the other by the whole lot size in the preceding process.

To shorten the first type of waiting time, line balancing must be achieved: production in each process must be the same in quantity as well as timing. Although the cycle or tact time must be the same in all processes on the assembly lines, there will be some variance in the actual operation time among processes depending on minor differences in workers' skills and capabilities. To minimize these differences, standardization of actions or operating routines is very important, and the supervisor or foreman must train workers to master the standard routines (Chapter 7).

At the same time, what Toyota calls *mutual relief movement* should be applied to make up for delays in some processes. At Toyota, the point connecting two workers or two processes is designed so that the workers will be able to help each other. This point is similar to the baton touch zone in relay races of track and field events. For example, when one part is completed by a team of workers in a certain line, the part must be handed on like a baton to the next worker. If the person in the subsequent process is delayed, the preceding worker should set up and take off the work on the subsequent machine. When the subsequent worker returns to his initial position, the preceding worker should hand the work to him immediately and go back to the preceding process. This same system would apply in reverse if the preceding worker were delayed. Human friendships may be cultivated through such teamwork under the mutual relief system.

The most serious problem with regard to line balancing is the existence of capacity differences among the machines used in each process. The full-work control system described in Chapter 2 is used to cope with such capacity differences.

To shorten the second type of waiting time, the conveyance lot must be minimized. This approach allows production with a large lot size for certain kinds of products, but it also requires that the product be conveyed to the subsequent process in minimal units. In other words, even if the product lot is made up of 600 units, if one unit is completed, that unit should be conveyed immediately to the next process. The effect of this approach is illustrated by the following example. Suppose there are three processes and each takes one minute to produce one unit. One unit of a product will require three minutes to go through the three processes. If 600 units must be produced, one process requires 600 minutes, or 10 hours, and all three processes will take 30 hours. However, if each single unit is conveyed to the subsequent process as soon as it has been processed by the preceding process, processes 2 and 3 can operate at the same time as process 1. Process 2 will have to wait while process 1 is processing the first unit, but only for one minute. Process 3 will also have to wait while process 2 is processing its first unit, but again only one minute. This relationship is depicted in Fig. 5.3.

Therefore, to produce 600 units through these three processes, the total time required is 600 minutes + one minute + one minute = 602 minutes. However, if processes 1 and 2 each had one unit of inventory of the finished output of its process on hand at the beginning of the month, the above waiting time of one minute each would disappear. Then it would be necessary to spend only 600 minutes to produce 600 units in three processes.

In a case in which lot production and lot conveyance are applied to n processes, the total processing time = n T, where T = processing time in each process. But if single-unit conveyance is applied to n processes with each preceding process having a single unit of inventory of finished output of its process, the total processing time will be only T; that is, it will be shortened by $1/n$.

If the conveyance lot is only a single unit, however, the frequency of delivery must be increased, and the problem of minimizing conveyance time arises.

Improvement of the conveyance operation

Improvement of the conveyance operation can be achieved in two steps: layout of machines and adoption of quick conveyance means. The layout of the different kinds of machines should be in accordance with the flow of processes of the products instead of by type of machine. If there are many kinds of products, common or similar processes for these various products should be grouped together. Next, quick means of conveyance such as the belt conveyor or chute or forklift should be used to connect the process. The use of the whirligig beetle system and the round-tour mixed-loading system by the subcontractor will help promote the continuous flow of products among processes. Finally, however, Toyota's ideal of small-lot production rests upon a crucial prerequisite: the shortening of setup time.

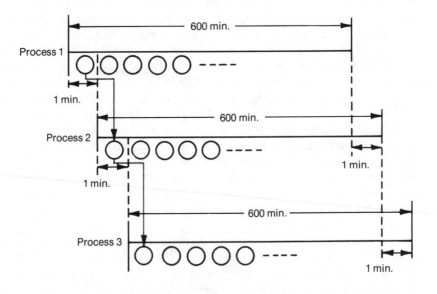

Fig. 5.3 Relationship between processes and processing times.

74

6
Reduction of Setup Time— Concepts and Techniques

In 1970, Toyota succeeded in shortening the setup time of an 800-ton punch press for the hood and fender to three minutes. This is called a *single setup,* meaning that the setup time has a single-digit number of minutes (within nine minutes, 59 seconds). At present the setup time has, in many cases, been reduced to less than a minute, or *one-touch setup.* American and European companies often spend from two to several hours, or at worst, an entire day on a setup action.

The need for Toyota to develop such an incredibly short setup time was recognized by Taiichi Ohno, former vice president of the company, who realized that by shortening setup time Toyota could minimize lot size and therefore reduce the stock of finished and intermediate products.

Through small-lot production, the production lead time of various kinds of products can be shortened, and the company can adapt to customer orders and demand changes very promptly. Even if the types of cars and delivery dates are changed in the middle of the month, Toyota can adapt quickly. From this viewpoint, too, the inventory of finished and intermediate products can be reduced.

The ratio of machinery utilization to its full capacity will be increased because of the reduced setup time. It should be noted, however, that the machinery utilization rate is allowed to be low since overproduction is considered to lead to waste, a worse situation than a low utilization rate. The minimization of stocks, job-order oriented production, and prompt adaptability to demand changes are the most important advantages of a single setup.

The single setup is an innovative concept invented by the Japanese in the field of industrial engineering. Its idea was developed by Shigeo Shingo, a consultant at Toyota, and one day it will be common knowledge in IE theory and practices of the world. The single setup should not be considered a technique. It is a concept that requires a change in attitude by all the people in a factory. In Japanese companies, the shortening of setup time is promoted not by the IE staff, but through the activities of small groups of direct laborers called QC circles or ZD (Zero Defect) groups. Achievement of improved setup time and the attendant morale boost enable workers to take on similar challenges in other areas of the factory; this is an important side benefit of setup time shortening.

Setup concepts

In order to shorten the setup time, four major concepts must first be recognized. Six techniques for applying these concepts are described herein. Most of these techniques were devised for applying concepts No. 2 and No. 3. To examine each concept and technique, the setup actions for the punch press operation will be used as a main example, but the same approach can be applied to all kinds of machines.

Concept 1: Separate the internal setup from the external setup. Internal setup refers to those setup actions that inevitably require that the machine be stopped. External setup refers to actions that can be taken while the machine is operating. In the case of a punch press, these actions can be taken before or after changing the die.

These two kinds of actions must be rigorously separated. That is, once the machine is stopped, the worker should never depart from it to handle any part of the external setup.

In the external setup, the dies, tools, and materials must be perfectly prepared beside the machine, and any needed repairs to the dies should have been made in advance. In the internal setup, only the removal and setting of dies must be done.

Concept 2: Convert as much as possible of the internal setup to the external setup. This is the most important concept regarding the single setup. Examples include:

- The die heights of a punch press or a molding machine can be standardized by using the liner (spacer) so that stroke adjustment will be unnecessary (Fig. 6.1).
- The die-casting machine can be preheated using the waste heat of the furnace that belongs to this machine. This means the trial shot to warm up the metal mold in the die casting machine can be eliminated.

Concept 3: Eliminate the adjustment process. The process of adjustment in

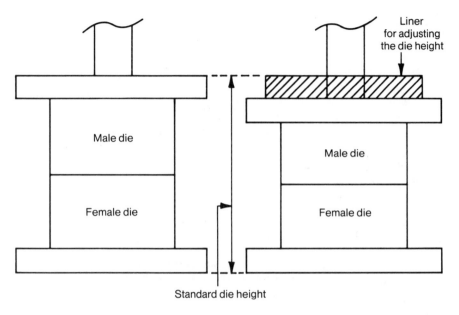

Liner
for adjusting
the die height

Male die

Female die

Standard die height

Male die

Female die

Fig. 6.1   Using a liner to standardize die height.

the setup actions usually takes about 50 to 70% of the total internal setup time. Reducing this adjustment time is very important to shortening the total setup time.

Adjustment is usually considered to be essential and to require highly developed skills, but these are mistaken notions. Setting operations such as moving the limit switch from the 100 mm position to the 150 mm position might be necessary. But once the limit switch has been moved to a certain position, further repetitive revision of the setting positions should be eliminated. Setting is a concept that should be considered independently of adjustment. Examples include:

- The maker of a punch press may produce a machine that is adjustable to various buyers' die-height requirements. But each particular company (each user) could standardize its die height at a certain size so that the stroking adjustment could be omitted (Fig. 6.1).
- Suppose the molding machine requires a different stroke of the knockout depending on the die used, so the position of the limit switch needs changing to adjust the stroke. In order to find the right position, adjustment is always necessary. In such a situation, instead of only the one limit switch, five limit switches can be installed at the five required positions. Furthermore, in the new device, electric current can be made to flow only to the necessary limit switch at a certain point in time with one-touch handling. As a result, the necessity to adjust the position is completely eliminated (Fig. 6.2).

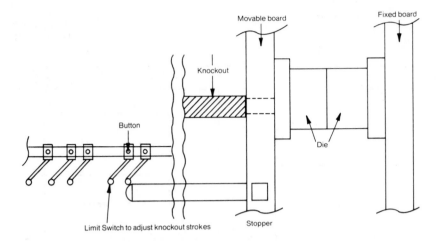

Fig. 6.2 Installing limit switches at all required positions speeds knockout stroke adjustment.

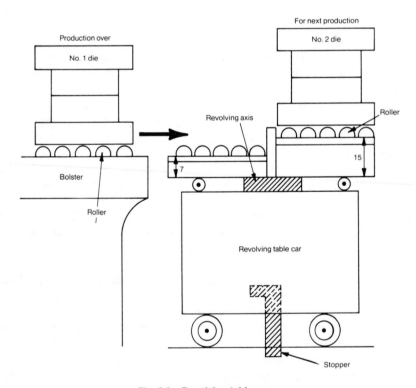

Fig. 6.3 Revolving table car.

- To exchange the dies on the stamping machine, a revolving table car can be prepared. The idea behind this revolving table car is the same as the principle of revolver (gun). The procedures follow (Fig. 6.3):
  a. Detach the No. 1 die from the die holder of the press (production by this die is finished).
  b. Push the table car to approach the press and then fix the stopper.
  c. Put the No. 1 die on the table car.
  d. Revolve only the upper part of the table car to set the No. 2 die onto the bolster.
  e. Detach the table car stopper and pull the table car far from the press and at the same time set the No. 2 die on the press. Fig. 6.4 is a view of the revolving table.

It should again be emphasized that although the machine might be capable of changing positions continuously, only a few finite, stepwise positions are needed. The examples of the five discrete limit switches (Fig. 6.2) and the revolving table car (Fig. 6.3 and 6.4) are based on this idea. The number of setting positions needed in the actual operations is quite limited. Such a system can be described as the *finite-settings built-in system*. This system will enable one-touch setup.

Concept 4: Abolish the setup step itself. To completely do away with the setup, two approaches can be taken: one, use uniform product design and use

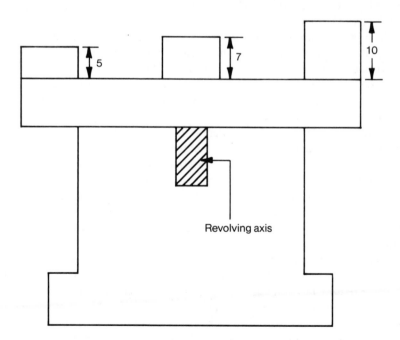

Fig. 6.4   Revolving table.

the same part for various products; two, produce the various parts at the same time. The latter can be achieved by two methods. The first method is the set system. For example, on the single die of the punch press, two different shapes of parts A and B were carved as a set. These two parts are separated after continuously punching both shapes at the same time.

The second method is to press the multiple parts in parallel using less expensive multiple machines. For example, one department uses a normal jack for a pressing function instead of the punch press. In this department, each worker handles this small jack while he is engaged in other jobs as a multi-functional worker. This jack is attached to a small motor for use and can perform the same function as a heavy punch press. If several jacks of this kind are available, they could be used in parallel for producing various types of parts.

Concept application

The following are six techniques for applying the four concepts explained before.

Technique 1: Standardize the external setup actions. The operations for preparing the dies, tools, and materials should be made into routines and standardized. Such standardized operations should be written on paper and pasted on the wall for workers to see. Then the workers should train themselves to master the routines.

Technique 2: Standardize only the necessary portions of the machine. If the size and shape of all the dies is completely standardized, the setup time will be shortened tremendously. This, however, would cost a great deal. Therefore, only the portion of the function necessary for setups is standardized. The liner explained under Concept 2 (Fig. 6.1) for equalizing the die height is one example of this technique.

If the height of the die-holders were standardized, the exchange of fastening tools and adjustments could be eliminated (Fig. 6.5).

Technique 3: Use a quick fastener. Usually, a bolt is the most popular fastening tool. But because a bolt fastens at the final turning of the nut and can loosen at the first turn, a convenient fastening tool that would allow only a single turning of the nut should be devised. Some examples are the use of the pear-shaped hole, the U-shaped washer, and the chipped nut and bolt as shown in Fig. 6.6.

A coil-winding operation was carried out by a certain company. The wound coil used to be pulled out after the nut and washer were removed. To shorten the time required to pull out a coil, the outside diameter of the nut was set at a size smaller than the inside diameter of the coil and a U-shaped washer was used. The coil could then be detached very quickly by loosening the nut by only one turn, pulling out the U-shaped washer, and then pulling out the coil without removing the nut.

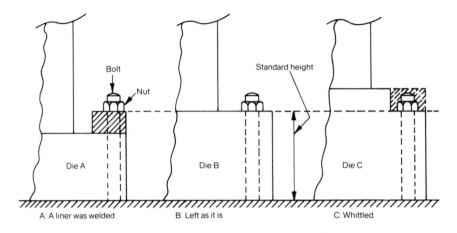

Fig. 6.5 Standardizing die-holder height
reduces the need to exchange fastening tools.

There were 12 bolts on the surrounding edge of the furnace. But the bolt hole of the lid was altered to a pear shape, and the U-shaped washer was used. As a result, when the nut is loosened by only one turn, the U-shaped washer should be pulled out and the lid must be turned to the left so that the lid can open through the bigger part of the pear-shaped holes without detaching the nuts from the bolts.

Three portions of the outside of the bolt must be chipped off, and corresponding to these portions, the screw of the nut inside also must be chipped off in three places. Then, when the nut is pushed down by matching the screw portions of the nut to the chipped portions of the bolt, the nut can fasten the machine in only one turn.

A cassette system that utilizes the setting-in idea will enable setup within a minute, or one-touch setup. An example is shown in Fig. 6.7. The sliding guide block shown in the figure was also devised and the size of the die holder was standardized. Fig. 6.7 also illustrates a device for die installation using a mountain-shaped guide.

Technique 4: Use a supplementary tool. It takes a lot of time to attach a die or a bite directly to the punch press or the chuck of a lathe. Therefore, the die or bites should be attached to the supplementary tool in the external setup phase, and then in the internal setup phase this tool can be set in the machine at one touch. For this method, the supplementary tools must be standardized. The revolving table car in Fig. 6.3 is another example of this technique.

Technique 5: Use parallel operations. The large punch press or the large molding machine will have many attachment positions on its left and right sides as well as on its front and back sides. The setup actions for such a machine will take one worker a long time. However, if parallel operations by

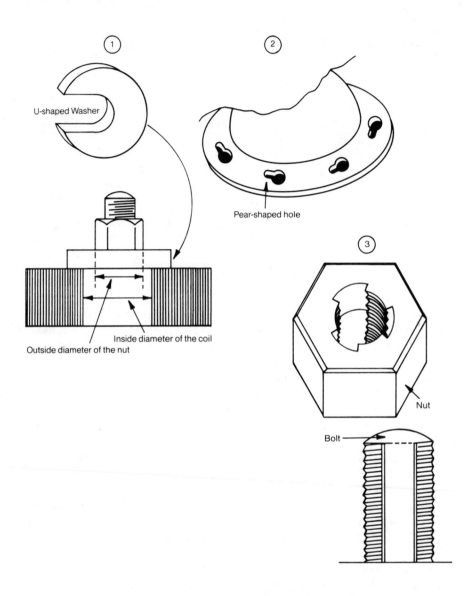

Fig. 6.6 Examples of quick fasteners (Technique 3):
1) U-shaped washer; 2) Pear-shaped bolt hole;
3) Nut and bolt with corresponding portions chipped off.

two persons were applied to such a machine, wasteful movements could be eliminated and the setup time reduced. Even though the total number of labor hours for the setup was not changed, the effective operating hours of the machine could be increased. If a setup time of one hour were reduced to three minutes, the second worker would be needed for this process for only three minutes. Therefore, specialists in setup actions are trained on the punch press, and they cooperate with the machine operators.

Technique 6: Use a mechanical setup system. To attach the die, oil pressure or air pressure could be used for fastening at several positions at a time by the one-touch method. Also, the die heights of a punch press could be adjusted by an electrically operated mechanism. However, although such mechanisms are very convenient, an expensive investment in them would be "putting the cart before the horse."

Although Toyota has reduced the setup time to less than ten minutes, that shortened time is the internal setup time. The external setup still requires half an hour or one hour even at Toyota. Without this time span, the die for the next lot cannot be changed. As a result, the lot size or the number of setups per day at Toyota is essentially constrained by the time span of external setup.

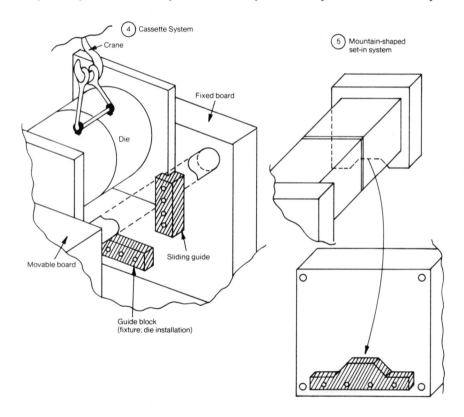

Fig. 6.7 **Setting-in systems for quick fastening (Technique 3):**
4) Cassette system with sliding guide block;
5) Die installation device with mountain-shaped guide.

In conclusion, for American and European companies, as well as companies of any other country, application of the Toyota production system might pose some difficulties, such as labor union or geographical problems. However, the approaches to reducing the setup time described here can definitely be applied in any company and will reduce in-process inventory and also shorten the production lead time, although not as greatly as they would if accompanied by the Kanban system. Reducing the setup times of many machines would be one of the easiest ways to introduce the Toyota production system.

7

Standard Operations
Can Attain Balanced Production
with Minimum Labor

The ultimate purpose of the Toyota production system is to reduce costs relating to production. To do so, Toyota tries to eliminate production inefficiencies such as unnecessary inventories and workers.

Standard operations is aimed at production using a minimum number of workers. The first goal of standard operations is achieving high productivity through strenuous work. "Strenuous work" at Toyota, however, does not mean forcing the workers to work very hard; instead, it means working efficiently without any wasteful motions. A standardized order of the various operations to be performed by each worker, called the *standard operations routine,* is important in facilitating this first goal.

The second goal of Toyota's standard operations is to achieve line balancing among all processes in terms of the timing of production. In this case, the cycle time concept should be built into standard operations.

The third and final goal is that only the minimum quantity of work-in-process will qualify as *standard quantity of work-in-process,* or the minimum number of units necessary for the standard operations to be performed by the workers. This standard quantity contributes towards eliminating excessive in-process inventories.

To attain the three goals, standard operations consists of the cycle time, standard operations routine, and standard quantity of work-in-process (Fig. 7.1).

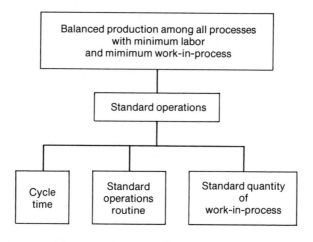

Fig. 7.1 Elements of standard operations.

In furthering these goals, the production of items is set to eliminate both the occurrence of accidents and the production of defects. As a result, the routine and positions to check the safety and quality of products are also standardized. Thus, safety precautions and product quality are subgoals of Toyota's standard operations.

Determining the components of standard operations

The components of standard operations are determined mainly by the foreman (supervisor). The foreman determines the labor hours required to produce one unit at each machine and also the order of various operations to be performed by each worker. Generally in other companies such standard operations are determined by the IE staff.

Toyota's method might seem unscientific; however, the foreman has an intimate knowledge of past performances of workers. In addition, the typical foreman also uses IE techniques, such as time and motion studies; therefore, such factors as the determined motion speed can be regarded as appropriate even by an impartial observer. Also, in order to teach the worker to understand and follow the standards completely, the foreman himself must master and recognize the standards perfectly. Standard operations are determined by the following:
1. Determine the cycle time.
2. Determine the completion time per unit.
3. Determine the standard operations routine.
4. Determine the standard quantity of work-in-process.
5. Prepare the standard operations sheet.

Determining the cycle time

The cycle time or tact is the time span in which one unit of a product must be produced. This cycle time is determined by the required daily quantity of output and the effective daily operating time in the following manner:

$$\text{Cycle Time} = \frac{\text{Effective Daily Operating Time}}{\text{Required Daily Quantity of Output}}$$

The effective daily operating time should not be reduced for any allowances due to machine breakdowns, idle time awaiting materials, rework, or for fatigue and rest time. Also, the necessary quantity of output should not be increased by allowing for defective output. By viewing the time spent in producing defective items as unnecessary, the consumption of such time is visible when it does occur in a process, and makes it possible to take immediate action to improve the process. The cycle time can be rather long compared to other companies which make allowances for fatigue time and defective items when determining the cycle time. Moreover, since it is necessary to determine both the number of different operations and the number of workers needed to produce a single unit of output within the cycle time, the number of workers in any department at Toyota's factory can be decreased if the cycle time is relatively longer.

Sometimes, the cycle time is determined erroneously by using the current machine-capacity and labor-capacity. Although this gives a probable time span for producing one unit of output, it does not give the necessary time-span needed for repositioning the workers. To be sure that the cycle time is determined properly, the effective daily operating time and the required daily output must be used.

Determining the completion time per unit

The completion time per unit of output has to be determined at each process and for each part. This time unit is always written on the *part production capacity sheet* which is filled out for each part (Fig. 7.2).

The *manual operation time* and the *machine automatic processing time* are both measured by a stopwatch. The manual operation time should not include the walking time at the process. The speed and the level of skill required for each manual operation are determined by the foreman.

The *completion time per unit* in the basic time column is the time required for a single unit to be processed. If two units are processed simultaneously, or one unit in every few units is inspected for quality control, the completion time per unit will be written on the reference column.

In the tool exchange column, the *exchange units* specify the number of units to be produced before changing the bite or tool. The *exchange time* refers to the setup time.

Part production capacity sheet

Part production capacity sheet	Item no.	Item name	Necessary quantity per day	Worker's name

Order of processes	Description of operations	Machine no.	Basic time — Manual operation time (min.)	(sec.)	Machine processing time (min.)	(sec.)	Completion time per unit (min.)	(sec.)	Tool's exchange — Exchange units	Exchange time	Production capacity (960 min)	References — manual operation / machine processing
1	center drill	CD-300		07	1	20	1	27	80	1'00"	655 units	
2	chamfer	KA-350		09	1	35	1	44	20	30"	549	
3	ream	KB-400		09	1	25	1	34	50	30"	606	
									20	30"		
4	ream	KC-450		10	1	18	1	28	40	30"	643	
									20	30"		
2-1	mill	MS-100		(20)	(2	10)	(2	20)	1,000	7'00"	820	$10''$ — $10''$ — $2'10''$
2-2	mill	MS-101		(15)	(2	10)	(2	15)	1,000	7'00"		$5''$ — $10''$ — $2'10''$
	(two stands of machines)			18								$\left[\dfrac{\text{manual operation}}{\text{time per unit}}\right] = \dfrac{20''+15''}{2} = 17.5'' \rightarrow 18''$
3	bore	BA-235		(08)		(50)		(58)	500	5'00"	1,947	
	(two units processing at a time)			04				29				$\left[\dfrac{\text{manual operation}}{\text{time per unit}}\right] = \dfrac{8''}{2} = 4''$
	gauge (1/5)			(18)								
4	(one unit inspection in every five units)			09								$\left[\dfrac{\text{manual operation}}{\text{time per unit}}\right] = \dfrac{18''}{2} = 9''$
	total											

Fig. 7.2 Part production capacity sheet.

88

The production capacity in the extreme right-hand column is computed by the following formula:

$$N = \frac{T}{C+m}, \quad OR \quad \frac{T-mN}{C}, \quad \text{Where } mN = \text{summation of total setup time}$$

Formula Notations:
N = Production capacity in terms of units of output
C = Completion time per unit
m = Setup time per unit
T = Total operation time

Determining the standard operations routine

After determining the cycle time and the manual operation time per unit for each operation, the number of different operations that each worker should be assigned must be calculated. In other words, the standard operations routine of each individual worker must be determined.

The *standard operations routine* is the order of actions that each worker must perform within a given cycle time. This routine serves two purposes. First, it provides the worker with the order or routine to pick up work, put it on the machine, and detach it after processing. Second, it gives the sequence of operations that the multi-functioned worker must perform at various machines within a cycle time.

At this point, it is important to differentiate between the "order of process" and the operations routine because these two orders are not identical in many cases. If the operations routine is simple, it can be determined directly from the part production capacity sheet (Fig. 7.2). In this case, the order of processes is actually identical with the operations routine. If the routine is complicated, however, it may not be easy to determine whether the automatic processing time of a certain machine will be finished before the worker handles the same machine in the next cycle of the tact time. As a result, the standard operations routine sheet is used to determine the exact operations routine (Fig. 7.3).

The procedure to prepare the standard operations routine sheet follows:
1. The cycle time is drawn with a red line on the operations time dimension of the sheet.
2. The approximate range of processes which one worker can handle should be predetermined. The total operations time, which is approximately equal to the cycle time in red, should be computed using the part production capacity sheet (Fig. 7.2). Some slack time for walking between machines must be allowed. The walking time should be measured using a stopwatch and recorded on some memo.
3. The manual operation and machine processing times for the first machine

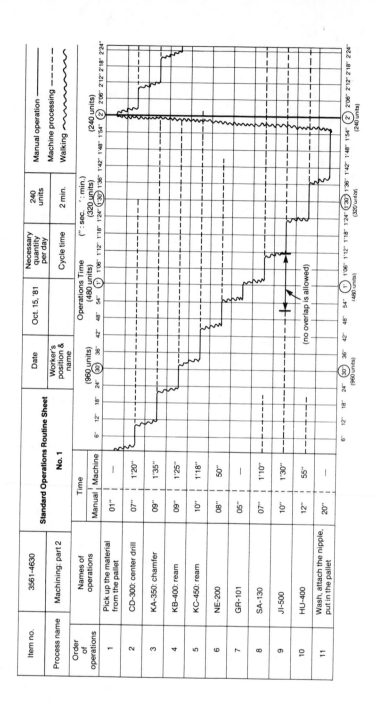

Fig. 7.3   Standard operations routine sheet.

90

are first drawn on this sheet by copying the data from the part production capacity sheet.

4. Next, the second operation of this worker must be determined. It should be remembered that the order of processes is not necessarily identical to the operations routine. Also, the walking distance between machines, the point at which product quality is checked, and specific safety precautions must be taken into account at this stage. If some walking time is necessary, its time must be drawn on the sheet by a wavy line from the ending point of the preceding manual operation time to the beginning point of the subsequent manual operation time.

5. Steps 3 and 4 are repeated until the whole operations routine can be determined. When performing these steps, if the dotted line of machine processing time reaches the unbroken line of the next manual operation, the operations sequence is not feasible and some other sequence must be chosen.

6. Since the operations routine was plotted to cover all of the estimated number of processes at step 2, the routine must be completed at the initial operation of the next cycle. If walking time is necessary for this winding up, the wave line must be drawn.

7. If the final wind-up point meets the red line of cycle time, the operations routine is an appropriate mix. If the final operation ends before the cycle time line, consider whether more operations can be added. If the final operation overflows the cycle time line, ways to shorten the overflow must be considered. This could be achieved by improving various operations of this worker.

8. Finally, the foreman should actually try to perform the final standard operations routine. If the foreman can comfortably finish it within the cycle time, the routine can then be taught to the workers.

The allocations of various operations among workers must be such that each worker can finish all of his assigned operations within the specified cycle time. Also, the layout of processes must be such that each worker has the same cycle so that production line balancing among various processes can be realized. A simplified scheme of this allocation of operations and layout of processes is shown in Fig. 7.4

If there is too much waiting time at the end of the operations routine in Fig. 7.3, a double cycle time could be set in order to have simultaneous operations by two or three workers subject to the same operations routine. This helps to eliminate slack in the cycle time (Fig. 7.5). Otherwise, by an improvement in the operations of the process in question, one more operation could be inserted into the cycle time.

Yo-i-don System

Yo-i-don means "ready, set, go." The Yo-i-don system is a method for balancing the production timing (synchronization) among various processes

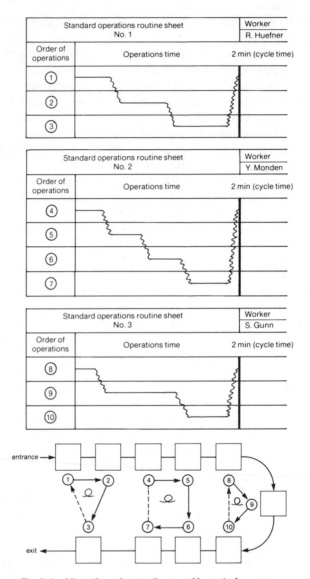

Fig. 7.4 Allocation of operations and layout of processes.

where there is no conveyor belt. It can also be used as a method of measuring the production capacity of each process.

Let's examine in detail the Yo-i-don system using Andon. In a body welding plant of Daihatsu Motor Company (a partner of Toyota), there are six *under-body* processes (U_1, U_2, ... U_6), six *side-body* processes (S_1, S_2, ... S_6), and four *main-body* processes (M_1, M_2, ... M_4), as depicted in Fig. 7.6. By companies, the body welding plant is also called a sheet-metal factory, a body assembly line, or simply a body line.

The body welding plant must produce one unit of its product in 3 min., 35 sec. (the cycle time of this factory). By dividing this cycle time into three equal portions accumulatively as $1/3$, $2/3$, and $3/3$ when time elapses, the standard time per unit of a product for completing each process is established. The table in Fig. 7.7 is called *Andon;* it is hung high from the factory ceiling for all workers to see.

The workers of the under-body processes must complete their operations from U_1 to U_6 within 3 min., 35 sec., and the laborers of the side-body processes also must finish their jobs from S_1 to S_6 within this time period. And, the workers in the main-body processes must complete their processes from M_1 through M_4 within the cycle time. At the starting point of a cycle, each worker sets the work to the first process he must handle. If each worker finishes his operations at all his responsible processes and transfers the finished work to the next process within the cycle time, then this body welding plant as a whole can produce one unit of finished product per 3 min., 35 sec.

The worker in each process will push his button when his job is finished, and after 3 min., 35 sec. have passed, the red lamp on Andon will only go on

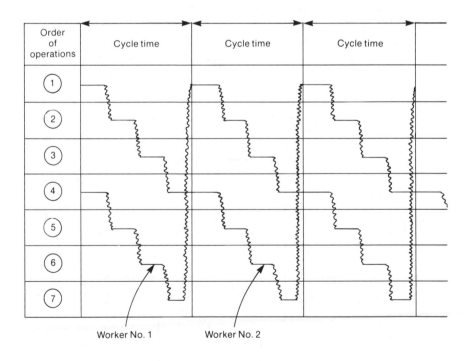

Fig. 7.5 Double cycle time for use by two workers.

automatically at those processes where the job is not yet completed. Since the red lamp indicates a delay in processing, the whole line stops operation while a red lamp is on.

For example, the red lamp might be turned on at processes U_4, S_5, and M_2. When this happens, the supervisor or nearby workers help the workers at these processes finish up their jobs. In most cases, all red lamps will go out within 10 sec.

At this stage, the next cycle time will start, and again the operations in all processes start together. This is called Yo-i-don, which will realize the balanced production among all processes. It utilizes Andon, cycle time, and the multi-process holding for a single-piece production and conveyance. The Andon in this case is also called the "process-completion display board," which is at times apart from the usual Andon board at Toyota.

In a sense, the Yo-i-don system is a modification of the so-called "Tact system." Under the ordinary Tact system, the supervisor will oversee the whole process, and when all workers finish their respective jobs, he signs to

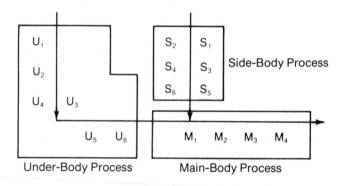

Fig. 7.6   Process in a body welding plant.

1/3		2/3		3/3	
U_1	U_2	U_3	U_4	U_5	U_6
S_1	S_2	S_3	S_4	S_5	S_6
M_1		M_2		M_3	M_4

Fig. 7.7   Andon of the body plant.

move the product of each process to the next process. However, under the Yo-i-don system at Toyota, such a function is replaced by the Andon. However, new considerations and expectations must be made for the introduction of welding robots, conveyor belts between processes, and central computer systems controlling the body-welding lines.

One shot setup

Machine sequencing is an important consideration in complex operation routines. If there are many different machines laid out in succession, how should the setup problem be handled?

Suppose, for example, that there are four different kinds of machines such as a bending machine (W), a punch press (X), a welding machine (Y), and a boring machine (Z) in succession at a certain machining process (Fig. 7.8). Assume that these four machines are handled by a multi-functioned worker and although he is now processing part A, he must next process part B in this multi-machinery process.

In order to change production from part A to part B in this situation, the worker will never setup these four machines after finishing the processing of all of part A at these machines. Such an approach would consume an appreciable amount of production lead time.

Instead, the worker should begin the setup of part B while part A is still in process. Note that only a single unit of a part can flow through each machine within a cycle time. Therefore, when the last unit of part A has been processed at the first machine W, "air" should be sent to machine W. While "air" is flowing through machine W, the setup action can be performed for this machine. In other words, machine W can be setup within a given cycle time.

As a result, all of these four machines can be setup by sacrificing production of just one piece of part B. If all of these four machines are handled by one multi-functioned worker, all of the machines can be setup within four cycle times. If each machine is handled separately by each different worker, all four machines can be setup in one cycle time of the first case. At Toyota, such a setup approach is called *one shot setup* (Fig. 7.8).

Determining the standard quantity of work-in-process

The standard quantity of work-in-process is the minimum necessary quantity of work-in-process within the production line; it consists principally of the work laid out and held between machines. It also includes the work attached to each machine. However, the inventory at the store of completed products of the line cannot be regarded as the standing holding quantity.

Without this quantity of work, the predetermined rhythmic operations of various machines in this line cannot be achieved. The actual standard holding quantity varies according to the following differences in machine layouts and

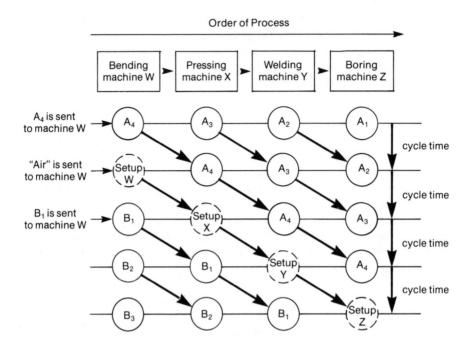

Order of Process

Fig. 7.8 One shot setup.

operations routines:

- If the operations routine is in accordance with the order of process flow, only the work attached to each machine is necessary; it will not be necessary to hold work between machines.
- However, if the operations routine is in an opposite direction to the order of processing, it must be necessary to hold at least one piece of work between machines.

Moreover, when determining the standard quantity of work held, the following points should also be taken into consideration:

- The quantity necessary for checking the product quality at necessary positions of the process.
- The quantity necessary to be held until the temperature of a unit from the preceding machine goes down to a certain level.

The standard quantity held should be kept as small as possible. Besides reducing holding costs, visual control in checking the product quality and improving the process would be made easier because defects would be more evident.

Preparing the standard operations sheet

The standard operations sheet is the final item needed for standardizing the operations at Toyota. This sheet (Fig. 7.9) contains the following items:

- Cycle time
- Operations routine
- Standard quantity of work-in-process
- Net operating time
- Positions to check product quality
- Positions to pay attention to worker safety

When a standard operations sheet is displayed where each worker of the process can see it, it can be useful for visual control in the following three areas:

1. It is a guideline for each worker to keep his standardized operations routine.

2. It helps the foreman or supervisor check to be sure each worker is following standard operations.

3. It allows the superior manager to evaluate the supervisor's ability, since standard operations must be revised frequently by improving operations of the process. If the unrevised standard operations sheet was up for a long time, the manager would note that the supervisor is not making an attempt to improve operations.

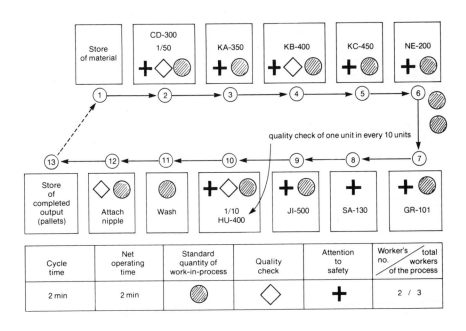

Fig. 7.9   Standard operations sheet.

Proper training and followup:
the key to implementing a successful system

Once the standard operations were set by the supervisor (foreman), he must be able to perform these operations perfectly, and then instruct his workers. The supervisor should not only teach the operations, but also explain the reasons the standards must be kept (i.e., the goals of standard operations). This provides the workers with the incentive to take responsibility for product quality.

In order to ensure that the workers thoroughly understand the standards, two sheets called the *operations keypoints note* and the *operations guidance note* are prepared and conveyed to the workers. The operations keypoints note describes the important points of each operation in the standard operations routine, while the operations guidance note will explain the details of each operation at each line and also methods for checking product quality. They also contain the data provided by the standard operations sheet. These sheets are also posted in each process.

The supervisor must always observe firsthand whether the standards are being followed in his department. If the standards are not being kept, he should immediately instruct the workers in the proper procedures. If the standards themselves are faulty, they must be revised promptly.

An electric board shows the actual and scheduled cumulative quantities of outputs at the completion of each cycle time in every process. The supervisor must check the results of implementing the standard operations, and if something abnormal is found in the process, he must investigate the reasons and take remedial actions. The supervisor's remedial actions are regarded as current control or operational control, but his performance in each month can be evaluated by the traditional budgetary control system.

Finally, it is important to revise the standard operations regularly, since they are always imperfect and operations improvements are always required in a process. The most fundamental idea behind the Toyota production system is summed up in the statement: "Progress of a company can be achieved only by continuous efforts on the part of *all* members of the company to improve their activities."

8

Machine Layout, Multi-Function Workers, and Job Rotation Help Realize Flexible Workshops

Toyota manufactures a variety of automobiles with many different specifications. Each type of car is always subject to fluctuations in demand. For example, the demand of car A might decrease, while at the same time, car B might increase in its demand. Therefore, the work load at each workshop in the plant must be frequently evaluated and periodically changed. Continuing an example, a number of workers at the workshop for car A would have to be transferred to the workshop of car B so that each shop can adapt to the change in demand with the minimum necessary number of workers.

Moreover, even though the demand of all types of products may be reduced simultaneously because of a general economic depression or some foreign export restriction, the company should still be able to reduce the number of workers at any workshop by taking out part-time workers or extra workers coming from related companies.

Shojinka: meeting demand through flexibility

Attaining flexibility in the number of workers at a workshop to adapt to demand changes is called *Shojinka*. In other words, Shojinka in the Toyota production system means to alter (decrease or increase) the number of workers at a shop when the production demand has changed (decreased or increased).

Shojinka has an especially significant meaning when the number of workers must be reduced due to a decrease in demand. For example, at a line, five workers perform jobs which produce a certain number of units. If the production quantity of this line was reduced to 80%, the number of workers must be reduced to four (= 5 × 0.80); if the demand decreased to 20%, the number of workers would then be reduced to one.

Obviously, then, Shojinka is equivalent to increasing productivity by the adjustment and rescheduling of human resources. What was called a flexible workshop in the title of this chapter is essentially a workshop which is achieving Shojinka. In order to realize the Shojinka concept, three factors are prerequisite:

1. Proper design of machinery layout.
2. A versatile and well-trained worker; i.e. a multi-function worker.
3. Continuous evaluation and periodic revisions of the standard operations routine.

The machinery layout for Shojinka at Toyota is combined U-form lines. Under this layout, the range of jobs for which each worker is responsible can be widened or narrowed very easily. However, this layout assumes the existence of multi-functioned workers.

Multi-functioned workers at Toyota are cultivated through the unique *job rotation system*. And, finally, the revision of the standard operations routine can be made through continuous improvements in manual jobs and machineries. The purpose of such improvements is to reduce the necessary number of workers even in the period of increased demand.

The relationship among these important prerequisites is shown in Fig. 8.1. This chapter is devoted to explaining the factors affecting the widening or narrowing of the range of jobs for each worker.

Layout design: the U-turn layout

The essence of the U-turn format is that the entrance and exit of a line are at the same position. The U-turn layout has several variations, such as the concave (⌷_⌷) and circle forms (Fig. 8.2). The most remarkable and important advantage of this layout is the flexibility to increase or decrease the necessary number of workers when adapting to the changes in production quantities (changes in demand). This can be realized by adding or reducing the number of workers in the inner area of the U-shaped workplace (Fig. 8.2).

Just-in-time pulling production also can be achieved in each process. One unit of material can pass into the entrance of the process when one unit of output leaves through the exit. Since such operations are performed by the same worker, the quantity of work-in-process within the layout can always be constant. At the same time, by keeping a standard inventory quantity at each machine, the unbalanced operations among workers will be visualized, so that improvements in the process can be evoked.

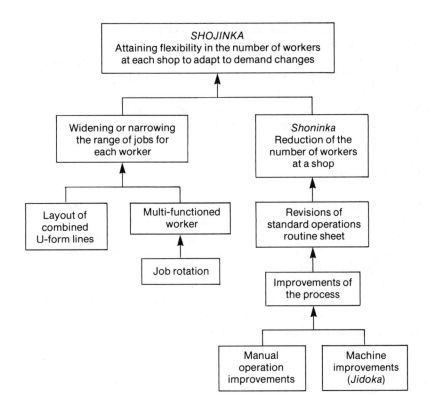

Fig. 8.1 Causal factors to realize Shojinka.

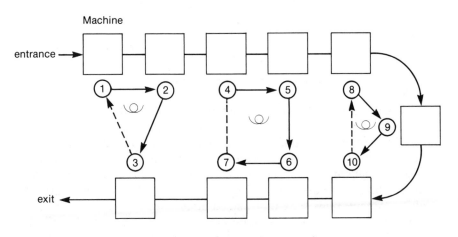

Fig. 8.2 U-form layout.

Finally, the U-turn format allows regions or areas to be developed for specific worker operations. Systems using automatic large scale machines often have workers located only at its entrance and exit. A chain hanger is one such example. If the positions for loading and unloading the material are different, two persons will always be needed, and each worker often has idle time or waiting time. However, if the loading and unloading positions are set at the same point of line, one worker can handle both the entrance and exit jobs.

Improper layouts

Improper layouts which Toyota has avoided can be divided into three major categories: bird cages, isolated islands, and linear layouts.

Bird cage layouts. The simplest form of machine layout calls for one worker assigned to one type of machine. This type of layout has a major disadvantage: the worker has waiting time after he has loaded the work piece into the machine and the part is in process. To avoid such waiting times, two or more stands containing the same type of machine can be laid out around the worker (Fig. 8.3). This type of layout is called a bird cage layout; they are usually triangular, rectangular, or rhombic in shape.

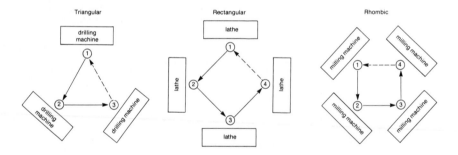

Fig. 8.3 Types of bird cage layouts.

By making each worker handle multiple machines of the same type, the production quantity per worker can be increased. Although this method is much improved over the single machine layout, the production quantity per worker increases; thus, the inventory of semi-finished or intermediate inventory produced at each station also increases. As a result, production balancing between stations is difficult to achieve and these semi-finished products cannot flow smoothly and continuously through the various production processes. *Synchronization* among stations is hardly achieved. In turn, the lead time to produce finished goods rises dramatically.

Isolated island layouts. In order to avoid excessive intermediate inventories from each station and decrease the conveyance time, the layout of machines must be improved to increase the speed of producing a finished product. Therefore, the layout of machines should be in accordance with the sequential order of processing a part (see Fig. 8.4). This layout assumes the existence of a multi-function worker, and enables a continuous, smooth flow of products among different types of machines; it also ensures a continuous walking route with the least distance for each worker. This type is an *isolated island* layout.

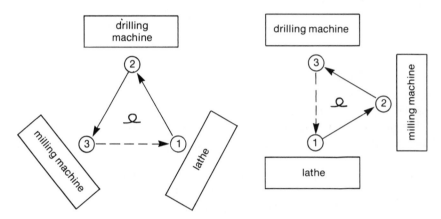

Fig. 8.4   Isolated island layouts.

Toyota rejects all types of the isolated island layout because of the following disadvantages:

• When the entire factory is under this layout, workers are separated from one another and, as such, cannot help each other. It is difficult to attain total balancing of production among the various processes. Unnecessary inventory still occurs among different processes. The mutual relief movement (Chapter 5) cannot be applied to isolated islands.

• Since the unnecessary inventory can exist among isolated islands, waiting time of a worker will be absorbed in producing this inventory. Thus, the reallocation of operations among workers to respond to the changes in demand is difficult in this process.

The layout of the isolated island is based on the methods engineering theory that a worker should never walk at all while working at a certain position. Such an idea was held even by Henry Ford. This idea is correct when productivity is viewed from the efficiency of individual workers; however, it is incorrect when viewed from line balancing within a whole factory and from minimizing the total number of laborers. Concerning the isolated island, the way of using a conveyor is also important. A conveyor is often used only to convey products from place A to place B. In this case, the worker at place A is separated from the worker at place B, and therefore they cannot help each other with the job. Toyota will remove the conveyor in such cases.

Linear layouts.   To overcome the demerits of an isolated island layout, different types of machines can be laid out in a linear form (Fig. 8.5). Under this layout, workers must walk between machines. This is one of the typical characteristics of Toyota's layout.

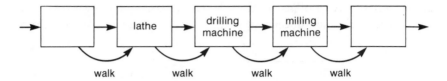

Fig. 8.5   Linear layout.

Using this linear layout, one of the major disadvantages of isolated islands (unnecessary stocking of outputs among processes) can be eliminated, thereby allowing products to flow smoothly and quickly among machines. One problem that cannot be eliminated using the linear layout, however, is the inability of reallocating operations among workers to adapt to changes in demand.

Another problem associated with this system is when machines are set out in a linear form, each line is independent from other lines. In this situation, the repositioning of operations among workers in accordance with the demand for products often requires a fractional number of workers, such as 8.5 persons. Since 0.5 manpower is not actually available, it must be rounded up to one person. As a result, the worker will have some amount of waiting time, or excessive production will occur.

As an example, one unit has been produced in a two-minute cycle time by only one worker. Assume that the demand of cars was increased and that the cycle time was reduced to 1.5 minutes per unit. In this case, if a worker can normally finish half of the total jobs for making one unit of product within one minute, then an additional worker must be introduced to this process to complete the other half of the total jobs. As a result, each of the two workers in this process must have 0.5 minutes of waiting time in every cycle time. Or, if the first worker performed more jobs in 1.5 minutes without any idle time, the second worker must have one full minute of idle time.

Combining U-form lines

In order to overcome this problem of fractional numbers of workers, Toyota eventually decided to combine several U-form lines into one integrated line. Using this combined layout, the allocation of operations among workers in response to variations in production quantities of automobiles can be accomplished by following the procedures of setting the standard operations routine.

The following example will show how Shojinka can be attained using this concept. Suppose there is a combined process which consists of six different lines (A—F), and each line is manufacturing a different gear (Fig. 8.6). According to the monthly demand of products in January, the cycle time of this combined process was one minute per unit. Under this cycle time, eight persons were working in this process (Fig. 8.7), and the walking route of each worker is described by the arrow line.

In February, however, the monthly demand for the products was decreased and the process cycle time was increased to 1.2 min per unit. As a result, all operations of this combined line were reallocated among the workers, and each worker now had to undertake more operations than in January. Fig. 8.8 shows that the walking route of each worker was expanded under the new allocation of operations. In this case, worker 1 will do, as an additional job, some of the operations which worker 2 was doing in January. Worker 2 will also undertake an additional job which was previously accomplished by worker 3 in January. The result of expanding the walking route of each worker is that workers 7 and 8 can be omitted from this combined line. Thus, the fractional manpower which might have occurred in a linear form layout was absorbed in various individual lines under this combined layout.

Attaining Shojinka through multi-function workers

Fig. 8.1 showed that the ability to widen or narrow the range of jobs performed by each worker is a key ingredient in achieving Shojinka. Carefully-designed machine layouts helps develop this ability, but machine layouts alone cannot achieve Shojinka.

Remember that the true meaning of Shojinka is the ability to quickly alter the number of workers at each shop to adapt to changes in demand. When viewed from the side of the individual worker, Shojinka demands that the worker must be able to respond to changes in cycle time, operations routines, and in many cases, the contents of individual jobs. In order to respond quickly, the worker must be multi-functioned; that is, he must be trained to be a skilled worker for any type of job and at any process.

Cultivating multi-function workers through job rotation

Obviously, cultivating or training the individual worker to become multi-functioned is an important part of achieving Shojinka. Toyota cultivates their workers using a system called *job rotation,* where each worker rotates through and performs every job in his workshop. After a period, the individual worker develops proficiency in each job and thereby becomes a multi-functioned worker.

The job rotation system consists of three major parts. First, each manager and supervisor must rotate through every job and prove their own abilities to the general workers in the shop. Second, each worker within the shop is rotated through and trained to perform each job in the shop. The final step is

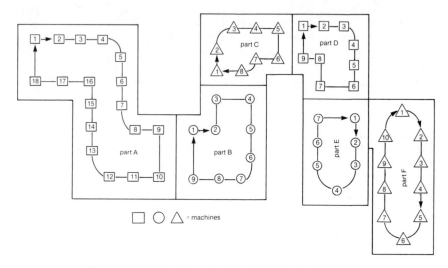

Fig. 8.6   Combined line of making six kinds of parts (A-F).

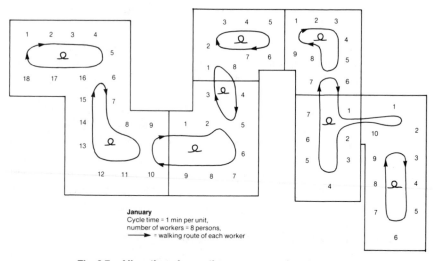

January
Cycle time = 1 min per unit,
number of workers = 8 persons,
→ = walking route of each worker

Fig. 8.7   Allocation of operations among workers in January.

scheduling the workers through job rotation at a frequency of several times each day.

Toyota first implemented a job rotation plan at their Tsutumi Factory (Machining Plant No. 2) where they process and assemble rear-wheel differential carriers. The organization of the plant is shown in Fig. 8.9. Notice that at each work's shop and line there are general foremen, foremen, and line chiefs, respectively. General workers are the responsibility of each line chief with a total of 220 employees working at the plant. Rotation of workers among jobs was implemented following the three steps previously discussed.

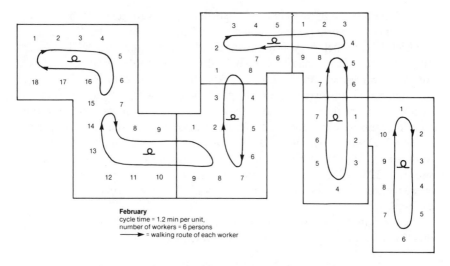

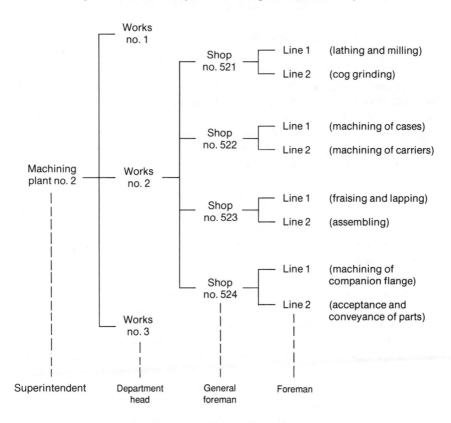

February
cycle time = 1.2 min per unit,
number of workers = 6 persons
⟶ = walking route of each worker

Fig. 8.8   Allocation of operations among workers in February.

Fig. 8.9   Organization of machining plant no. 2.

107

Step 1: Rotation of supervisors. In order to cultivate general laborers into multi-function workers, the managers and supervisors must first display themselves as models or examples of the multi-functioned worker. As a result, all of the general foremen, foremen, and line chiefs (about 60 persons as a total) were rotated among each work's shop and line in this plant. The foremen were transferred among shops of the same works. Since the rotation of all managers and supervisors took three years to accomplish, the job-rotation plan was implemented as part of a long-range planning program.

Step 2: Rotation of workers within each shop. To accomplish this step, a job-training plan must be scheduled for general workers as was planned for shop no. 523 in Fig. 8.10. This plan was set by the general foreman so that every worker in his shop could master any kind of operation at every process in the shop.

To promote the training plan, a multi-function worker rate for each shop must be formulated using the following formula:

$$\frac{\sum_{i=1}^{n} \text{number of processes each worker (i) has mastered}}{\text{total number of processes within the shop x n}}$$

Where n = total number of workers at the shop.

Toyota's goal for this rate was 60% for the first year (1977), 80% for the second year (1978), and 100% for the third year (1979). However, the actual average rate attained in 1979 at the Tsutsumi Plant was 55%. This low figure was due to the physical health and strength of the typical worker, the number of extra workers from outside-related companies, and the number of part-time seasonal and newly-employed laborers. The actual training time for a worker to master each job usually varies from several days through several weeks.

Step 3: Job rotation of several times per day. When the aforementioned multi-function worker rate became high, Shojinka could be realized, and job rotation could be made every week, or in many cases every day. In some advanced cases, all workers could be rotated among all processes of the line in two- or four-hour intervals.

An example of this advanced job rotation occurred in line 2 of shop no. 523. In this line, the 160 θ differential carriers are assembled by eight workers (excluding the line chief as a relief man) within its cycle time of 26 seconds. The layout and the standard operations routine of each worker are depicted in Fig. 8.11. Keep in mind that each process means the standard operations routine, or in other words, the walking route of each worker. Such a walking route will not change unless the cycle time of this line will be changed.

The manual operations time to complete one unit at each process was about 26 seconds for all workers except at process 8. The job characteristic and fatigue rank of each process in this line are described in Fig. 8.12. The grade of

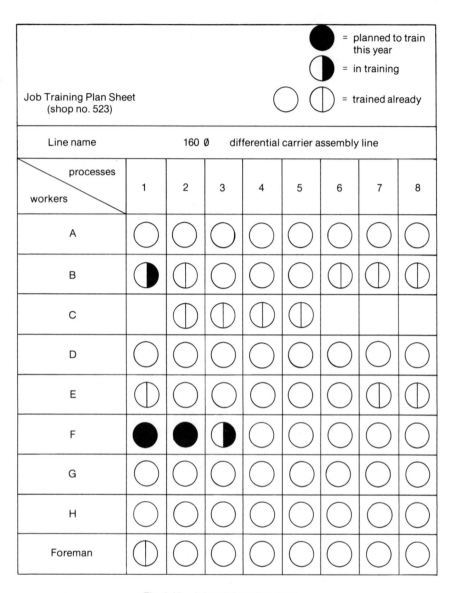

Fig. 8.10 Job training plan sheet.

fatigue at each process will be different depending on differences of the contents of the operations.

Job rotation at shop 523 is accomplished in intervals of two hours. First, a predetermined job rotation schedule must be planned for the five days of the following week. When planning this type of schedule, it should be noted that the allocation of the various processes among workers must be fair; also, the training program for the newcomer must also be considered.

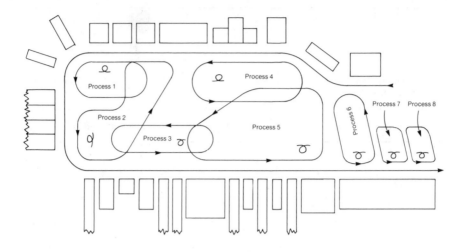

Fig. 8.11 Layout and standard operation routines.

Process No.	Contents of the job at each process	Characteristic of operations	Manual operations time	Fatigue rank
1	Differential case	Skill of finger work is required	26″	4
2	Cover assy	Skill and knowledge of quality check are required	26″	5
3	Can adjust	Long walking distance	26″	3
4	Ring gear assy	Finger work, and heavy work by right arm	26″	1
5	Pre-load adjustment	Long walking distance with heavy material	26″	2
6	Bearing assy	Sensitivity of hand and finger is required	26″	6
7	Back-rush holding	Skilled work, and heavy work by waist and arms	26″	7
8	Rock-bolt assy	Waiting time of 2 sec. exists	24″	8

Fig. 8.12 Job characteristics and fatigue rank
of each process.

Each morning, the general foreman listens again to the health conditions and desires of all workers, and also reexamines the proper way to introduce extra workers onto the line. Finally, he determines the job rotation schedule (Fig. 8.13).

In this job rotation schedule, the following conditions of the workers H, B and C should be considered:

- Worker H is a veteran, but yet sickly.
- Worker C is a long-term extra worker from outside of the company.
- Worker B is still in a training stage for process 1. Therefore, when worker B works at process 1 in his fifth rotation time, veteran worker D will support him as a nearby worker.

Job-Rotation Schedule   (shop no. 523)

Times of rotation	Time interval	160 Ø differential carrier assembly line							
		1	2	3	4	5	6	7	8
1	8AM - 10AM	A	B	C	D	E	F	G	H
2	10AM - 12AM	G	A	B	C	D	H	E	F
3	1PM - 3PM	E	G	C	A	B	F	D	H
4	3PM - 5PM	D	C	G	B	A	H	F	E
5	5PM - 7PM	B	D	C	F	E	A	G	H

Fig. 8.13   Job rotation schedule for workers A - H.

At this shop, all workers except C and H will engage in different kinds of jobs in each two-hour interval. Since this workshop has a smaller cycle time (26 seconds), the worker must have a narrower range of jobs; this is the principal reason for assigning a two-hour interval to this shop. In the event the cycle time was longer, however, workers could handle a wider range of jobs, and thus a four-hour interval could be applied. Some shops even have eight-hour intervals (or, one-day interval).

Additional advantages of job rotation

Among the advantages of job rotation documented by Toyota at their Tsutsumi Plant include:

- The workers' attitudes are refreshed and muscular fatigue can be prevented; as a result, workers were more attentive and careful in avoiding labor accidents. The frequency of shop accidents is actually decreasing at this plant.
- The feeling of unfairness that veterans must have heavy works will disappear. Also, at the beginning of each rotation, there are some conversations between rotating workers. Through these conversations, the human relationship between workers improves, and the mutual relief

movement will be further promoted.

- Since senior workers and supervisors teach their own skills and knowledge to their younger workers and subordinates, the skills and know-how are dispersed throughout the shops and kept on standard operations sheets.
- Since each worker participates in every process within the shop, he feels responsible for all goals of the shop, such as safety, quality, cost, and also production quantity.
- At new shops and processes, all people (irrespective of supervisors or subordinate workers) take a fresh approach and, through this new viewpoint, can isolate problems or points for improvements. Thus, ideas and suggestions to improve the process will increase remarkably.

The various benefits can best be summarized with the simple words: respect for humans. This is a considerably different attitude from traditional schemes where mass production yields a division of labor and, in turn, specialization of labor, simplification of jobs, and, finally, human alienation.

Importance of the line chief: giving rest time and job rotation to workers

One of the most important elements affecting the success of the job rotation system is the role of the line chief. Aside from guidance, the line chief also allows workers to take rest time while still permitting job rotation. The line chief or foreman can always replace a worker in the line, whether the worker is taking a rest or exchanging jobs with another worker.

Suppose worker A wishes to take a rest (or another kind of job). At this time, he calls his line chief or foreman and explains his desire. The line chief will then take worker A's job, and worker A can take a rest. After taking a rest, worker A may go to worker B and ask to exchange jobs. Worker B then leaves his process and worker A engages in B's job. If worker B does not want to have a rest, he may request to change jobs with another worker. The other worker can in turn take a rest when worker B takes his new job.

In this way any worker can take a rest and still exchange his job with another worker. This process can occur quite freely whenever a worker desires, even though the job rotation schedule (Fig. 8.13) has been established and there is no allowance for a rest time in the standard operations routine sheet.

America vs. Japan: the multi-function worker

The multi-functioned worker is not unique to Toyota; in fact, the concept of the multi-function worker is prevalent in many companies throughout Japan. A question that comes to mind is: "How can the multi-function worker be prevalent in Japanese companies but hardly exist in American companies?" To understand the reason for this difference, it is best to analyze a case study involving a company that seems typical of the American business climate: the Caterpillar Tractor Company, for example. In its large-parts machine line for their type D-8 tractor, there are various kinds of jobs and numerous workers (Fig. 8.14).

Labor grade	Kinds of jobs	Number of workers
A	Sweeper	1
B	Cleaner	1
C	Production scraper	2
D	Mill	5
E	Multi-driller	1
F	Multi-driller	1
F	Radial-driller	10
G	Boring machinist	5
H	Salvage welder	5
H	Salvage welder	5

**Fig. 8.14 Job types at a machining line
in the Caterpillar Tractor Company.**

The left side of this figure displays the grade for the company (letters A – H). The rank of each labor grade increases with ascending letters of the alphabet. A wage rate per hour is determined for each labor grade. Even for the same kind of job, such as multi-driller, there are separate ranks and wage rates; in this case, E and F. Fig. 8.15 shows the basic hourly wage rate for each labor grade.

Labor grade \ Pay raise steps	1	2	3	4
A	4.69			
B	4.69	4.77		
C	4.77	4.86		
D	4.86	4.96		
E	4.86	4.96	5.07	
F	4.96	5.07	5.35	
G	5.07	5.19	5.35	
H	5.07	5.19	5.35	5.57
J	5.19	5.35	5.57	5.83
K	5.35	5.57	5.83	6.15
L	5.57	5.83	6.15	6.49

Fig. 8.15 Hourly basic wage rate of each labor grade (as of 1976; dollar unit).

113

Fig. 8.14 shows that there are some laborers who work specifically as sweeper, cleaner, or production scraper. These classes of workers seem unusual in Japanese eyes, because in Japan it is quite natural that the individual driller or welder sweeps his own area, as well as sets up and scrapes his workpiece. In the Caterpillar Tractor Company, the boring machinist specializes only in boring, and he has his own wage rate based on his labor grade.

The facts here show the following features about the American business community:

- In American companies, job classification is excessive compared with Japanese companies. This seems to be based on an American ideology for standardization, which has resulted in an extremely fine division of labor.
- Most American workers are single-function workers. Even if the worker is versatile, he still works as a specialist of a certain type of job. This seems partly based on the fact that there are many kinds of craft unions in the same factory.

Such excessive classification and specialization in jobs increase the cost of products. For example, suppose that an electric welding operation needed only 20 seconds to make one unit, and the job must be done at a specific welding place. If one part is made each minute of cycle time, the welder will process this part in 20 seconds and have a waiting time of 40 seconds; otherwise, the worker will engage in lot production, which creates a large inventory from the welding process. This creates a long lead time as a whole.

Other reasons why the multi-function worker has not been cultivated in American companies are:

- Wage system based on labor grades.
- Lack of on-the-job-training programs for cultivating blue-collar workers into multi-function workers.
- Difficulty of transferring blue-collar workers among the various kinds of jobs in a plant.

Looking at the first of these factors, the wage rate of each labor grade cannot be increased once it has reached its final step (Fig. 8.15). After that step, the only pay raises possible are those designed to overcome inflation. In order for blue-collar workers to increase their wages beyond this point, they must take either of two approaches: change job type within the same company or change companies.

The first approach, changing jobs within the same company, has two negative aspects. First, American companies rarely give on-the-job-training (like Toyota's Job Rotation System) to blue-collar workers. At the Caterpillar Tractor Company, for example, a sweeper (Fig. 8.14) will remain in his present job unless he personally studies to become a driller or boring machinist.

Second, and more important, American companies rarely transfer blue-collar workers among the various kinds of jobs within the same company, as the Japanese do in their companies. For example, the management of the Caterpillar Tractor Company appear very reluctant to implement a job-rotation system for the following reasons:

- Without a vacancy at the job in question, transfer cannot take place.
- Without a proposal or request from some worker, management cannot determine who should be transferred.
- The transfer of workers is normally determined automatically in accordance with seniority out of those workers desiring transfers.
- Many of the workers requesting transfers often want to take simpler, easier jobs.

As a result of these negative aspects, American workers seeking to increase their wage rates quite often will transfer to another company. This is best observed by the labor mobility rates for Japan and the United States. The labor mobility rate is essentially a percentage of the total work force that changes companies (enter or leave). During 1978, the average monthly labor mobility rate for Japan was 1.4%, while the rate for the U.S. was 3.9%. Therefore, the annual rate for the U.S. was 47%, nearly 2.8 times the rate for Japan. This seems to indicate that nearly one half of the U.S. labor moves to a new company each year.

Japanese business climate: ideal for the multi-function worker

In Japan, a laborer's wages are basically connected to each individual worker, not to a specific labor grade. His wage rate will be increased mainly on the number of years he has been employed by the company. Also, the typical Japanese company teaches many different jobs to workers by means of on-the-job-training programs. These wage rates and OJT systems help motivate workers to stay in the same company until retirement. As a result, a multi-function worker can be developed that is also loyal to the company.

The labor-grade wage system has not been adopted in Japan as a principal criterion to determine wages. Although this wage system is partially adopted, the pay-raise period is very long; this is partly based on the Japanese value of group consciousness. Also, the typical Japanese firm has only an enterprise union in each company, instead of having many different craft unions in one plant.

The life-time employment system kept by Japanese management is another strong factor why typical Japanese employees are motivated to be versatile workers. Under this employment system, the company often has a favorable return on investment in educating the laborer as a multi-function worker.

At Toyota, overtime work seems to be a buffer for keeping such stable employment. By realizing Shoninka and Shojinka, Toyota has only the minimum number of workers necessary at each workshop, and all workers usually realize overtime. If demands were decreased or robotics were introduced, the overtime would be decreased without dismissing or laying off any workers.

Moreover, seasonal part-time workers and also the business groups are behind the life-time employment system. The firms within a certain business group will help each other; therefore, a depressed company can transfer its workers to prosperous companies within this business group. Such a Japanese business environment undoubtedly supports this type of employment system.

The Japanese employment system, wage system, the system of transferring workers among various departments, and the OJT system for cultivating versatile workers are all based on the principal Japanese value of group consciousness. For the purpose of attaining total system effectiveness in a society which had no additional frontiers, excessive individualism had to be restrained. Only an educational system would be effective in changing the social value over a long period of time.

9

Improvement Activities Help Reduce the Workforce and Increase the Workers' Morale

The Toyota production system attempts to increase productivity and reduce manufacturing costs. Unlike other such systems, however, it reaches its goal without a loss in the human dignity of the worker. As has often been pointed out in connection with the conveyor belt system developed by Henry Ford, attempts to increase productivity are usually accompanied by an increased demand on the individual worker. To increase productivity, one must either maintain the same level of production while reducing the size of the workforce or produce more and more with the existing number of workers. Traditionally, either alternative has involved an unacceptable sacrifice in human terms—a dehumanization of the worker. At Toyota, however, the conflict between productivity and human concerns has been resolved by initiating positive improvements at every workplace through small groups called *quality control circles*.

The improvements are varied: refinement of manual operations to eliminate wasted motion, introduction of new or improved machinery to avoid the uneconomical use of manpower, and improved economy in the use of materials and supplies. All three types of improvements are evolved by means of small group meetings in which a suggestion system similar to that employed in other countries plays a prominent part.

In addition, the Kanban system also functions to promote improvements in productivity. In all likelihood, it is the only production control system that

117

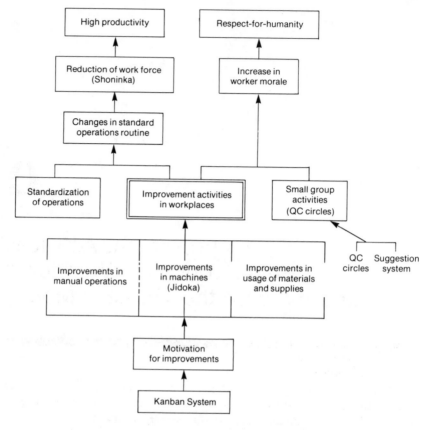

Fig. 9.1 Framework of improvement activities.

also provides a motivation for improved productivity. Fig. 9.1 shows the relationship between the Kanban system and the various improvements in the workplace together with their relationship to the quality control circle and increased productivity and morale.

Improvements in manual operations

In any factory, all manual operations fall into one of the following three categories:

Pure waste. Actions altogether unnecessary and should be eliminated immediately; i.e., waiting time, stacking of intermediate products, and "double transfer" (Fig. 9.2).

Operations without "value added." Operations that are essentially wasteful but may be necessary under present operating procedures. They include walking long distances to pick up parts, unpacking vendor parcels,

118

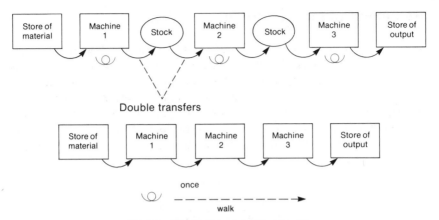

Fig. 9.2   Elimination of double transfer.

shifting a tool from one hand to another, etc. To eliminate such operations, it would be necessary to make changes in the layout of the line or arrange for vendor items to be delivered unpackaged—none may be practicable at the present time.

Net operations to increase "value added." Conversion or processing operations that increase the value of raw materials or semi-finished products by adding manual labor; i.e., subassembly of parts, forging raw material, tempering gears, painting bodywork, etc.

Also, remedial operations—operations to repair or remove defective products, tools, or equipment can be found in the factory.

Net operations to increase value added typically constitute only a small portion of total operations, the large part of which serve only to increase costs (Fig. 9.3). By raising the percentage of net operations to increase value added, labor required per unit can be reduced, thus reducing the number of workers at each workplace. The first step is to eliminate pure waste. Next, reduce operations without value added as far as possible without incurring unreasonable costs. Finally, examine even net operations to increase value added to see if they can be further increased as a proportion of total operations by introducing some type of automatic machinery to take the place of operations currently being carried out by hand.

Manual operations		
Pure waste	Operations	
	Operations without value added	Net operations with value added

Fig. 9.3   Categories of operations.

Reduction of the workforce

When making improvements to reduce the number of workers on its combined U-form lines, Toyota eliminates wasteful operations, reallocates operations, and reduces the workforce. The three steps are really parts of a cyclical process: elimination of purely wasteful operations (waiting time) leads immediately to reallocation of operations among the workers at the workplace and a partial reduction in the workforce. The three steps may be repeated several times before all possible improvements to the line have been made (Fig. 9.4).

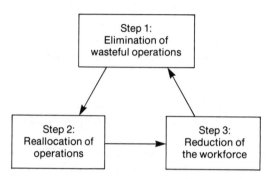

Fig. 9.4   Cycle for reducing the number of workers.

The first step toward reducing the number of workers is to determine the waiting time for each worker and revise the standard operations routine to eliminate it. Waiting time is often hidden behind over production and so never comes to light. In such cases, large amounts of inventory are behind or between processes. As a result, actions such as moving and stacking inventory, which occupy much of a worker's waiting time, are often regarded as part of his job. At Toyota, however, such actions are classified as a waste of over production, and the Kanban system, which serves to reduce inventory levels, makes the waste of overproduction obvious. Kanban plays as important a role in the elimination of wasteful operations as the standardization of operations.

To illustrate how elimination of waiting time and reallocation of operations leads to a reduction in the workforce, consider the following example. Seven workers, A through G, are all working at the same workplace. The standard operating time for the operations assigned to each worker must be measured. By subtracting the standard operating time for each worker from the cycle time, waiting time during each cycle for each worker can be determined. If, for example, the cycle time is one minute per unit of production and the total standard operations assigned to worker A take 0.9 minutes, he will have 0.1 minutes of waiting time. In most cases, each of the other workers will also have waiting times of varying length (Fig. 9.5).

To eliminate waiting time, some of worker B's operations must be

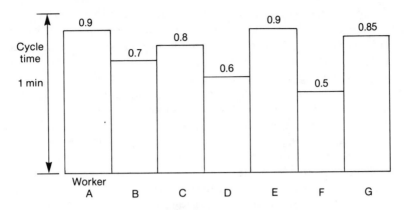

Fig. 9.5   Each worker has waiting time.

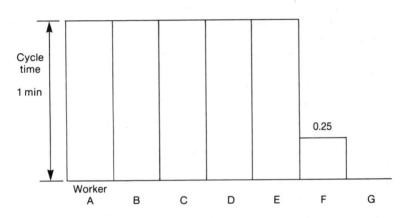

Fig. 9.6   Reallocation of operations among workers.

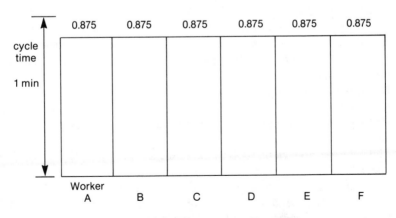

Fig. 9.7   Wrong allocation of operations.

121

transferred to worker A, some of worker C's operations to worker B, and so forth until enough operations have been reallocated to eliminate the waiting time for workers A through E. At this point, worker G's job will have been eliminated altogether (Fig. 9.6).

When reallocating operations among workers, either to bring about improvements in manual operations or to compensate for changes in production levels the following three rules should be observed:

1. When the waiting time for each worker is being measured, he should stand without doing anything at all after he has finished the operations assigned to him. If worker B, for example, finishes his job in 0.7 minutes, he should simply stand idle at his work station for the remaining 0.3 minutes. In this way, everyone will be able to see that he has free time, and there will be less resistance if he is assigned one or two more jobs.

2. When reducing the number of workers at a workplace, the best worker(s) should always be removed first. If a dull or unskilled worker is moved, he may resist, his morale may suffer, and he may never develop into a skilled worker. An outstanding worker, by contrast, is usually more willing to be moved since he has more self-confidence and may welcome the opportunity to learn other jobs in the factory.

3. After operations have been reallocated to workers A through E, the 0.75 minutes of waiting time for worker F should not be disposed of by distributing it equally among the six workers remaining on the line. If it were, it would simply be hidden again, since each worker would slow down his work pace to accommodate his share of the waiting time. Also, there would be resistance when it came time to revise the standard operations routine again (Fig. 9.7). Instead, a return to step 1 is necessary to see if there are further improvements that can be made in the line to eliminate the fractional operations left for worker F.

All three types of manual operations must be examined, including net operations to increase value added which might be omitted through introduction of an automatic machine. At this state, however, it is important to choose the least expensive plan, since only 0.25 minutes of manual operating time needs omitting. Less expensive improvements include:

• Move supplies of parts closer to the worker or introduce chutes to shorten walking distances.

• Use smaller pallets that can be placed beside workers who need only a small number of parts at a time.

• Redesign a tool to eliminate the wasted motion in changing it from one hand to the other.

• Make it easier to pick up tools by hanging them in racks with their handles uppermost.

• Introduce some simple tools to streamline operations.

• When a worker operates more than one machine, locate the on/off switch between the two machines so he can push it while he is walking from one machine to the other.

By means of one or more of the aforementioned devices, it should be possible to eliminate the 0.25 minutes of operating time remaining for worker F and so remove him from the line. Thus, in our example, it would be possible to eliminate two out of seven workers. Look at the line again for previously overlooked wasteful operations and attempt to remove another worker by eliminating other operations without value added. Improvements to the line at this point are difficult; some improvements that are intrinsically worthwhile may be held in reserve until a sales or model change makes it possible to alter the cycle time or the design of the workplace.

Improvements in machinery

In any manufacturing process, two kinds of improvements exist: improvements in manual operations and improvements in machinery. The first involves definition of standard operations, reallocation of operations among workers, relocation of stored parts and semi-finished products, etc. The second type of improvement involves introduction of new equipment such as robots and automatic machines. At Toyota, improvements in manual operations are always undertaken before making improvements in machinery. The reasons follow:

- From a cost-benefit standpoint, machine improvement may not pay. Remember that the purpose of any improvement is to reduce the number of workers. If the same purpose can be achieved through improvements in manual operations, it will not pay to install a new schedule.

- Changes in manual operations can be reversed if necessary, while those in machinery cannot. Thus, if a machine improvement ends in failure, the machine is a total loss. The cost of improvements in manual operations, on the other hand, are at least partially recoverable.

- Improvements to machinery often fail if they are made before improvements in manual operations. Since an automatic machine is inflexible in its operation, it can be successfully integrated into a line only if all manual operations have already been standardized. Otherwise, improper processing of the workpiece and operation of the machine may result in any unacceptable number of defective parts and the machine itself may break down frequently. If an automatic punch press, for example, was installed where the wrong types of material might be placed in the machine, the die could be permanently damaged and the machine along with it. As a result, it would be necessary to assign a watchman to the machine and its value as a labor-saving improvement would be reduced considerably.

Policies in promoting Jidoka

Autonomation or "Jidoka" is essentially improvements in machinery which serve to reduce the number of workers. There are two problems, however, that should be considered when promoting Jidoka:

1. Even if the introduction of an automatic machine reduces manpower requirements by 0.9 persons, it cannot actually reduce the number of workers on the line unless the remaining 0.1 person (which is often the watchman for the machine) can also be eliminated. As a result, introduction of the machine serves only to increase manufacturing costs and thus the cost of the product. To put the matter a different way, a reduction in the man-hours required to produce a unit ("Shoryokuka") is not the same thing as a reduction in the workforce. For this reason, a true reduction in the workforce is called Shoninka at Toyota to distinguish it from Shoryokuka. Only Shoninka can reduce the cost of an automobile.
2. Jidoka often has the undesirable effect of fixing the number of workers who must be employed at a given workplace; i.e., while Jidoka replaces manual operations, it may also require certain number of workers to help the machine by performing operations that cannot be automated. As a result, the same number of workers must always be present to operate the machine regardless of production quantity. At Toyota, this phenomenon is called a *quorum system* ("Te-i-in-se-i"), which is an undesirable phenomenon in any business.

In both respects, then, introduction of Jidoka may actually limit the ability to reduce the number of workers—a matter of some concern, since it is always essential to be able to reduce the workforce, especially when demand decreases. How can the two problems be solved? How can Shojinka (flexibility in the number of workers) be maintained when introducing Jidoka? Toyota has two policies:

1. Automatic machines should be introduced only when a strong need exists, not simply because the manual operation in question can be replaced by a machine.
2. The work stations at a machine should always be located as close together as possible, especially when the machine occupies a large area, as is the case with a transfer machine. Too often, the work stations are widely separated, and each worker's operation time at the machine per cycle is fractional. As a result, it is impossible to combine fractional manpower operations into integer operations when the workforce must be reduced.

Job improvements and respect for humanity

When making job improvements, respect for humanity can be maintained by observing the following rules:

Give the worker valuable jobs. Reductions in the workforce are sometimes regarded as a way of forcing hard work on the workers without considerations for their humanity. This criticism, however, is based on a misunderstanding of the nature of job improvements or in cases where the wrong procedure has been adopted. When operations at a workshop are improved, each worker must understand that the elimination of wasteful actions will never lead to harder work. Instead, the goal of the improvement program is to increase the number of net operations with added value that can be performed with the same amount of labor. For example, suppose a worker on a trimming line must walk five or six steps to pick up a part and climb in and out of the car several times during each cycle. The function of job improvement is to eliminate such wasteful actions and use the time instead to perform net operations with added value, thus reducing the total standard operations time and the number of workers. Unless this point is fully understood, the Toyota production system is hard to apply, especially in an environment where the labor union is strong.

At Toyota, then, respect for humanity is a matter of allying human energy with meaningful, effective operations by abolishing wasteful operations. If a worker feels that his job is important and his work significant, his morale will be high; if he sees that his time is wasted on insignificant jobs, his morale will suffer as well as his work.

Keep the lines of communication within the organization open. The approach used to promote job improvements is very important. A mere injunction to "Reduce the number of workers!" or "Improve the process!" is not enough to solve the problem. Every work shop has its problems and the workers are usually interested in solving them. A worker may complain, for example, that his operation is hard to do because of crowded conditions at his work station or that the machine is hard to adjust and leaks oil. When the worker notifies his supervisor about such problems, however, the supervisor may not pay attention or repair personnel may not attend to the problem on a timely basis. When this happens, an exceptional worker may try to solve the problem himself—and fail, especially if the solution requires that a machine be redesigned or modified. In most cases, however, the worker will simply lodge a complaint with the labor union and resistance to the manager will come out. (A representative case is clearly described in terms of experiences in an American automobile factory: see Runcie [1980].) If, on the other hand, the supervisor responds quickly and effectively, the worker will trust his supervisor and feel that he has an active role in efforts to improve the shop.

A relationship of trust and credibility is most important in promoting improvements. In order to establish such a relationship, however, the formal lines of communication from the lower level workers through to the foreman and general foreman up to the superintendent must be well drawn and open since any problem must be solved through these channels. If the supervisors and IE staff respect proposals from the workshop and promote improvements together with the workers, each individual in the factory will have high morale and an awareness of his role in improvement activities. No one will feel alienated, and every worker will feel that his work is an important part of his life.

The suggestion system

Although the stated purpose of any suggestion system is to draw upon the ideas of all employees to improve company operations, its real purpose is often quite different. In such cases, the suggestion system is intended simply to give an employee the sense that he is recognized by his company or his superior or to build loyalty and company pride by allowing him to draw up plans as if he were a member of management. In other words, the real purpose of a suggestion system in most companies is labor or personnel management.

At Toyota, however, both the purpose and spirit of its suggestion system are expressed in the slogan: "Good products, good ideas"—that is, its goal is to draw upon the ideas of all employees in order to improve product quality and reduce costs so the company can continue to grow in the world automobile market. This is not to say that Toyota is oblivious to the effect of a suggestion system on labor relations, but it is some index of the seriousness with which Toyota takes its employees' suggestions that most of the improvement activities described in this chapter were initiated through a company-wide suggestion system.

Individual improvement schemes are devised and introduced by an individual worker or by small groups called *QC circles*, which are composed of the workers at each work place and are led by the supervisor. When one of the members of the group calls a problem to the attention of the supervisor, the supervisor takes the following steps:

1. *Definition of the problem.*   In considering the problem, the supervisor should attempt to determine the exact nature of the difficulty and its effect(s) on other operations and workers.
2. *Examination of the problem.*   Present conditions must be examined in detail to determine the causes of the problem. In the process, other related problems may also come to light.
3. *Generation of ideas.*   The supervisor should encourage the worker to generate ideas for solving the problem. For example, suppose a worker has pointed out that it takes him a great deal of time to count the number of units on a pallet and that the pallet often contains several different kinds of parts. The worker might then suggest that frames be installed in the pallet to make it easier for him to count the number of parts it contains and to separate one kind of part from another (Fig. 9.8). Or an equally good solution may be evolved by the group as a whole. In either case, the supervisor should always show respect for his subordinates' ideas.
4. *Summary of ideas.*   The supervisor should summarize the various proposed solutions to the problem and allow his subordinates to select the best scheme.
5. *Submission of the proposal.*   One member of the group should write the selected scheme on a suggestion sheet and put it in the suggestion box.

Although many suggestions for improvements are generated by means of

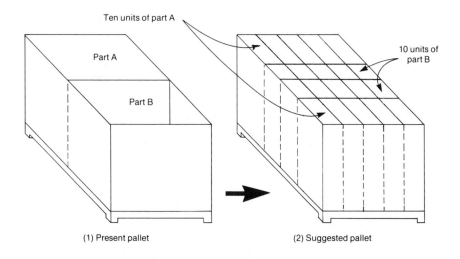

Ten units of part A

Part A

Part B

10 units of part B

(1) Present pallet

(2) Suggested pallet

Fig. 9.8 Example of suggestion scheme.

the QC circles, individual ideas for improvements can be submitted at any time without consulting with the supervisor or another group member. Nor is it necessary for a problem to arise in order for the group to operate as a source for suggested improvements. Toyota uses the following check list of topics:

Improvements in manual operations:
1. Is it appropriate to store materials, tools and products in the present way?
2. Is there any easier way to manage machine handling or machine processing?
3. Can you make your job easier and more efficient by changing the layout of machines and conveyance facilities?

Savings in materials and supplies:
1. Are you using oil, grease, and other supplies efficiently?
2. Is there anything that can be done to reduce leakage of steam, air, oil, etc.?
3. Can you reduce the consumption of materials and supplies by improving materials, machining methods, and jigs?

Improving efficiency in the engineering department and in offices:
1. Are there jobs in your office that overlap?
2. Are there any jobs that could be eliminated?
3. Could you improve the present voucher system?
4. Could you standardize your job?

Improving the work environment to increase safety and prevent dangerous accidents:
1. Are the lighting, ventilation, and temperature conditions good?
2. Are dust, gas, and bad odors fully removed from the work area?
3. Is your safety equipment appropriate: Does it function well?

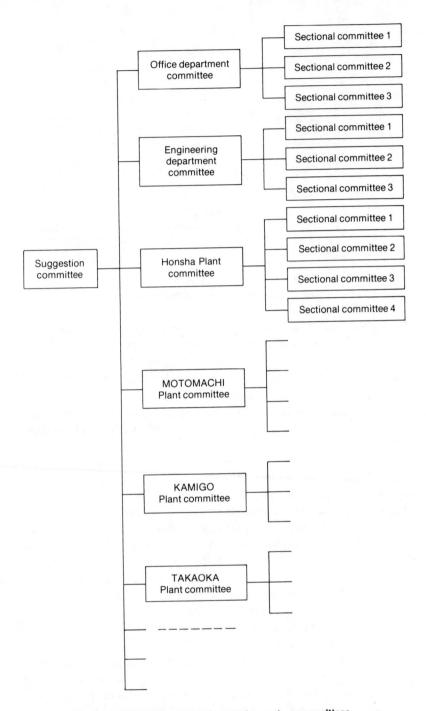

Fig. 9.9   Organization of suggestion system committees.

Improving efficiency and uniformity of the automobile itself:
1. Can the quality of the automobile be improved by changing its design and manufacture?
2. Is there any way to increase the uniformity of the product?

Although the procedure for proposing improvements is much the same at Toyota as it is in America and in European countries, the system for evaluating the proposals is quite different and far more effective because it is carried out in a rapid and orderly fashion. The assessment of proposals follows the path through the organization shown in Fig. 9.9 and consists of the following steps:
1. All suggestions are gathered at the plant office on the first day of each month and recorded in the suggestion ledger.
2. Each Plant Sectional Committee examines the suggestions by the twentieth of the month, and determines which plans deserve rewards of 5,000 yen or less.
3. The Plant Committee or Department Committee then examines plans which deserve a reward of at least 6,000 yen.
4. Plans which deserve a reward of at least 20,000 yen are examined professionally by a corporate-wide Suggestion Committee.
5. An official announcement of the results of the examination is published in the evaluation result table and in the Toyota newspaper.

All plans that have been adopted are implemented immediately. In some cases, a plan will be designated "pending" and examined again the following month. Other plans, designated "reference," may be improved by committee members or managers and used later. If any type of plan contains patentable material, the committee notifies the person responsible for the suggestion and then submits the plan to an Invention Committee for appropriate action. All patents are applied for under the company name. The rewards are usually kept by each group and used for recreational activities such as trips or fishing parties.

In addition to monetary rewards, other kinds of commendations are awarded:
*   For outstanding proposals, the company gives a testimonial to the person or persons responsible at a ceremony held each month.
*   On a yearly basis, commendations are awarded to the person with the largest total amount of rewards, the largest average reward per suggestion, etc.
*   Any employee who has been given yearly commendations for three years in a row is given a special testimonial and a commemorative gift.
*   A yearly testimonial and trophy can also be awarded to outstanding groups.

The suggestion system at Toyota was introduced in June, 1951. Fig. 9.10 shows the number of proposals in recent years. It does not show, however, that there were 48,757 workers at Toyota in 1980, including office workers.

Thus, on the average, each worker suggested more than ten improvement plans, most of which (94%) have been adopted.

In summary, the suggestion system has the following advantages:

- The system operates through individual workers or QC circles, where the supervisor of each group can give his subordinates' problems and proposals sincere and immediate attention.
- Proposals are examined every month on an orderly schedule and the results are announced immediately.
- The evaluation process establishes a close relationship between the workers and the professional staff. For example, if a suggested improvement involves a change in design, a professional engineer will examine it immediately.

Year	Number of suggestions	Adoption rate
1976	463,422	84%
1977	454,522	84
1978	527,718	88
1979	575,861	91
1980	859,039	94

Fig. 9.10   Number of proposals in recent years.

Kanban and improvement activities

Everyone wants to take it easy, and, in this respect, the Japanese are no different from people in other countries. When inventory levels are high, things seem to go better for everyone: if a machine breaks down or the number of defective parts increases suddenly, subsequent operations need not stop so long as there is sufficient stock in inventory; and when the required number of units are not produced during regular working hours, it is usually unnecessary to schedule overtime in order to meet production goals. As long as problems like these are hidden behind high inventory levels, however, they cannot be identified and eliminated. As a result, they will continue to be responsible for various kinds of waste: wasted time, wasted labor, wasted material, etc.

By contrast, when inventory is minimized by Just-in-time withdrawals under the Kanban system, such problems are impossible to ignore. If, for example, a machine breaks down or begins producing defective parts, the whole line will stop and the supervisor must be called in. In many cases, it will be necessary to schedule overtime hours in order to make up for lost production time. As a result, activities to correct the problems will take place in the appropriate QC group, plans for improvements will be devised, and productivity will rise. The function of the Kanban system is not merely to control production levels. Its more important role lies in its ability to stimulate

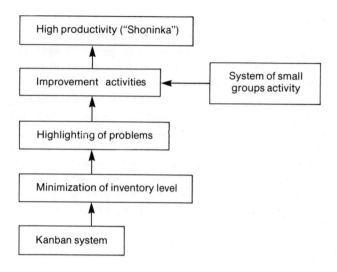

Fig. 9.11   Relationship between Kanban system and improvement activities.

improvements in operations that eliminate waste and improve productivity. Fig. 9.11 shows the relationship between the Kanban system and improvement activities.

In recent years, Toyota has expanded its improvement activities to all departments, including indirect divisions. At Toyota Motor Corp., there are 48,000 employees, 20,000 of whom are manual laborers in the factories. The performance of the remaining 28,000 people, in indirect departments, however, has an important effect on what happens in the workplace. The jobs at departments such as quality control, cost control, product design, and production control, for example, all affect the performance of direct departments.

Thus, in correcting individual problems at the workplace, Toyota has more than once found it necessary to make improvement in indirect departments as well. As a result, improvement activities in manufacturing operations have brought with them company-wide improvements.

Reductions in the workforce brought about by workshop improvements may seem to be antagonistic to the worker's human dignity since they take up the slack created by waiting time and wasted action. However, allowing the worker to take it easy or giving him high wages does not necessarily provide him an opportunity to realize his worth. On the contrary, that end can be better served by providing the worker with a sense that his work is worthwhile and allowing him to work with his superior and his comrades to solve the problems they encounter.

QC Circles

A *QC circle,* or *quality control circle,* is a small group of workers that study quality control concepts and techniques spontaneously and continuously in order to provide solutions to problems in their workplace. At Toyota, the ultimate purpose of QC circle activities is to promote a worker's sense of responsibility, provide a vehicle to achieve working goals, enable each worker to be accepted and recognized, and allow improvement and growth in a worker's technical abilities. The purpose of the QC circle is somewhat different from that of the suggestion system outlined previously. The evaluation for QC circle activities is hardly made in terms of the monetary amount of improved effects, but rather by how positive the circle is acting, how well the subject (topic) is pursued, and to what degree the members are participating.

Structure of the QC Circle

The QC circles at Toyota have a direct relationship with the formal organization of the workplace; therefore, all employees must participate in some QC circles. The QC circles are made up of a foreman ("Hancho") and his subordinate workmen (Fig. 9.12). However, the QC circle may take a form of a *united circle,* where members of other circles participate, or a *mini-circle,* which consists of some members of the whole circle, each depending on the topic to be solved. The department head ("Kocho") and the supervisor ("Kumicho") will be the advisor and the subadvisor, respectively.

Each plant or division has its own QC promoting committee (Fig. 9.13). At Toyota, QC circle activities are supported by the highest responsible person at each plant. The personnel division and the education division recently have begun promoting QC circle activities. As of 1981, about 4,600 groups of QC circles were active at Toyota; each group averaged 6.4 members.

QC Topics and Achievements

The subjects QC circles select as problems to be solved are not confined to product quality; cost reduction, maintenance, safety, industrial pollution, and alternative resources are considered as well. In 1981, the subject breakdown was: product quality, 35%; maintenance, 15%; cost reduction, 30%; and safety, 20%. The number of achieved topics in each circle averaged 3.4 per year. Since the economic effect itself is not the only purpose, 3-4 subjects are settled as a goal to be achieved each year.

The number of circle meetings actually held was 6.7 times per year for each topic, and each topic required an average of 6.4 hours. Therefore, each meeting was approximately one hour in length. It is considered best at Toyota to have the circle meeting twice or three times each month and approximately

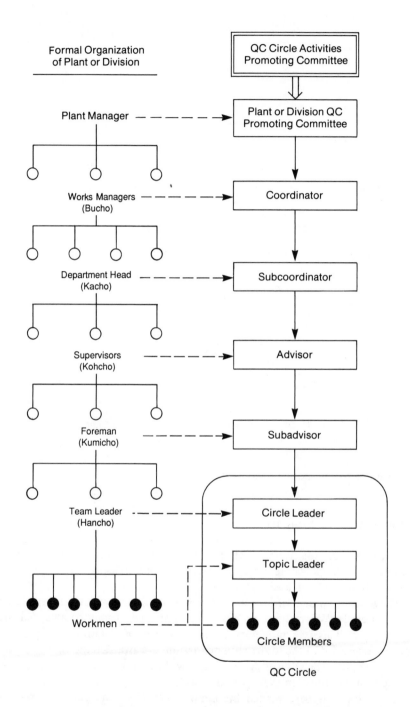

Fig. 9.12   Structure of the QC circle and its relationship to the formal organization.

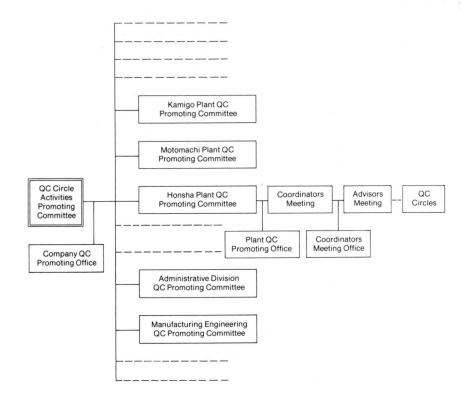

Fig. 9.13   Organization for promoting QC circle activities.

30 minutes to one hour in duration.

Fig. 9.14 details how QC circles are implemented.

Commendation Systems

The commendation systems at Toyota consist of three classes: topics commendation, QC circle commendation, and QC circle–Toyota prize. Each class includes various levels of awards.

The *topics commendation* awards the individual topic which was registered by each circle. When the topic has been completed, it may be awarded the *effort prize*. This is a monetary reward given each month or every other month. One third of the topics commendations are awarded the *advisor prize,* and one third of the advisor prize winners will be given the *coordinator prize.* These awards are given every six months.

One topic will be awarded the commendation of the plant promoting committee for each workshop within the plant in question. Furthermore, each

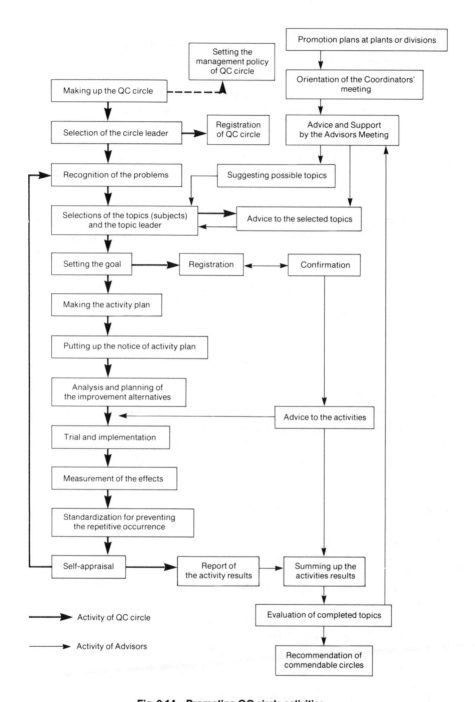

Fig. 9.14 Promoting QC circle activities.

plant committee will recommend about four topics (responding to quality, costs, maintenance, and safety) for their receiving the company commendations called the *Gold prize* and the *Silver prize*. Because there are thirteen plants and divisions and four topics are recommended, about 150 circles are usually awarded Gold or Silver prizes twice a year.

The above commendation system accompanies the *presentation system*. In other words, each level of awards is given just after the circle's presentations are made at the plant. The *QC circle commendation* awards the overall performance of a circle's one-year activities. This class of commendations also includes the advisor prize, coordinator prize, and plant committee prize.

A circle that has performed excellent activities for three years will be requested by the works manager to summarize its activities and give a presentation at the *plant-wide presentation contest*. Then, at the *first selection contest,* the production control managers from thirteen plants and divisions will hear thirteen presentations and select five circles as the final candidates for the *QC circle-Toyota prize*. These five circles must make presentations before the chairman of the company QC promoting committee and the engineering vice-president. Eight circles not given the Toyota prize can still be awarded the *Excellence prize*.

Two circles out of the five Toyota prize winners will then participate in the regional QC circle contest outside the Toyota Motor Corp. Then, if passed, they will participate in the *All-Japan QC Circles Contest.*

The suggestion system previously described is different from the QC circle's commendation systems. However, the monetary reward from the suggestion system will be given if the QC circle proposes improvement techniques. In average, about eleven proposals are suggested to the suggestion system from one circle per year. In this case, because the suggestion plan is the group proposal, the reward will be saved by the circle and used for its own purposes, such as a softball game or fishing contest.

Education Systems for QC Circles

At Toyota, several education programs promote QC circle activities. The following courses are held on a continuous basis:
- *Problem-solving course* for the foreman and supervisor.
- *Advisor course* for the department head and supervisor. (These two courses are also open to the supplier's employees.)
- *Trainer course* for department heads. The department heads must take this course when they are promoted.
- Various presentation contest within and outside the company.
- Participation in the shipboard school which goes to Hong Kong or Formosa.
- Participation in the inspection tour for field supervisors to go to the United States or Europe for three weeks.

10

"Autonomous Defects Control" Assures Product Quality

In Japan, quality control (QC) or quality assurance (QA) is defined as the development, design, manufacture, and service of products that will satisfy the consumer's needs at the lowest possible cost. As the definition implies, the customer's satisfaction with product quality is an end in itself at Toyota. At the same time, however, product quality is an indispensable part of the Toyota production system, since without quality control the continuous flow of production (synchronization) would be impossible.

The evolution of the Japanese approach to quality control and its application to specific needs and problems within the Toyota production system will be examined in this chapter. As Fig. 10.1 shows, quality control began with independent inspectors and statistical sampling methods but soon moved to a "self-inspection of all units" method which is based on autonomous control of defects within the manufacturing process itself. Quality control has now become a company-wide concern that extends outward from manufacturing to Toyota's functional management units.

Until 1949, quality control activities in Japan were largely a matter of rigorous inspections carried out by specialized inspectors: an approach that has been all but abandoned in present-day quality control programs. Today, fewer than 5% of the factory employees in Japan are inspectors and in the top companies fewer than 1%. By contrast, in America and Europe, where quality control activities are seldom entrusted to workers on the line, nearly 10% of all factory employees are inspectors.

In Japan, inspections by specialized inspectors have been minimized for a number of reasons: Inspectors whose activities stand outside the manufacturing process perform operations with no value added and thus add to production costs without increasing productivity. Also, feedback from the inspectors to the manufacturing process usually takes so long that defective parts or products continue to be produced for some time after a problem is discovered.

Under the present system, the manufacturer or manufacturing process is itself responsible for quality control; those most directly affected by defective parts are immediately aware of problems and charged with the responsibility for correcting them. As a result, few inspection procedures are assigned to specialized inspectors; usually the final inspections are made from the point of view of the consumer or management, not inspections for defects that would affect the flow of production.

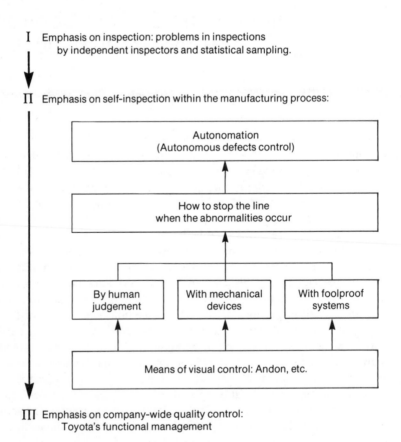

I Emphasis on inspection: problems in inspections
   by independent inspectors and statistical sampling.

II Emphasis on self-inspection within the manufacturing process:

Autonomation
(Autonomous defects control)

How to stop the line
when the abnormalities occur

By human
judgement

With mechanical
devices

With foolproof
systems

Means of visual control: Andon, etc.

III Emphasis on company-wide quality control:
    Toyota's functional management

Fig. 10.1 Evolution of quality control activities at Toyota.

Statistical quality control

Statistical quality control (SQC) originated in America in the 1930s as an industrial application of the control chart devised by Dr. W. A. Shewhart. It was introduced to Japanese industry after World War II, largely as the result of a lecture tour by Dr. W. E. Deming in 1950.

Although statistical quality control is still an important technique in Japanese QC systems, it too has certain drawbacks:

* In SQC, the acceptable quality level (AQL) which determines products that are passed but are of the minimum acceptable quality, is fixed at 0.5 or 1.0%. Either level, however, is unsatisfactory from the point of view of companies that aim for very high producer quality; e.g., a defect rate of one in a million. At Toyota, for example, the goal of quality control is to obtain 100% good units or a defect rate of 0. The reason for this is quite simple: even though Toyota may produce and sell millions of automobiles, an individual customer buys only one. If his car has defects, he will feel— and tell his friends—that Toyotas are "pieces of junk."

* Under the Toyota production system, excess inventory is a type of waste and thus is not permitted. Furthermore, Just-in-time production or the ability to meet demand changes with a minimum of lead time also makes it necessary to minimize inventory. If defective workpieces occur at any stage in the process, the flow of production will be interrupted and the entire line will stop.

For both reasons, then, Toyota is unable to rely on statistical sampling alone and has been forced instead to devise inexpensive means of conducting inspections for all units ("total inspection") to ensure zero defects.

Statistical sampling is still practiced at certain departments where lot production takes place. At a high-speed automatic punch press, for example, where lots of 50 or 100 units are kept in a chute, only the first and last units in the chute are inspected. If both units are good, *all* units in the chute are considered good. If the last unit is defective, however, a search will be made for the first defective unit in the chute, all defective units in the chute will be removed, and remedial action taken. So that no lot will escape inspection, the punch press is set to stop automatically at the end of each lot.

Use of statistical sampling is in effect a total inspection since it is used only when an operation has been fully stabilized through careful maintenance of equipment and tools and sporadic defects do not occur. In such cases, the distribution of the product's data variation (6 x the standard deviation) will be relatively small compared to the designed tolerance, and the bias of the data mean from the central value of the designed specification will also be small (Fig. 10.2). Under such conditions, the sampling inspection plan will guarantee the quality of all units in the chute.

In effect, then, all units inspection or its equivalent has been substituted for ordinary statistical sampling, just as inspections within the manufacturing process itself have been developed to replace inspections by independent inspectors. In both cases, more traditional methods of quality control have been replaced by self-inspection of all units in the interest of further reducing the number of defective units. This approach to quality control is called Jidoka or Autonomation.

Autonomation

In Japanese, *Jidoka* has two meanings and is written with two different ideograms (Fig. 10.3). One ideogram means automation in the usual sense: to change from a manual process to a machine process. With this kind of automation, the machine operates by itself once the switch is thrown but has no feedback mechanism for detecting errors and no device for stopping the process if a malfunction occurs. Because this type of automation can lead to large numbers of defective parts in the event of a machine malfunction, it is considered unsatisfactory.

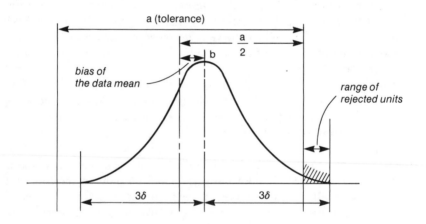

Process capability index (Cp) = $\dfrac{a}{6\delta}$

Degree of bias $(\beta) = \dfrac{b}{a/2}$

Condition for not producing the rejectable units:

$$b + 3\delta < a/2$$

or

$$Cp\,(1 - \beta) > 1.$$

$Cp \geq 1.33$ in the Toyota group.

Fig. 10.2   Process capability for quality and the bias.

$$\text{Jidoka} = \begin{cases} 1. & \text{自動化} = \text{Automation} \\ 2. & \text{自働化} = \text{Autonomation} \end{cases}$$

Fig. 10.3 Two meanings of Jidoka.

The second meaning of Jidoka is "automatic control of defects," a meaning coined by Toyota. To distinguish between the two meanings of Jidoka, Toyota often refers to the second type of Jidoka as *Ninbennoaru* Jidoka or, literally translated, "automation with a human mind." Jidoka translates to autonomation in English.

Although autonomation often involves some type of automation, it is not limited to machine processes but can be used in conjunction with manual operations as well. In either case, it is predominantly a technique for detecting and correcting production defects and always incorporates the following devices: a mechanism to detect abnormalities or defects; and a mechanism to stop the line or machine when abnormalities or defects occur. In short, Autonomation at Toyota always involves quality control since it makes it impossible for defective parts to pass unnoticed through the line. When a defect occurs, the line stops, forcing immediate attention to the problem, an investigation into its causes, and initiation of corrective action to prevent similar defects from occurring again. Autonomation also has other equally important components and effects: cost reduction, adaptable production, and increased respect for humanity (Fig. 10.4).

Cost reduction through decreases in the work force. With equipment designed to stop automatically when the required quantity has been produced or when a defect occurs, there is no need for the worker to oversee machine operations. As a result, manual operations can be separated from machine operations, and a worker who has finished his work at machine A can go on to operate machine B while machine A is still running. Autonomation thus plays an important role in refining the standard operating routine: the worker's ability to handle more than one machine at a time makes it possible to reduce the workforce and thus the cost of production.

Adaptability to changes in demand. Since all machines stop automatically when they have produced the required number of parts and produce only good parts, autonomation eliminates excess inventory and thus makes possible Just-in-time production and ready adaptability to changes in demand.

Respect for humanity. Since quality control based on autonomation calls immediate attention to defects or problems in the production process, it stimulates improvement activities and thus increases respect for humanity.

141

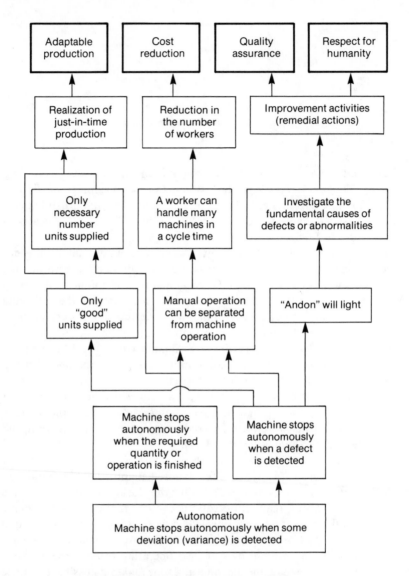

Fig. 10.4 How autonomation attains its purposes.

Autonomation and the Toyota production system

Having examined the purposes of autonomation, we next consider its application to the Toyota production system; i.e., the specific types of devices used to stop the line when defects occur, the techniques employed to accustom the workers to autonomated production, and the means for monitoring production and correcting abnormalities when they occur.

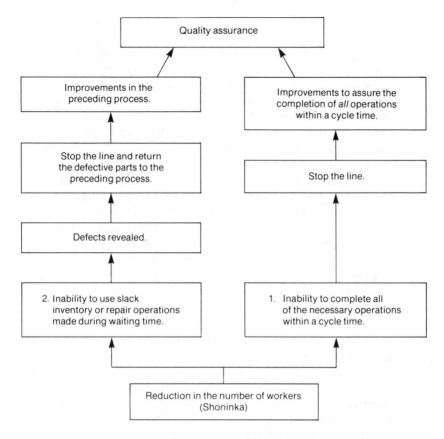

Fig. 10.5 Causal relationships in line stoppages.

Methods for stopping the line

In general, there are two ways to stop the line when abnormalities occur: by relying on human judgement and by means of automatic devices.

Each worker has the power and the responsibility to stop the line if all operations are not or cannot be performed in accordance with the standard operations routine. The causes are either a reduction in the number of workers (Shojinka), which results in a cycle time that is too short, or defective units produced at the preceding process, making it necessary for the worker at the next process to stop the line. If, for example, it takes a worker 80 seconds to complete his assigned operations and his cycle time is 70 seconds, he must stop the line for ten seconds at each cycle. Otherwise, he will be unable to finish his work and defects will occur. When the line stops, supervisors and engineers must investigate the problem and undertake improvement activities in order to reduce the actual operations time from 80 to 70 seconds. Such activities may include elimination of wasteful actions, shortening of walking distances, etc.

Defective units produced at the preceding process usually appear when reductions in intermediate inventory under the Kanban system or reductions in the workforce make it impossible to replace the defective units from inventory or repair them during waiting time. As a result, the line must stop when the defects appear, which calls attention to the problem and presents an opportunity for further improvement activities. Design defects, for example, or continually omitted operation at the previous process may surface in this way (Fig. 10.5).

With line stoppages due to defective units or revision of the standard operations routine, the supervisor's responsibility is twofold. First, he must teach the workers to stop the line whenever defects occur so that only good units are delivered. Second, he must discover and correct the cause of the defects that have stopped the line. In the case of defective workpieces delivered from the preceding process, for example, he must return the parts to the previous station, investigate the cause of the problem, and, if necessary, institute changes to prevent the defects from occurring again.

The key to preventing defects via human judgement is that every worker has the power to stop the line. In this respect Toyota's production system is not only more effective in controlling quality than Henry Ford's conveyor line, but more humanistic as well.

When the author described Toyota's system to American industrial engineers at conferences in 1981, many of those attending said their employees could not be trusted to such an extent and would stop the line simply to avoid work. In Japan, the problem is just the opposite. Because the workers' morale is so high, they often fail to stop the line when they should and even enter the next process to complete their assigned operations; i.e., they force themselves to finish their jobs in spite of the supervisor's instructions to stop the line if they are delayed or become tired.

Similar problems may also develop with part-time or seasonal full-time workers, who often send products on without installing all of the parts or without fully tightening fasteners. In either case, quality control methods based on human judgement alone may fail as a result of the worker's reluctance to slow production and call attention to himself by stopping the line. A series of devices were installed to stop the line automatically if the worker fails to complete his assigned operation in the allotted time.

Mechanical checks in aid of human judgement

On one line, for example, the workers carry out their operation while walking along beneath an overhead conveyor. Between processes is a mat like those that open doors automatically in supermarkets and airports. If the worker exceeds the distance allotted for completion of his work, he steps on the mat and the line stops. In a similar operation, the tool used to install lugnuts on wheels is suspended from an overhead rail and moves with the worker as he walks along the line. If the tool holder passes a certain point on the rail, the line stops automatically to prevent the worker from entering the next process to finish his job.

At first, workers resisted even such limited forms of automatic controls because they were forced to complete their jobs within the assigned cycle time. Thus, it was necessary for the supervisors to explain the purpose of the system and its advantages for the worker: to free him from the burden of wasted actions by identifying and correcting various problems in the line. As a result, the workers fully accepted the system, quality control improved, and the total time consumed by line stoppages was actually reduced.

Foolproof systems for stopping the line

Foolproof systems are similar in operation to the mechanical checks described here and are widely used in both machine and manual operations. Unlike the mechanical checks, however, foolproof systems are used to eliminate defects that may occur due to an oversight on the worker's part, not to lack of time in the cycle or unwillingness to stop the line.

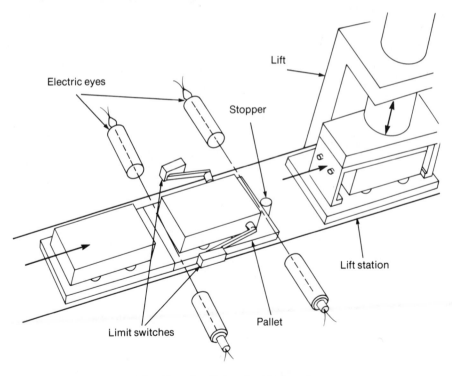

Fig. 10.6   Contact method foolproof.

A foolproof system consists of a *detecting* instrument, a *restricting* tool, and a *signaling* device. The detecting instrument senses abnormalities or deviations in the workpiece or the process, the restricting tool stops the line, and the signalling device sounds a buzzer or lights a lamp to attract the worker's attention. In the packing process shown in Fig. 10.6, for example, the lift or the product may be damaged if the product is off center on the pallet. To prevent this, a pair of limit switches detects the side-to-side position of the product and a pair of electric eyes checks its position front to rear. If the product is incorrectly positioned, a stopper prevents the pallet from continuing along the line to the lift and a buzzer sounds to call the problem to the worker's attention. In this case, the limit switches and electric eyes are the detecting instruments, the stopper is the restricting tool, and the buzzer is the signalling device.

Generally, detecting devices fall into one of three categories and are dictated by the type of foolproof method in use.

Contact method. Limit switches or electric eyes like the ones shown in Fig. 10.6 are used to detect differences in the size or shape of the product and thus to check for the presence of specific types of defects. For the purpose of using the contact method, uniqueness of shape or size is sometimes intentionally designed into essentially similar parts. Devices that distinguish

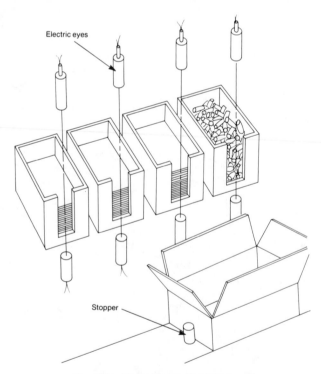

Fig. 10.7 Altogether method foolproof.

146

one color from another are also part of the contact method, even though the "contact" is made with reflected light instead of a limit switch or electric eye.

Altogether method. Unlike the contact method, which is used mainly to check for the presence of a particular feature or to ensure that a specific step has been performed correctly, the altogether method is used to ensure that all parts of an operation have been successfully completed. An altogether system is used, for example, to be sure that the worker puts all of the required parts and an instruction sheet into the shipping box (Fig. 10.7). To construct the foolproof, electric eyes were installed in front of each parts bin so that the worker's hand interrupts the light beam when he removes a part or instruction sheet from its bin. Unless all of the beams have been interrupted, the stopper will not release the box and allow it to leave the worker's station.

Other processes controlled by the altogether method use a counter to prevent oversights. At a spot welding station, for example, a counter records the number of welds and sounds a buzzer if there is a discrepancy between the number it has counted and the number required.

Action step method. The action step method is so named because, unlike other foolproof methods, it requires the worker to perform a step which is not part of the operations on the product. Consider, for example, the station where metal fittings are attached to seats. Since the same department would often process as many as eight different kinds of seats in a mixed schedule, a Kanban was attached to each seat so that the worker would know which metal fittings to attach. Even so, improper metal fittings continued to be installed several times each month. As a result, the following action step foolproof was devised. At the lower edge of each Kanban is a piece of aluminum foil. When a seat arrives at the worker's station, the worker picks up the Kanban and inserts it in a specially installed *Kanban inserting box.* When the Kanban is inserted in the box, a sensor detects the position of the aluminum foil, turns on a red lamp over the proper box of metal fittings, and opens the box. The worker than removes a set of fittings from the open box and installs them on the seat.

The aforementioned is an example of the advantages of a foolproof system over methods based on human judgement alone. Both methods fulfill the major purposes of autonomation: quality assurance, cost reduction, realization of just-in-time delivery, and increased respect for humanity. Foolproof systems, however, not only guarantee product quality, but contribute to greater respect for humanity by relieving the worker of constant attention to worrisome details.

Visual controls

In implementing autonomation, various visual controls monitor the state of the line and the flow of production. Some of the visual controls have been mentioned in connection with various types of quality control devices. Most foolproof systems, for example, use a light or some other type of signal to indicate an abnormality in the production run. Other visual controls include: Andon and call lights, standard operations sheets, Kanban tickets, digital display panels, and storage and stock plates.

Andon and call lights. Each assembly and machining line is equipped with a call light and an Andon board. The call light is used to call for a supervisor, maintenance worker, or general worker. Usually it has several different colors of lights, each of which is used to summon a different type of assistance. On most lines the call light is suspended from the ceiling or otherwise located so that supervisors and maintenance workers can see it easily.

Andon is a nickname for the indicator board that shows when a worker has stopped the line. As explained earlier, each worker at Toyota has a switch that enables him to stop the line in the event of a breakdown or a delay at his station. When this happens, a red lamp on the Andon over his line will light to indicate which process is responsible for the stoppage. The supervisor then goes immediately to the workstation to investigate the problem and take the necessary corrective action. Fig. 10.8 shows a call light and Andon boards with the switch used to control the lamps. In the figure, the call lights are mounted on the Andon; at some stations, however, the two are installed at separate locations (Fig. 10.9).

In many cases, the Andon has different colored lights to indicate the

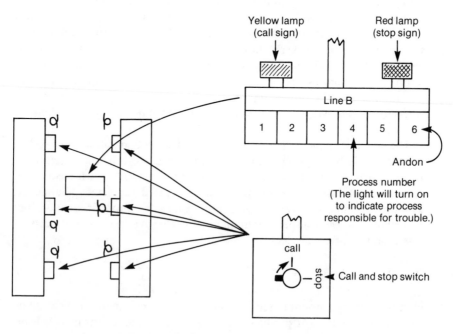

Fig. 10.8 Call light, Andon, and stop switch.

148

condition of the line. A green light, for example, indicates normal operation, and a yellow light that a worker is calling for help with a problem. If the trouble is not corrected, a red light will come on to show that the line has stopped. At other locations, Andon boards may have even more lights and use a different color code to indicate the condition of the line. The board usually has five colors with the following meanings:

Red Machine trouble
White End of a production run; the required quantity has been produced
Green No work due to shortage of materials
Blue Defective unit
Yellow Setup required (includes tool changes, etc.)

All types of Andons are turned off when a supervisor or maintenance person arrives at the workstation responsible for the delay.

Standard operations sheets and Kanban tickets. As explained in Chapter 7, a standard operation at Toyota consists of a cycle time; a standard

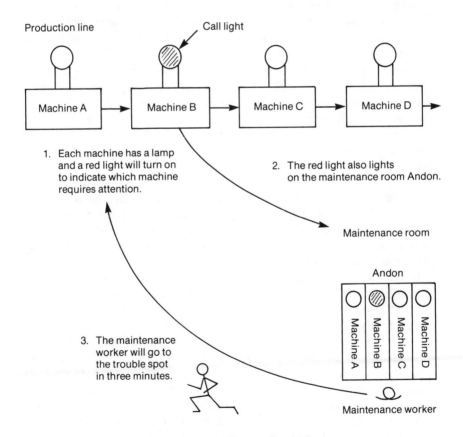

Fig. 10.9 Machine-maintenance Andon.

operations routine, including assigned checks for quality and safety; and a standard quantity of work in process. All three of these elements are included in a standard operations sheet, which is posted at the line where each worker can see it easily. When a worker cannot perform his standard operations within the cycle time, he must stop the line and call for help to resolve the problem. The standard operations sheet thus works together with other types of visual controls to achieve standard operations, eliminate waste, and prevent defects.

Like the standard operations sheet, Kanban tickets also serve as a visual control over abnormalities in production. If, for example, products find their way into the storage area behind the line with no Kanban attached, it is a sign of overproduction that should be investigated immediately. Either the cycle time has been set too long, the worker has excessive waiting time, or the line has been stopped frequently at the next process. In any case, the absence of the Kanban should act as a signal for immediate investigation and elimination of the problem.

In addition to their role in overproduction control, Kanban tickets serve other visual control functions as well. By checking the number of the production ordering Kanban, for example, the supervisor can tell which products are in process and determine whether overtime will be necessary or not.

Digital display panels. The pace of production is also shown in digital display panels which indicate both the day's production goal and a running count of the units produced so far. Thus, by watching the panels, everyone on the line can tell whether production is going too slowly to meet the day's goal and can work together to keep production on schedule. Like call lights and Andons, the digital display plates also serve to alert supervisors to problems and delays at various points along the line.

Store and stock indicator plates. Each storage location is assigned an "address" which is shown both on a plate over the storage location (Fig. 10.10) and on the Kanban. As a result, carriers can always deliver parts to the proper location by comparing the address on the Kanban to that on the store plate. In addition to the storage address, the stock plate also indicates the standard quantity of stock as an aid to inventory control.

While visual control systems are effective in achieving autonomation, they, like other quality control methods, function only to detect abnormalities (Fig. 10.11). Remedial action to correct the defects or abnormalities remains in the hands of the supervisor and his workers, who must always follow a prescribed sequence of events: standardization of operations, detection of abnormalities, investigation of causes, improvement activities through QC circles, and restandardization of operations. Ultimately, however, the goal of autonomation must be unmanned production, where even remedial action to correct defects is taken autonomously. Before going on to examine other types of quality control, it may be useful to look at robotics—its use and its potential impact on the Toyota production system.

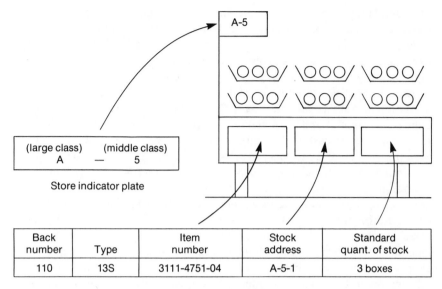

Back number	Type	Item number	Stock address	Standard quant. of stock
110	13S	3111-4751-04	A-5-1	3 boxes

Stock indicator plate

Fig. 10.10   Store plate and stock plate.

Robotics

Like their American counterparts, Japanese automobile manufacturers are installing industrial robots on a large scale, especially in processes that involve welding, painting, and machining of parts. The reasons are many, including: increased safety, increased product quality, and increased productivity with,

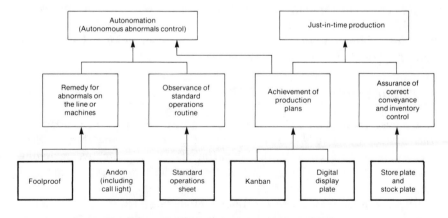

Fig. 10.11   Framework of the visual control systems.

of course, reduced costs. As safety and product quality are concerned, the advantages of robotics are obvious. Robots can relieve human workers of hazardous jobs in areas where they are exposed to dangerous fumes and other environmental threats. Since robots can perform repetitious operations with high accuracy and without fatigue, they also contribute to improved quality control. Increased productivity, on the other hand, is less simple to assess.

At present, a skilled laborer in Japan earns about 4 million yen per year with annual increases of approximately 6 to 7 percent. While wages continue to rise, however, the cost of the simplest robot is approximately 2 million yen; even the most complex robots can be purchased for 15 to 20 million yen. Since a painting robot, for example, can do the work of 1.5 men, the long-term savings in labor costs from robotics are obvious and hard to ignore. In addition, robots are more easily adaptable to increased product diversity than a human labor force since they require fewer changes in the layout of processes when designs change. A production system composed of robots and machines, for example, can often be adapted to new models simply by a change in tools and a change in the robot's memory. With men-machine systems, on the other hand, a model change often involves large investments in new equipment and training for human operators.

Robots and the Toyota production system

Whatever the impact of robotics on employee relations, it is important to see that its introduction is not an abandonment but a logical extension of the Toyota production system. In fact, the principal goals of robotics are fully in keeping with those of the system in general cost reduction, quality assurance, flexible production, and respect for humanity. How robotics contributes to the first three goals has already been described. Its contribution to respect for humanity is not only to relieve human workers of risky, severe jobs but to extend in various ways the prevailing use of machines and technology in the Toyota production system—namely, to replace men with machines only when it will free the worker from repetitive tasks and make more time available for meaningful human action. In short, robots, like any other kind of technology must remain the tool of men and not the other way around.

Company-wide quality control

The phrase Total Quality Control (TQC) was first used by Dr. Feigenbaum of the United States in *Industrial Quality Control* magazine (May, 1957). According to Feigenbaum, all departments of a company, including marketing, design, production, inspection, and delivery must participate in QC.

Feigenbaum assigns the central role in promoting TQC to QC specialists. Japanese QC, however, which is often called Company-Wide Quality

Control (CWQC) to distinguish it from Feigenbaum's TQC, is not conducted by QC specialists. If it were, line employees in each department would very likely reject the suggestions of the QC staff because line connections are very strong in Japanese companies. Instead, QC is the responsibility of workers at every level and in every department of the organization, all of whom have studied QC techniques.

According to Dr. Kaoru Ishikawa, promoter of the Japanese QC movement, CWQC has the following three characteristics: all departments participate in QC, all types of employees participate in QC, and QC is fully integrated with other related company functions.

All departments participate in QC

In order to assure product quality, all departments—product planning, design, testing, purchasing, suppliers, manufacturing engineering, inspection, sales, and service, etc.—must participate in QC activities. Quality analyses at the product development and product design stages, for example, are essential to establishing overall product quality, since it is impossible to correct errors made at either stage once the product reaches manufacturing and inspection departments. At the same time, however, each of the other departments also has an important role of its own to play. At this point, it may be useful to recall the definition of quality control with which the chapter began: In Japan, quality control (QC) or quality assurance (QA) is defined as the development, design, manufacture, and service of products that will satisfy the consumer's needs at the lowest possible cost.

Satisfaction of the consumer's needs is predominantly the concern of new product development and design, which must identify customer needs such as high gas mileage and trouble-free performance and be sure that the product satisfies them. Quality control at this level ensures that the Japanese automobile will continue to be popular throughout the world and thus, ultimately, that sales and profits will continue to be high. Quality control during manufacturing (through autonomation and other techniques described in this chapter) decreases production costs by reducing defects and thus guarantees both low cost to the consumer and company profitability. And finally, quality control in customer service in the after market is important for maintaining the automobile in good working order and so confirming the customer's confidence in the product and the company. The same points are made in pamphlets issued by Toyota Motor Sales, USA.

All employees participate in QC

People at all levels of the organizational hierarchy participate in quality control—from the president of the company, the directors, and departmental managers to blue collar workers and salesmen. Furthermore, all suppliers, distributors, and other related companies also take part in QC activities.

Although the term "QC circle" is very popular in other countries, it should be recognized that QC circle activities are merely a part of CWQC. Without CWQC and without the obvious participation of top management, departmental managers and their staffs, QC circles would lose much of their effectiveness and might cease to exist altogether.

QC is fully integrated with other related company functions

To be effective, quality control must be promoted together with cost management and production management techniques. These include profit planning, pricing, production and inventory control and scheduling, each of which has a direct impact on quality control. Cost control techniques, for example, can help identify wasteful processes that can be improved or eliminated and can measure the effect of QC activities once undertaken. Pricing determines not only the level of quality built into the product but the customer's expectations about quality as well. And various kinds of production control data can be used to measure defect rates, establish target areas for QC activities, and promote QC in general.

11

Functional Management to Promote Company-Wide Quality Control and Cost Management

As described in Chapter 10, CWQC is possible only if quality control activities and quality-related functions are carried out in all departments and at all levels of management. Furthermore, the activities of each department must be planned so they are reinforced by other departments. Additionally, they will benefit from quality-related functions throughout the company. The responsibility for establishing communication links between the various departments at Toyota and ensuring cooperation in implementing QC programs is given to an organizational entity known as a *functional meeting*. Functional meetings do not serve as project teams or task forces. Rather, they are formally constituted, decision-making units whose power cuts across department lines and controls broad corporate functions. Consisting typically of department directors from all parts of the company, each functional meeting will consider such corporate-wide problems as cost management, production management, and quality assurance, respectively. The meeting then communicates their policy decision and plans for implementation to each department for action. Such management through functional meetings is called *functional management* ("Kinohbetsu Kanri") at Toyota.

In this chapter, we will examine the structural relationships between the functional meetings and the more formally developed organizations at Toyota, how business policy is made and administered through functional management, and some of the advantages to be gained from the functional management concept. Although the Toyota production system in a narrow sense does not include the product planning and design steps, the author includes functional management in the broad overview of the system. The reader should realize that the most important aspects for increasing productivity or decreasing costs and improving quality are the QC and cost reduction activities in the product development and design steps.

Historically, functional management is the outgrowth of a long process of trial and error. The QC Promoting Office at Toyota took the first steps toward company-wide quality control in 1961 by defining various important functions to be performed by the company. Each department, in turn, collaborated to determine and arrange the contents of the functions. By the addition, integration, and abolition of these inputs, the defined functions were classified and selected into the two most necessary rules for the entire company: quality assurance and cost management. Rules were then established to define what kinds of activities each department must undertake to properly perform these two functions.

Quality assurance

Quality assurance, as defined in this rule at Toyota, is to assure that the quality of the product promotes satisfaction, reliability, and economy for the consumer. This rule outlines the activities of each department for quality assurance at all phases from product planning to sales and service. Further, the rule specifies when and what should be assured by whom at where.

The rule defines *when* as applicable eight steps in a series of business activities from planning through sales: product planning, product design, manufacturing preparation, purchasing, manufacturing for sales, inspection, sales and service, and quality audit. The term by *whom at where* means the specific department manager and the name of his department. *What* consists of items to be assured and the operations for assurance. Table 11.1 defines the quality assurance rule as it pertains to the steps in the business activities defined here and the primary operations of each department.

Cost management

Toyota utilizes cost management to develop and perform various activities to attain a specific profit goal, evaluate results, and take appropriate action as necessary. In other words, cost management is not simply confined to cost reduction. It also covers company-wide activities to acquire profit. This rule specifically outlines the activities of each department level to maintain cost management. The framework of this cost management evolves from the following four categories: cost planning, capital investment planning, cost maintenance, cost improvement.

Cost planning has been regarded as especially important because most of the cost is determined during the development stages of the product. A cost

156

Functional Steps	Person in Charge	Primary Operations For QA	Contribution
Product Planning	• Sales Department Manager • Product Planning Department Head	1. Forecasts of demands and market share	△

		2. Obtain the quality to satisfy marketing needs
		  a. Set and assign proper quality target and cost target.
		  b. Prevent recurrence of important quality problems.
			◎

Product Design	• Design Department Manager • Body-Design Department Manager • Engineering Department Managers • Product Design Department Manager	1. Design of prototype vehicles a. Meet quality target	◎

		b. Test and examine car for:
		    Performance
		    Safety
		    Low Pollution
		    Economy
		    Reliability
			○

		2. Initial design to confirm necessary conditions for QA	○
Manufacturing Preparation	• Engineering Department Managers • QA Department Manager • Inspection Department Managers • Manufacturing Department Manager	1. Preparation of overall lines to satisfy design quality	◎
		2. Preparation of proper inspection methods	○
		3. Evaluation of initial prototypes	○
		4. Develop and evaluate a plan of initial and daily process control	△
		5. Preparation of line capacities	◎
Purchasing	• Purchasing Department Managers • QA Department Manager • Inspection Department Managers	1. Confirmation of qualitative and quantitative capabilities of each supplier	△
		2. Inspect initial parts supplied for product quality	△
		3. Support in strengthening QA system of each supplier	△
Manufacturing	• Manufacturing Department Managers • Production Control Department Manager	1. Match product quality to established standards	○
		2. Establish properly controlled lines	○
		3. Maintain necessary line capacities and machine capacities	○
Inspection	• Inspection Department Manager • QA Department Manager	1. Inspect initial product for quality	○
		2. Decision whether to deliver product for sale	◎
Sales and Service	• Sales Department Manager • Export Department Manager • QA Department Manager	1. Prevention of quality decline in packaging, storage and delivery	○
		2. Education and public relations for proper care and maintenance	△
		3. Inspection of new cars	△
		4. Feedback and analysis of quality information	◎

Table 11.1 Quality assurance summary.

Functional Steps	Related Departments	Cost Management Operations	Contri-bution
Product Planning	• Corporate Planning • Product Planning Office • Production Engineering Departments • Accounting Departments	1. Set target cost based on new product planning and profit planning, then assign this target cost to various cost factors 2. Set target investment figures 3. Allocate target cost to various design departments of individual parts *(cost planning)* 4. Allocate target investment amounts to various investment planning departments *(capital budgeting)*	◎ ◎ ○ ○
Product Design	• Product Planning Office • Engineering Departments	1. Cost estimate based on prototype drawing 2. Evaluate possibility of attaining target costs 3. Take necessary steps to minimize deviations between target costs and estimated costs through Value Engineering (VE)	◎ ◎ ○
Manufacturing Preparation	• Product Planning Office • Engineering Departments • Manufacturing Engineering Departments • Production Control Department	1. Establish cost estimate by considering line preparation and investment plans 2. Evaluate possibility of attaining target costs 3. Take actions to minimize deviations 4. Evaluate facilities investment plans 5. Evaluate production plans, conditions and decisions to make or buy parts	◎ ◎ ◎ ○ ○
Purchasing	• Purchasing Departments	1. Evaluate procurement plans and purchasing conditions 2. Establish control of supplier prices (comparison of target reduction and actual reduction amounts, analyze variances and take appropriate action) 3. Investigate improvement of supplier costs (apply Value Analysis (VA), establish support to promote supplier cost improvement activities)	○ ○ ◎
Manufacturing Inspection	• Related Departments • Accounting Department	1. Instigate cost maintenance and improvements through: a. budgeting fixed costs (Manufacturing and Managerial Departments) b. cost improvements in primary projects (classified for each type of vehicle and cost factor) c. increased cost consciousness of employees through suggestions systems, case presentation seminars, reward or incentive programs, etc.	○ ○ ◎
Sales and Service	• Related Departments • Accounting Department	1. Measure actual costs of new products through overall evaluation 2. Participate in analyses and discussions at operations check, cost management functional meetings, cost meetings, and various committee meetings	○ ○

Table 11.2   Cost management summary.

planning manual assigns primary responsibilities and tasks at each phase of product development. Establishing a target cost to be followed during all development stages promotes activities to reduce costs, while maintaining minimum quality standards.

Cost maintenance and improvement are cost management processes at the manufacturing level. These are promoted by a company-wide budgeting system and the improvement activities described in Chapter 9. To maintain these functions, each department has its own departmental budgeting manual and cost improvement manual.

The contents of cost management activities are specified in detail in the cost management operations assignment manual. Table 11.2 summarizes the cost management rule with respect to related departments and cost management operations.

Relations among departments, steps in business activities and functions

In order to effectively promote functional management, it must be clearly understood how each step to be performed by each department contributes to its function. Because equal emphasis cannot be placed on all operations, each step must be graded for relative contribution. Thus, the right-hand column in Tables 11.1 and 11.2 describes the relative contribution for each managerial function, as noted by the following symbols:

◎ Defines factors with critical influence on the function

○ Defines factors with some influence that could be remedied in later steps

△ Defines factors with relatively small influence

Such assessments were made for all functions. The relationships between departments and functions are summarized in Table 11.3.

The final business purpose at Toyota is to maximize long-range profit under various economic and environmental constraints. This long-range profit will be defined and expressed as a concrete figure through long-range business planning. Therefore, each function must be carefully selected and organized to be helpful in attaining the long-range profit.

If the number of functions was too high, then each function would begin to interfere with other functions, frustrating attempts to produce a new product in a timely and cost effective manner. Further, too many functions will foster strong independence of certain functions to the point that each departmental management might be enough to perform the function.

Conversely, if the number of functions was too small, too many departments would be related in a single function. Managing so many departments from a certain functional standpoint would be very complicated, if not impossible.

Toyota regards quality assurance and cost management as paramount functions, or *purpose functions,* and calls them the two pillars of functional management. Other functions are regarded as *means functions.* Thus, product planning and product design are integrated into an engineering function;

Table 11.3 Summary of various functional managements.

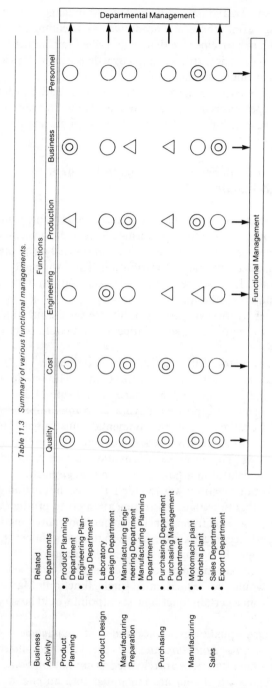

Table 11.3 Summary of various functional managements.

manufacturing preparation and manufacturing into a production function; and sales and purchasing into a business function.

As a result, six functions remain in the Toyota functional management system (Table 11.3). In summary, each function in new product development, manufacturing technique, and marketing philosophy is not identical with other functions in its character or priority.

Organization of the functional management system

At Toyota, each director of the company is responsible for a certain department. Since each department involves more than one function, each director must participate in multiple functions (Table 11.3). No single director is responsible for a single function; he serves as a member of a team. Conversely, not all department directors participate in all functions. This would create difficulties managing each functional meeting because of too many members. For example, although there are thirteen departments involved in product planning and product design, only one or two directors will attend a QA functional meeting.

As previously stated, the functional meeting is the only formal organizational unit in functional management. Each functional meeting is a chartered decision-making unit charged to plan, check, and decide remedial actions required to achieve a functional goal. Each individual department serves as a line unit to perform the actions dictated by the functional meeting.

Fig. 11.4 details the framework of the top management organization at Toyota. Each department is managed by a managing director or common director, whereas each functional meeting consists of all directors, including six executive directors. Since each executive director is responsible for integrating the actions of various departments, he will participate as chairman in those functional meetings that have close relationships with his integrated departments. By necessity, even a vice president may participate in a functional meeting. A functional meeting typically numbers about ten members.

The quality assurance and cost management functional meetings are normally conducted once a month. Other functional meetings are usually held every other month. A functional meeting should not be convened without a significant agenda.

Functional meetings are positioned below the management meeting which consists of all managing directors and the standing auditor. The management meeting is an executive organization that gives final approval to the decision items of the functional meeting. However, the essential decision-making authority remains with each functional meeting because implementation of the decision begins at the functional meeting. As long as there are no special objections in the management meeting, the decision made by the functional meeting will be treated as a company decision.

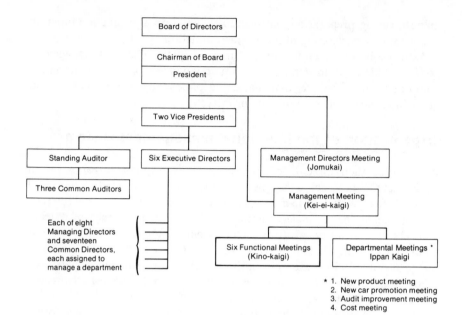

```
                    ┌─────────────────────┐
                    │  Board of Directors │
                    └──────────┬──────────┘
                    ┌──────────┴──────────┐
                    │  Chairman of Board  │
                    │      President      │
                    └──────────┬──────────┘
                               │
                    ┌──────────┴──────────┐
                    │ Two Vice Presidents │
                    └──────────┬──────────┘
```

Board of Directors

Chairman of Board
President

Two Vice Presidents

Standing Auditor

Three Common Auditors

Six Executive Directors

Management Directors Meeting
(Jomukai)

Management Meeting
(Kei-ei-kaigi)

Each of eight
Managing Directors
and seventeen
Common Directors,
each assigned to
manage a department

Six Functional Meetings
(Kino-kaigi)

Departmental Meetings *
Ippan Kaigi

* 1. New product meeting
  2. New car promotion meeting
  3. Audit improvement meeting
  4. Cost meeting

Fig. 11.4   Framework of Toyota management organization (as of 1981).

The *departmental meetings* shown in Fig. 11.4 provide each department with a vehicle to discuss implementation of decisions made by the functional meeting. Note that the departmental meeting is not positioned as a substructure of the functional meeting. As with the functional meetings, plans for implementation generated within departmental meetings are subject to review and approval by the management meeting.

Occasionally, a problem arises such as a need to achieve a certain quality characteristic within a short-term period that cannot be resolved by only one functional meeting. By necessity, man-hours and costs must increase to improve the quality. At this time, a *joint functional meeting* is found to combine quality and production functions. Further, in order to cope with a new legal restriction for safety and pollution, most of the functions, such as QA, cost, engineering, and production, must consider the restriction together. In this case, an *enlarged functional meeting* is formed to consider the problem. Note that these are not permanent organizational entities.

Another example involves a *cost management functional meeting*. Just after the oil shock in 1973, the profitability of the Toyota Corolla showed a marked decrease because of cost increases due to oil prices. At that time, the plant manager of Corolla made the following proposals to the cost functional meeting:

1. Promotion of a company-wide cost reduction movement for Corolla.
2. Organization of a Corolla Cost Reduction Committee chaired by the plant manager.

3. As substructures to this committee, organization of the following sectional meetings:
   a. production and assembly
   b. design and engineering
   c. purchasing
4. Establish a cost reduction of 10,000 yen (about $40) per automobile.
5. Goal to be achieved within six months.

Through a concerted effort by all departments based on the decisions of the cost management function meeting, the actual result of the plan was 128% attainment of the goal at the end of six months (May 1975).

Business policy and functional management

Since the introduction of the CWQC concept, a business policy has been developed and published. The policy applies to the operations level and includes each function previously discussed. The six elements of the business policy are shown in Fig. 11.5 and defined in the following paragraphs.

1. *Fundamental policy* is the business ethic principle, or fundamental directions, of the company. Once established, it will not change for many years. An example is "Toyota wishes to develop in the world by collecting all powers inside and outside the company." The expression is abstract, but represents a business philosophy of top management. The fundamental policy is used to guide long-range planning.

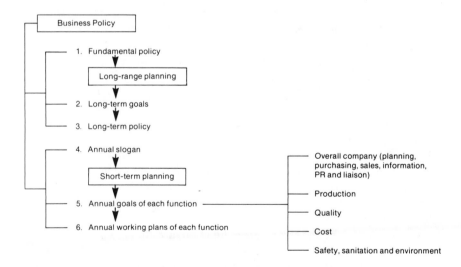

Fig. 11.5   Six elements of business policy at Toyota.

2. *Long-term goals* are goals to be attained within five years as an output of long-range planning. These goals are concrete figures expressed for production quality, sales quality, market share and ROI, etc.
3. *Long-term policy* is the strategy used to achieve the long-term goals, and is expressed in more concrete detail than the fundamental policy. It covers several items common to the overall company. For example: "In order to manage the overall company in a scientific manner, policies, goals, and plans must be prepared for each department and a control point must be clearly defined and directed."
4. *Annual slogan* is a means for Toyota to emphasize annual policies. It consists of two types of slogans. The first type remains the same every year, such as "Assure the quality in every Toyota." The second type emphasizes the policy for the year. For example, the slogan for 1974 just after the oil shock was "Build Toyotas for the changing age." Also: "It is time to use scarce resources effectively." The purpose of these slogans is to encourage a sound mental attitude in all employees.
5. Accepting the long-term goals described above, the *annual goals of each function* to be achieved within the current year must be expressed in specific figures. These goal figures are established for each function. Each functional meeting, in turn, decides how to achieve these goals. The items included as annual goals for each function follow:
   a. Overall company: ROI, production quantity, and market share.
   b. Production: Rate of reduced manpower to previous year's manpower level.
   c. Quality: Rate of reduction of problems in market.
   d. Cost: Total amount of costs to be reduced, plant and equipment investment amount, and margin rates of the preferentially developed automobiles.
   e. Safety, sanitation, and environment: Number of closures for holidays, etc., at business and plants.
6. Once annual goals are established for each function, *annual working plans of each function* must be determined by the appropriate functional meeting. Implementation of these working plans then becomes the responsibility of the department meeting.

Classification of the functions shown in Fig. 11.5 is somewhat different than shown in Table 11.3 because the business policy must describe all the important topics to be achieved in the current year. The business function in Table 11.3 is incorporated into the overall company function shown in Fig. 11.5 which also includes information and public relations. Further, although the safety, sanitation, and environment functions are not shown in Table 11.3, nor is there a functional meeting, safety and environment are included with the production functional meeting, while sanitation is included with both the production and personnel functions.

Extension of business policy

Formal announcement of the business policy at Toyota is made by the president in his New Year's greetings to the employees. Extension plans of each function will then be issued to each department by the office of the functional meeting. Department policies and plans are then formulated by the department meeting.

After implementation of these plans, the results of actual performance will be evaluated during the middle and at the end of the current year. Feedback from these evaluations will be used to form the policies for the next year. Such checks and evaluations are made at three levels within the organization: operations checks of selected topics by top management, functional checks by each functional meeting chairman, and department checks by each department manager or director. Fig. 11.6 shows the organization planning and control system employed at Toyota.

Critical considerations for functional management

Four critical considerations demand special attention in order to achieve a successful functional management program:

1. Selection of important functions should be made using special caution to properly balance department participation. Too many departments in the same functional meeting leads to confusion and difficulties in managing the meeting. Too few member departments create a need for many individual functions that will begin to overlap responsibilities, again creating confusion and management problems.
2. Functional management should not be regarded as an informal system. The position and guidelines of functional meetings in the top management scheme must be clearly defined. The function meeting must be given the necessary authority to implement its decisions as company policy.
3. Each line department must have a strong structure in place to execute the plans put forth by the various functional meetings.
4. The director in charge of each function is also responsible for an individual department. However, he must not view the function for his department alone, but rather formulate and direct the function for the overall company.

Advantages of functional management

Functional management as implemented at Toyota offers certain advantages not found in other management systems. For example:

- Both policies and implementation are decisive and rapidly instituted. This results because the functional meeting is a substantial decision-making

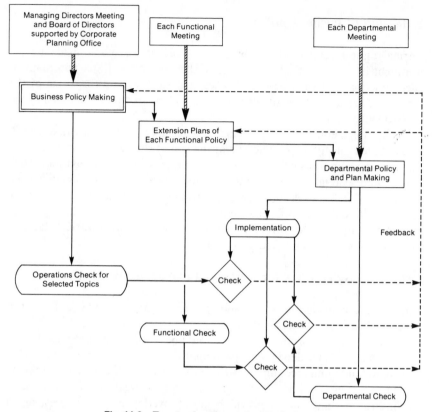

Fig. 11.6 Toyota planning and control system.

entity with responsibilities and authority directed from top management. Additionally, communication to executing line departments is rapid since the members of the functional meeting are also directors responsible for the related departments.

- *Nemawashi* is unnecessary at Toyota. The original meaning of Nemawashi comes from the preparations for transplanting a large tree. You must dig around the roots and cut the big roots so as to influence the small roots to run to secure its new position. Nemawashi, as applied to business, relates to the persuasion of related individuals, such as management executives, in advance of a formal decision meeting to accept some proposal. At Toyota, the functional meeting itself becomes the Nemawashi negotiation.

- The functional meetings serve to greatly enhance communications and human relations among the various departments because all sides are brought together to achieve a common goal.

- Communications from subordinate employees to the functional meetings are easily achieved because there is no need for Nemawashi. These employees need only to bring their suggestions and ideas to their department manager for discussion at the functional meeting.

166

Appendix 1

Determination of the Number of Kanban Pertinent to the Alternative Withdrawal Systems

The Toyota Kanban system is a pulling system: a withdrawal system where a manufacturing process withdraws parts from a preceding process and then the preceding process begins to produce as many units as withdrawn. In a sense, the subsequent process orders the necessary parts from the preceding process in the right quantity at the right time. As a result, the Kanban system can be examined from the viewpoint of inventory control systems.

Two types of inventory control systems exist: the *constant order-quantity system* and the *constant order-cycle system*. Under the constant order-quantity system, the predetermined fixed quantity will be ordered when the inventory level recedes to the reorder point (which is the expected usage during lead time). Although the order quantity is fixed, the reorder date is irregular. Under the constant order-cycle system, however, the reorder date is fixed and the quantity ordered depends on the usage since the previous order was placed and the outlook during the lead time. This outlook occurs after the order is placed but before it is received.

In the Kanban system, the total number of each part finally stored at the subsequent process and the number of Kanban delivered to the preceding process at each withdrawal point in time are determined by these two kinds of inventory models. At Toyota, two kinds of withdrawal systems correspond to these two different inventory systems: the *constant quantity, nonconstant cycle withdrawal system* and the *constant cycle, nonconstant quantity withdrawal system*.

Although basic similarities exist between the Kanban system and the

167

inventory control systems, many significant differences are evident. For example, when using Kanban, there is no need to examine the inventory quantity continuously; however, this is required in the constant order-quantity system. In the constant order-cycle system, the inventory quantity must be examined at each order time. At the same time, this amount must be subtracted from the standard quantity. With Kanban, the number of withdrawal Kanban detached at the subsequent process since the previous order is what must be ordered. Inventory calculations become very simple in Kanban systems.

With these points in mind, the Kanban can be defined as a medium of information for dispatching the right quantity of the right item at the right time. Standard inventory control systems will not have the means of conveying such information although the contents of such information is provided as logic. The Kanban system is a complete information system to control inventory.

The Kanban system is an indispensable subsystem of Toyota's total production system. To implement the Kanban system, the overall preparations in the production systems must include scheduling a smoothed sequence of products at the final assembly line, designing a layout of machines, standardizing operations, and shortening the setup time, etc. Further, as explained in Chapter 2, the Kanban system is a very powerful means for improving each production process.

Constant quantity, nonconstant cycle withdrawal system

At Toyota, the processes within the Toyota Motor Corp. plants normally use the constant quantity withdrawal system, whereas the supplier Kanban exclusively uses the constant cycle withdrawal system. This is due to the geographical distance. Within the Toyota plant, for example, the lead time is relatively short because of the short distance between processes and also the well improved processes. However, the total lead time for a supplier's products is relatively long because of the greater distances from the supplier, resulting in a longer conveyance time. The Kanban system has some similarity to the *two-bin* system, which is a type of constant order quantity inventory system, although it is not a derivative of this type of system.

The following formulas are used in constant order-quantity inventory system:

The order-quantity at each order or lot-size (Q) is determined by the EOQ model as follows:

(A-1) $Q = \sqrt{\dfrac{2AR}{ic}}$ (Notations are omitted)

The reorder point, which is the quantity level that automatically triggers a new order, is determined as:

(B-1)   Reorder Point

= average usage during lead time + safety stock
– orders placed but not yet received,

where the average usage during lead time = avg. usage per day × lead time

The lead time in this formula is simply the time interval between placing an order and receiving delivery. Also the last term in (B-1) is usually zero.

Kanban number under constant quantity withdrawal system

The constant quantity system at Toyota will not use the EOQ model to determine the lot size. To reduce the production lead time, the lot size must be minimized and setup times per day must be increased. However, there is a constraint for reducing the lot size: the necessary time span for the external setup (Chapter 6). Although the internal setup time at Toyota has been reduced to less than ten minutes, the external setup still requires one half to one hour. Without this minimum time span, you cannot step to the next lot. As a result, the lot size, or the number of setups per day at Toyota, must be determined by the constraint of the time span of external setup. Some efforts to reduce the external setup time must be made. For example, using a crane to fix the die on the bolster takes much time, so some method must be devised to do away with the crane.

Thus, although the lot size at Toyota is different among the various plants, the lot of 2 or 2.5 shifts use are very prevalent. Suppose the body line assembles 400 units per shift of a particular body style. Then a lot size of 2.5 shifts used for this body style means 1,000 units (= 2.5 x 400). If the SPH (stroke per hour) of the punch press is 500, it must run two hours for this lot size, and then the setup must be done. Since the lot size at Toyota is determined as shown here, it is not changed frequently. However, the reorder point is often changed because the daily average usage will change due to seasonal fluctuations.

There are three applications of Toyota's constant quantity withdrawal system. In the case where the lot size is fairly large, or the setup action is not sufficiently improved, the following formula is applied:

(A-2)   Total Number of Kanban

$$= \frac{\text{economic lot size} + (\text{daily demand} \times \text{safety coefficient})}{\text{container capacity}}$$

OR

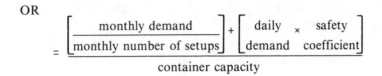

$$= \frac{\left[\dfrac{\text{monthly demand}}{\text{monthly number of setups}}\right] + \left[\text{daily demand} \times \text{safety coefficient}\right]}{\text{container capacity}}$$

In this instance, the signal Kanban is used in the die-casting, punchpress and forging processes. The position of a triangular Kanban is then computed by the formula:

(B-2)   Position of the Triangular Kanban

$$= \frac{\text{average daily demand} \times \text{lead time} \times (1 + \text{safety coefficient})}{\text{container capacity}}.$$

Some companies in the Toyota group are also using the following formula:

(B-3)   Position of the Triangular Kanban

$$= \left[\!\!\left[\frac{\text{daily average demand}}{\text{container capacity}}\right]\!\!\right] + 1,$$

Where $[\![\ ]\!]$ means the minimum integer not less than the figure in it.

Where the setup methods are improved and the distance between the subsequent and preceding processes is short, the "constant quantity" will be equivalent to one pallet or one cart which corresponds to a sheet of Kanban. When the subsequent process withdrew one box of parts (fixed quantity), the preceding process must pick up the one empty box and immediately begin to produce the number of parts to be contained in this box. However, each withdrawal time cannot be known by the preceding process. The "whirligig beetle" explained in Chapter 2 is an example of this case.

In such cases, the maximum necessary inventory is equal to the reorder point. Therefore, the total number of Kanban which must correspond to the maximum inventory follows:

(A-3)   Total Number of Kanban

$$= \frac{\text{average daily demand} \times \text{lead time} \times (1 + \text{safety coefficient})}{\text{container capacity}}$$

Where, the lead time = processing time + waiting time
+ conveyance time + Kanban collecting time.

The ideal condition for Just-in-time production is that each process can produce only one piece, convey it one at a time, and also have only one piece in stock both between the equipment and the processes. This is known as one-piece production and conveyance. This type is a synchronization or a total conveyor-line production system connecting all the external and internal processes with invisible conveyor lines.

Suppose, that, in the equation (A-3):

the safety coefficient	= 0,
the waiting time	= 0,
the Kanban collecting time	= 0,
and, the container capacity	= 1.

Then, the Kanban system, which connects the two processes, is nothing but a conveyor line. In such a case, there is no need to use Kanban between two adjacent processes. If plural processes are connected very closely with each other, one sheet of Kanban is used commonly by these plural processes. This is the case of a *through* Kanban (also called *tunnel* Kanban), which is similar to the through ticket used between two adjacent railways.

Constant cycle, nonconstant quantity withdrawal system

In the constant order-cycle system for inventory control, the following formula is used to calculate necessary quantity for the period of order cycle plus lead time. This necessary quantity is called standard quantity:

(C-1)   Standard Quantity

= daily demand × (order cycle + lead time) + safety stock,

where the order cycle is the time interval between an order time and the next order time, and the lead time is simply the time interval between placing an order and receiving delivery. The order cycle plus the lead time is often called the replenishment lead time.

Theoretically, the order cycle is determined by the formula:

$$\text{Order Cycle} = \frac{\text{economic lot size for expected demand}}{\text{daily average demand}}$$

However, the order cycle is often determined by an external constraint such as steps in the monthly production scheduling or a contract between the supplier and the paternal maker.

171

Next, the order quantity in this system is measured by the formula:

(D-1)   Order Quantity

= (standard quantity – existing inventory)
  – (orders placed but not yet received),

where the last term (orders placed but not yet received) is sometimes equal to zero.

Kanban number under constant cycle withdrawal system

In the case of Toyota's Kanban system using the constant cycle withdrawal approach, the following formula is used for computing the total number of Kanban:

(C-2)   Total Number of Kanban

$$= \frac{\text{daily demand} \times (\text{order cycle} + \text{lead time} + \text{safety period})}{\text{container capacity}},$$

where the lead time = processing time + waiting time
                     + conveyance time
                     + Kanban collecting time

When analyzing this formula, it is important to note the following:

- The *order cycle* is the time interval (measured by days) between instructing production order to the line and instructing the next production order. Also called a *Kanban cycle.*

- The *processing time* is the time interval (days) between placing a production order and completing its production. This time interval corresponds to the number of Kanban of the work-in-process being kept or processed within the line.

- The *Kanban collecting time* is the time interval (days) between picking up Kanbans from the post, which were detached at the subsequent process, and placing the production order to the preceding process. This is equivalent to the total number of Kanbans kept in (1) the withdrawal Kanban post, (2) the Kanban receiving post, and (3) the production-ordering Kanban post in Fig. 2.9 of Chapter 2.

- The *safety inventory period* corresponds to the stock kept at the store. This inventory is to respond to the defective products and machine troubles, etc. To determine the level of safety inventory, the probabilities of occurrence of each trouble factor must be estimated respectively.

Next, by using the following formula, the order quantity under this Kanban system is determined:

(D-2)   Order Quantity

= (number of Kanban detached by the time of regular Kanban collection since the previous collection) × container capacity

Therefore, there is no need to compute the order quantity by using the formula (D-1). Under this type of Kanban system, the order quantity is automatically specified by the number of Kanban detached by the time of regular Kanban collection since the previous collection.

The reason which validates the equation (D-2) is due to the following relationship:

$$
\text{(D-3)} \quad \begin{pmatrix} \text{Number of Kanbans} \\ \text{detached by the regular} \\ \text{point in time} \\ \text{since the previous} \\ \text{collection of Kanban} \end{pmatrix} + \begin{pmatrix} \text{Number of Kanban} \\ \text{still kept in the} \\ \text{preceding process} \end{pmatrix}
$$

$$
= \begin{pmatrix} \text{Total number} \\ \text{of Kanbans} \end{pmatrix} - \begin{pmatrix} \text{existing number of Kanban} \\ \text{attached to the existing} \\ \text{inventory at the subsequent} \\ \text{store, at a regular point} \\ \text{in time} \end{pmatrix}
$$

This relationship is equivalent to the formula (D-1).

Changing the cycle time of standard operations routine instead of the number of Kanban

Even if the total number of each Kanban is calculated by computer using each pertinent formula described before, the computed number should not be applied automatically without exercising the improvements recommended by the supervisor. In other words, the factors in the right-hand side of each formula should not be regarded as constant, given conditions. During the implementation phase to apply the computed number of Kanban, the final authority to change the number of Kanban is delegated to the supervisor of each shop.

The variables which determine the total number of Kanban in any formula follow:

1. Average daily demand
2. Lead time
3. Safety coefficient or safety stock
4. Container capacity

At first, the average daily demand is determined by the smoothed amount per day derived from a monthly demand quantity. When the monthly demand has changed, the total number of Kanban per day would also be changed. At Toyota plants, however, changing lead time is more important and more often made than revising the total number of Kanban. Such an idea is unique when compared with ordinary inventory systems. Toyota recognizes that an increase of inventory level is not only the worst phenomenon among various wastes, but it is also the ultimate origin of all kinds of wastes. Thus, the total number of each Kanban is kept rather constant at Toyota. When the average daily demand increases, the lead time should decrease. This means that the cycle time of a standard operations routine (Chapter 7) can be reduced by changing the allocations of workers in the line. For example, suppose it is expected that the average daily demand of next month will be two times the demand of the current month. Then, according to the formulas (A-2) and (A-3), the total number of Kanban will be doubled under ceteris paribus conditions. At Toyota, however, the cycle time is cut in half and the turnover (circulation speed) of Kanban is doubled, resulting in the total number of Kanban being unchanged. This approach can hardly be adopted under the constant cycle withdrawal system unless the regular withdrawal cycle is changed.

Under Toyota's approach, if a workshop is incapable of sufficient improvement, it will have overtime or line-stop because the number of Kanban is fixed. As a result, the Kanban system can quickly visualize the trouble. Such troubles will evoke immediate improvement actions. However, incapable shops might increase the safety stock or the total number of Kanban to adapt to demand increase. Therefore, the size of safety stock is an indicator of the shop's ability to improve.

In the case of a demand decrease, the cycle time of the standard operations routine will be increased. However, the probable idle time of workers must be avoided by reducing the number of workers from the line (Chapter 8). Moreover, in order to reduce inventory level, the container capacity should also be minimized. Since this is a minimum lot size, it must be determined by considering the process ability of each station to approach a one-piece production and conveyance scheme.

In order to grasp the up-to-date nature of Kanbans, it is important to understand the master files of Kanbans in Toyota's plant. When the supervisor of each process makes some improvements that changed the data and factors in the implementation phase, the new data will be introduced to the master file for adjustment each month.

The influence of the supervisor on the total number of Kanban

The actual number of Kanbans at each process within Toyota's factories is not determined automatically by the specific formula. The supervisor influences the number of Kanbans in the system. In fact, each supervisor is given very specific instructions: "You can have as many Kanban as you want. You should reduce the number of Kanban (i.e., inventory level) one sheet by one sheet down to your minimum possible limit as you are able to improve your process."

The goal of this system is that when the subsequent process withdraws its parts, the inventory level at the product store of the preceding process would be zero and the next replenishment would be made immediately. This goal is somewhat hard to achieve.

When it is found that the present number of Kanban is not suitable and causes trouble in the shop, the number of Kanban should be changed (increased) immediately. In a sense, this is a trial-and-error method; but this approach is very practical and useful for motivating the supervisor and workers to reduce the number of Kanban and improve their process.

While reducing the number of Kanban, the size of the safety inventory or the safety coefficient has some influence on the worker's attitude. If the safety stock level is too small, it will be regarded as too tight or too severe, and the workers will lose their motivation to attain its level. On the contrary, if the safety level is too big, it will be accepted as too loose or indulgent, and the worker will again lose his motivation. Therefore, the tightness of the number of Kanban is very important for the motivation of workers. The level which is somewhat tight but attainable would be the best level for attaining good performance.

Constant withdrawal cycle system for the supplier Kanban

Since the cooperative supplier companies are located somewhat distant from the paternal manufacturer, the total lead time, including conveyance tme, is relatively long and therefore the constant quantity withdrawal system might cause a shortage of parts. As a result, only the constant cycle, nonconstant quantity withdrawal system is used for the supplier Kanban.

Moreover, the parent manufacturer is withdrawing many varieties of parts from various vendors at the same time. If the maker applied the constant quantity withdrawal system to these suppliers, the order time to each supplier would be varied, and thus it would be unfeasible to withdraw small quantities of parts very frequently from various, distant vendors. As a result, the round-tour, mixed-loading system explained in Chapter 2 has been used by the subcontractors under the constant withdrawal cycle system. It can gather the various parts ordered to different suppliers at each regular point in time.

Also, the total number of each supplier Kanban is definitely computer-calculated by a paternal maker. However, the number of Kanban to be delivered to the supplier at each regular cycle is still subject to the paternal maker's production situation.

Now, returning to the formula (C-1) of the constant order-cycle system, the total number of each supplier Kanban will be computed by the following formula:

(C-3)　　Total Number of Kanban

$$= \frac{\text{daily demand} \times \left(\begin{array}{l} \text{order cycle} \\ \text{to the} \\ \text{supplier} \end{array} + \begin{array}{l} \text{production} \\ \text{lead time of} + \\ \text{the supplier} \end{array} \begin{array}{l} \text{safety} \\ \text{coefficient} \end{array} \right)}{\text{container capacity}}.$$

The *order cycle* (or Kanban cycle) to the supplier is the time interval (measured by days) between placing one order with the supplier and placing the next order. In other words, the order cycle corresponds to the number of hours set by the paternal maker to bring the supplier Kanban to the supplier. The order cycle is calculated by using the following formula:

(C-3-1)　Order Cycle to the Supplier

$$= \frac{[[\text{number of days spent for one-time conveyance}]]}{\text{number of times of conveyance per day}},$$

where [[ ]] means the minimum integer not less than the accurate figure in it. Therefore even though a conveyance time may only be two hours, it must be counted as one day.

The *production lead time of the supplier* is the time interval between placing the production order by the supplier to his line and completing his production. This time interval is measured by the following formula:

(C-3-2)　Production Lead Time of the Supplier

$$= \text{order cycle to the supplier} \times \text{conveyance interval},$$

where the conveyance interval can be understood through the following example. Suppose there are several Kanban conveyances per day from the paternal manufacturer to the vendor. Then, how many times of Kanban conveyances must be required by the vendor to be able to deliver the ordered quantity to the paternal maker after the maker has placed the order in question at a certain point in time? This times of Kanban conveyance is the conveyance interval in this formula. It is essentially based on the processing time of the supplier.

The order cycle and the conveyance interval is usually written on the supplier Kanban, such as the description of *"1.6.2"* at the bottom of a supplier delivered six times a day and the actual withdrawals of parts must be made two times later after the Kanban is brought at a certain point in a withdrawal time. Thus, using the equations (C-3-1) and (C-3-2), the following relationship can be developed:

$$
\text{(C-3-3)} \quad
\begin{bmatrix} \text{order cycle} \\ \text{to the} \\ \text{supplier} \end{bmatrix}
+
\begin{bmatrix} \text{production lead} \\ \text{time of} \\ \text{the supplier} \end{bmatrix}
$$

$$
= \left[\begin{bmatrix} \text{number of days spent} \\ \text{for one-time} \\ \text{conveyance} \end{bmatrix}\right]
\times \left(\frac{1 + \text{conveyance interval}}{\text{number of conveyance times per day}} \right)
$$

As a result, the equation (C-3) can be transformed as:

(C-4)   Total Number of Kanban

$$
= \frac{\text{daily demand}}{\text{container capacity}} \times
\left\{ \left[\begin{bmatrix} \text{no. of days} \\ \text{spent for} \\ \text{one-time} \\ \text{conveyance} \end{bmatrix} \right] \times \right.
$$

$$
\left. \left(\frac{1 + \dfrac{\text{conveyance interval}}{}}{\begin{array}{c}\text{no. of times} \\ \text{of conveyance} \\ \text{per day}\end{array}} \right) + \begin{array}{c}\text{safety} \\ \text{coefficient}\end{array} \right\},
$$

where the safety coefficient or the level of safety inventory is dependent on the supplier's ability to cope with the following disturbances:
1. Since the supplier Kanban is delivered on the constant

withdrawal-cycle system, the quantity withdrawn must be varied at each withdrawal time. For example, the customer-maker (Toyota) may pull five pallets of parts at a certain point in time, but may withdraw seven pallets at another point in time. However, if the daily withdrawn quantity out each time is leveled because of the smoothed production by the customer-manufacturer, the constant cycle system is almost the same as the constant quantity system.

2. Even if the daily production level is averaged, the actual monthly production quantity based on the actual daily dispatchings from Toyota through Kanban may deviate from the predetermined monthly production plan sent from the customer-maker. This difference is usually $\pm 10\%$. This also means the actual daily demand may deviate from the planned average daily quantity by $\pm 10\%$.

3. The variance in the number of Kanban brought to the supplier may sometimes be due to the driver's error that he forgot some of the Kanbans. However, this can be avoided by the driver's care.

4. Machine breakdowns may occur.

5. Traffic accidents may occur on the road to the customer-client. This probability may increase in proportion to the length of the conveyance period or the value of the equation (C-3-3).

The supplier's ability to cope with the above disturbances will be summarized by the worker's ability to adapt to demand increases, the shop's ability to reduce the lead time by changing the cycle time, and the ability of equipment maintenance.

Let us take a numerical example for the formula (C-4):

Suppose,
the number of days spent for one-time conveyance = 1 day,
the number of times of conveyance per day = 6 times,
the conveyance interval = 2 times later after the original
conveyance of Kanban,
the average daily demand = 100 units,
the container capacity = 5 units, and
the safety coefficient = 0.2.

Then,

the total number of Kanban

$$= \frac{100}{5} \times \left\{ \left[1 \times \left(\frac{1+2}{6} \right) \right] + 0.2 \right\}$$

$$= 20 \times (0.5 + 0.2) = 14$$

Finally, the withdrawal quantity to be made at a regular point in time is determined by the number of Kanban detached since the previous conveyance. That is, the equations (D-2) and (D-3) explained previously can also be used for the supplier Kanban.

Appendix 2

Sequencing Method for the Mixed-Model Assembly Line to Realize Smoothed Production

The procedure for designing a mixed-model assembly line involves the following steps:

1. Determination of a cycle time.
2. Computation of a minimum number of processes.
3. Preparation of a diagram of integrated precedence relationships among elemental jobs.
4. Line balancing.
5. Determination of the sequence schedule for introducing various products to the line.
6. Determination of the length of the operations range of each process.

Appendix 2 deals with the fifth step: The problem of sequencing various car models on the line.

Goals of controlling the assembly line

The sequence of introducing models to the mixed-model assembly line is different due to the different goals or purposes of controlling the line. There

Appendix 2 is based on the presentation by Mr. Shigenori Kotani (staff of the production control department at Toyota Motor Corporation) at the conference of Japan Operations Research Society, March 25, 1982, and his abstract (pp. 149-150) in the proceedings of this conference. This appendix is also based on followup discussions with Mr. Masuyama, Mr. Terada, and Mr. Kotani of Toyota Motor Corporation. The numerical examples here except Fig. A2.5 are made by the author.

are two goals:
1. Leveling the load (total assembly time) on each process within the line.
2. Keeping a constant speed in consuming each part on the line.

Goal 1

Concerning Goal 1, it is important to note that a product might have a longer operation time than the predetermined cycle time. This is due to the fact that the line balancing on the mixed-model line is made under the condition that the operation time of each process, which was weighted by each quantity of mixed models, should not exceed the cycle time. This condition (constraint) will be described as the following formula:

$$\max_{l} \left\{ \frac{\sum\limits_{i=1}^{\alpha} Q_i T_{il}}{\sum\limits_{i=1}^{\alpha} Q_i} \right\} \leq C,$$

Q_i = planned production quantity of the product A_i $(i=1,\ldots,\alpha)$

T_{il} = operation time per unit of product A_i on the process l

C = cycle time = $\dfrac{\text{total operation time per day}}{\sum\limits_{i=1}^{\alpha} Q_i}$.

As a result, if products with relatively longer operation times are successively introduced into the line, the products will cause a delay in completing the product and may cause line stoppage. Therefore, a heuristic program can be developed for the assembly line model-mix sequencing problem to minimize the risk of stopping the conveyor (for example, see Okamura and Yamashita [1979]).

Although this first goal is also considered in Toyota's sequencing program, it is incorporated in the solution algorithm which mainly considers the second goal. As a result, Toyota considers most important the second goal of the sequence schedule: keeping a constant speed in consuming each part.

Goal 2 and the sequencing model

In the Kanban system used at Toyota, preceding processes supplying the various parts or materials to the line are given greatest attention. Under this "pulling" system, the variation in production quantities or conveyance times at preceding processes must be minimized. Also, their respective work-in-process inventories must be minimized. To do so, the quantity used per hour (i.e., consumption speed) for each part in the mixed-model line must be kept as constant as possible. Toyota's sequencing method is designed to reach this second goal. To understand this sequencing method, it is important to define several notations and values:

Q = Total production quantity of all products A_i ($i=1,\ldots,\alpha$)

$$= \sum_{i=1}^{\alpha} Q_i, \quad (Q_i = \text{production quantity of each product } A_i)$$

N_j = Total necessary quantity of the part a_j to be consumed for producing all products A_i ($i=1,\ldots,\alpha$; $j=1,\ldots,\beta$)

X_{jk} = Total necessary quantity of the part a_j to be utilized for producing the products of determined sequence from first to Kth.

With these notations in mind the following two values can be developed:

N_j/Q = Average necessary quantity of the part a_j per unit of a product.

$\dfrac{K \cdot N_j}{Q}$ = Average necessary quantity of the part a_j for producing K units of products.

In order to keep the consumption speed of a part a_j constant, the amount of

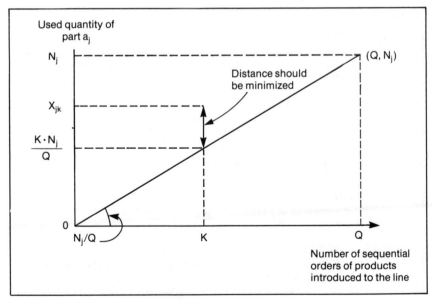

Fig. A2.1   Relationship between X_{jk} and $K \cdot N_j/Q$.

X_{jk} must be as close as possible to the value of $\dfrac{K \cdot N_i}{Q}$. This is the basic concept underlying Toyota's sequencing algorithm and is depicted in Fig. A2.1.

It can now be further defined that:

A point $G_k = (K \cdot N_1/Q, \; K \cdot N_2/Q, \; \ldots, \; K \cdot N_\beta/Q)$,

A point $P_k = (X_{1k}, \; X_{2k}, \; \ldots, \; X_{\beta k})$.

In order for a sequence schedule to assure the constant speed of consuming each part, the point P_k must be as close as possible to the point G_k. Therefore, if the degree is measured for the point P_k approaching the point G_k by using the distance D_k:

$$D_k = \left\| \; G_k - P_k \; \right\| = \sqrt{\sum_{j=1}^{\beta} \left(\frac{K \cdot N_j}{Q} - X_{jk} \right)^2} \; ,$$

then, the distance D_k must be minimized. The algorithm developed on this idea by Toyota is called the *Goal-Chasing Method* (Fig. A2.2).

Fig. A2.2   Goal-Chasing Method I

Denote:

    $b_{ij} =$ Necessary quantity of the part a_j ($j=1,\ldots,\beta$) for producing one unit of the product A_i ($i=1,\ldots,\alpha$).

Other notations are already defined.

Then,

Step 1   Set $K=1$, $X_{j,k-1}=0$, ($j=1,\ldots,\beta$), $S_{k-1} = \{\, 1, 2, \ldots, \alpha \,\}$.

Step 2   Set as Kth order in the sequence schedule the product A_{i^*} which minimizes the distance D_k. The minimum distance will be found by the following formula:

        $D_{ki^*} = \min\limits_{i} \{\, D_{ki} \,\}$, $i \in S_{k-1}$,

        where $D_{ki} = \sqrt{\sum_{j=1}^{\beta} \left(\dfrac{K \cdot N_j}{Q} - X_{j,k-1} - b_{ij} \right)^2}$.

Step 3   If all units of a product A_{i^*} were ordered and included in the sequence schedule, then

    Set $S_k = S_{k-1} - \{\, i^* \,\}$.

    If some units of a product A_{i^*} are still remaining as being not ordered, then set $S_k = S_{k-1}$.

Step 4   If $S_k = \emptyset$ (empty set), the algorithm will end.

    If $S_k \neq 0$, then compute $X_{jk} = X_{j,k-1} + b_{i^* j}$ ($j=1,\ldots,\beta$) and go back to Step 2 by setting $K = K + 1$.

Goal-Chasing Method: a numerical example

To fully understand Toyota's Goal-Chasing Method, it is best to review an example. Suppose the production quantities Q_i (i = 1, 2, 3) of each product A_1, A_2, and A_3, and the required unit b_{ij} (i = 1, 2, 3; j = 1, 2, 3, 4) of each part a_1, a_2, a_3 and a_4 for producing these products are as shown in Table A2.1:

Table A2.1   Production Quantities Q_i and Parts Condition b_{ij}

Products A_i	A_1	A_2	A_3
Planned Production Quantity Q_i	2	3	5

Parts a_j / Products A_i	a_1	a_2	a_3	a_4
A_1	1	0	1	1
A_2	1	1	0	1
A_3	0	1	1	0

Then, the total necessary quantity (N_j) of the part a_j (j = 1, 2, 3, 4) for producing all products A_i (i = 1, 2, 3) can be computed as follows:

$$[N_j] = [Q_i] [b_{ij}]$$

$$= [2, 3, 5] \begin{bmatrix} 1 & 0 & 1 & 1 \\ 1 & 1 & 0 & 1 \\ 0 & 1 & 1 & 0 \end{bmatrix} = [5, 8, 7, 5]$$

Further, the total production quantity of all products A_i (i = 1, 2, 3) will be:

$$\sum_{i=1}^{3} Q_i = 2 + 3 + 5 = 10$$

Therefore,

$$[N_j/Q] = [5/10, \ 8/10, \ 7/10, \ 5/10]$$
$$(j = 1, 2, 3, 4)$$

Next, applying the values of $[N_j/Q]$ and $[b_{ij}]$ to the formula in step 2 of the above algorithm, when K = 1, the distances D_{ki} can be computed as follows:

for i=1, $D_{1,1}$ =

$$\sqrt{\left(\frac{1\times5}{10}-0-1\right)^2+\left(\frac{1\times8}{10}-0-0\right)^2+\left(\frac{1\times7}{10}-0-1\right)^2+\left(\frac{1\times5}{10}-0-1\right)^2}$$

= 1.11.

for i=2, $D_{1,2}$ =

$$\sqrt{\left(\frac{1\times5}{10}-0-1\right)^2+\left(\frac{1\times8}{10}-0-1\right)^2+\left(\frac{1\times7}{10}-0-0\right)^2+\left(\frac{1\times5}{10}-0-1\right)^2}$$

= 1.01.

for i=3, $D_{1,3}$ =

$$\sqrt{\left(\frac{1\times5}{10}-0-0\right)^2+\left(\frac{1\times8}{10}-0-1\right)^2+\left(\frac{1\times7}{10}-0-1\right)^2+\left(\frac{1\times5}{10}-0-0\right)^2}$$

= 0.79.

Thus, $D_{1,i*}$ = min $\{1.11, 1.01, 0.79\}$ = 0.79

$$\therefore i* = 3$$

Therefore, the first order in the sequence schedule is the product A_3.

Proceeding to Step 4 of the algorithm,

$$X_{jk} = X_{j,k-1} + b_{3,j}:$$

$$X_{1,1} = 0 + 0 = 0 \qquad\qquad X_{3,1} = 0 + 1 = 1$$

$$X_{2,1} = 0 + 1 = 1 \qquad\qquad X_{4,1} = 0 + 0 = 0$$

Thus, the first line in Fig. A2.3 was written based on the above computations.

Fig. A2.3   Sequence Schedule

K	D_{k1}	D_{k2}	D_{k3}	Sequence Schedule	X_{1k}	X_{2k}	X_{3k}	X_{4k}
1	1.11	1.01	0.79*	A_3	0	1	1	0
2	0.85	0.57*	1.59	$A_3\ A_2$	1	2	1	1
3	0.82*	1.44	0.93	$A_3\ A_2\ A_1$	2	2	2	2
4	1.87	1.64	0.28*	$A_3\ A_2\ A_1\ A_3$	2	3	3	2
5	1.32	0.87*	0.87	$A_3\ A_2\ A_1\ A_3\ A_2$	3	4	3	3
6	1.64	1.87	0.28*	$A_3\ A_2\ A_1\ A_3\ A_2\ A_3$	3	5	4	3
7	0.93	1.21	0.82*	$A_3\ A_2\ A_1\ A_3\ A_2\ A_3\ A_3$	3	6	5	3
8	0.57*	0.85	1.59	$A_3\ A_2\ A_1\ A_3\ A_2\ A_3\ A_3\ A_1$	4	6	6	4
9	1.56	0.77*	1.01	$A_3\ A_2\ A_1\ A_3\ A_2\ A_3\ A_3\ A_1\ A_2$	5	7	6	5
10	—	—	0*	$A_3\ A_2\ A_1\ A_3\ A_2\ A_3\ A_3\ A_1\ A_2\ A_3$	5	8	7	5

*Indicates smallest distance D_{ki}

Next, when k=2, then

for i=1, $D_{2,1}$ =

$$\sqrt{\left(\frac{2\times5}{10} - 0 - 1\right)^2 + \left(\frac{2\times8}{10} - 1 - 0\right)^2 + \left(\frac{2\times7}{10} - 1 - 1\right)^2 + \left(\frac{2\times5}{10} - 0 - 1\right)^2}$$

= 0.85.

for i=2, $D_{2,2}$ =

$$\sqrt{\left(\frac{2\times5}{10} - 0 - 1\right)^2 + \left(\frac{2\times8}{10} - 1 - 1\right)^2 + \left(\frac{2\times7}{10} - 1 - 0\right)^2 + \left(\frac{2\times5}{10} - 0 - 1\right)^2}$$

= 0.57.

for i=3, $D_{2,3}$ =

$$\sqrt{\left(\frac{2\times5}{10} - 0 - 0\right)^2 + \left(\frac{2\times8}{10} - 1 - 1\right)^2 + \left(\frac{2\times7}{10} - 1 - 1\right)^2 + \left(\frac{2\times5}{10} - 0 - 0\right)^2}$$

= 1.59.

Thus, $D_{2,i*}$ = Min { 0.85, 0.57, 1.59 }

$$= 0.57.$$

$$\therefore \ i^* = 2.$$

Therefore, the second order in the sequence schedule is the product A_2. Also, X_{jk} will be computed as:

$$X_{jk} = X_{j,k-1} + b_{2,j} :$$
$$X_{1,2} = 0 + 1 = 1$$
$$X_{2,2} = 1 + 1 = 2$$
$$X_{3,2} = 1 + 0 = 1$$
$$X_{4,2} = 0 + 1 = 1$$

This procedure was used to develop the second line of Fig. A2.3. The remaining lines in Fig. A2.3 can also be written by following the same procedures. As a result, the complete sequence schedule of this example will be:

$$A_3, \ A_2, \ A_1, \ A_3, \ A_2, \ A_3, \ A_3, \ A_1, \ A_2, \ A_3.$$

Evaluation of the Goal-Chasing Method

The values of $K \cdot N_j / Q$ and X_{jk} for each part a_j in the previous example are depicted as graphs in Fig. A2.4. The figure shows that all parts a_1, a_2, a_3 and a_4 are attaining optimality.[1]

Fig. A2.4 How X_{jk} approached to $K \cdot N_j / Q$.

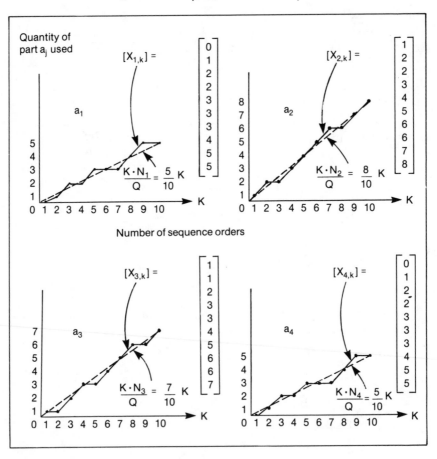

---

1. The meaning of "optimality" in this section is as follows: Suppose $[[K \cdot N_j / Q]]$ denotes the integer which is closest to $K \cdot N_j / Q$.

Then, if $X_{jk} = [[K \cdot N_j / Q]]$ holds for the part a_j, the optimality is achieved in this part. Fig. A2.4 shows all parts attaining optimality in this meaning.

To further evaluate this algorithm, the mean and the standard deviation of the values:

$$\left| \frac{K \cdot N}{Q} - X_{jk} \right| \quad \text{for each part } a_j$$

were computed.

Then, the following results were found:
1. Even when the number of items of parts was increased, the mean and the standard deviation hardly changed.
2. If the number of product-models was increased, the values of both the mean and standard deviation became small; in other words, the degree of production smoothing became increasingly better.

Another general approach for verifying the usefulness of this hueristic algorithm is expressed by the following procedure. Suppose the total production quantity $Q (= \sum Q_i)$ is large (1,000 units, etc.). Then, the sequence determined by this algorithm can be divided into 16 equal ranges, with each range corresponding to approximately one hour of production. The quantity of each part contained in each range will be computed, and its standard deviation will be computed. The actual distribution of these values shows that the variation (δ) per each hour is fairly small. (Fig. A2.5).

Fig. A2.5 Distribution of each kind of front axle used.

Range / Kinds of front axles	1	2	3	4	5	6	7	8	9	10	11	12	13	14	15	16	$\bar{x}$	δ
a_1	9	7	7	9	8	7	8	8	8	8	7	8	9	7	7	8	7.8	.73
a_2	6	5	7	6	5	6	7	5	7	6	5	7	6	6	5	6	5.9	.75
a_3	5	6	5	5	6	6	4	6	4	6	6	5	4	6	5	6	5.3	.77
a_4	3	3	3	2	3	3	3	3	3	2	3	3	3	2	3	3	2.8	.33
a_5	2	2	2	2	3	2	2	2	2	3	2	1	3	2	2	2	2.1	.48
a_6	1	1	1	1	1	2	1	1	2	0	2	1	1	1	1	1	1.1	.48

The Toyota approach: a simplified algorithm

To decrease computational time, a simplified algorithm known as Goal-Chasing Method II (Fig. A2.6) can be developed. This simplified algorithm is evolved from Step 2 of Goal-Chasing Method I (Fig. A2.2) and is based on the following proposition:

Among a product A_b and the other product A_c,

if $D_{k,b} \leq D_{k,c}$, then the relationship:

$$\sum_{j_b \in B_b} \left(\frac{K \cdot N_{jb}}{Q} - X_{jb,K-1} \right) \geq \sum_{j_c \in B_c} \left(\frac{K \cdot N_{jc}}{Q} - X_{jc,K-1} \right)$$

will hold and vice versa, and where B_b is a set of constituent parts a_{jb}, for the product A_b. This equivalence relationship can hold under the condition that the number of items of parts used for each product must be the same among different products and that the necessary quantity of each part used for one unit of each product must be the same among different products.[2]

Fig. A2.6   Goal-Chasing Method II

$$E_{ki} = \max \{ E_{ki} \}, i \in S_{k-1}$$

$$\text{where } E_{ki} = \sum_{j_i \in B_i} \left(\frac{K \cdot N_{ji}}{Q} - X_{ji,k-1} \right)$$

(B_i is a set of constituent parts a_{ji} for the Product A_i)

Applications of the simplified algorithm. The goal of the simplified algorithm is to keep a constant speed in the utilization of each part on the mixed-model assembly line. However, another goal to escape successive proceedings of the products which have a larger load of assembly time has also been considered.

In general, the kind of product that has a larger load is different when a different process is considered for the product in question. Toyota's line-balancing is designed so that the car model which has a larger assembly-time always has larger loads at every process in the line. To avoid introducing successively the same product requiring a longer operation time, all automobiles on the line are classified according to large (a_l), medium (a_m), or small (a_s) total assembly times. Each a_j $(j = l, m, s$ in this situation) must be introduced to the line so as to keep the speed constant on the line. This goal can be achieved by using the same simplified algorithm for keeping the speed constant of utilizing each part a_j on the line.

---

[2]The process to prove this proposition is as follows:

Denote:

    W = necessary quantity of each item of part for a unit of a product, then,

$$D_{k,c}^2 - D_{k,b}^2$$

$$= \sum_{j_c \in B_c-B_b} \left\{ \left(\frac{K \cdot N_{jc}}{Q} - X_{jc,k-1} - W \right)^2 - \left(\frac{K \cdot N_{jc}}{Q} - X_{jc,k-1} \right)^2 \right\}$$

$$+ \sum_{j_b \in B_b-B_c} \left\{ \left(\frac{K \cdot N_{jb}}{Q} - X_{jb,k-1} \right)^2 - \left(\frac{K \cdot N_{jb}}{Q} - X_{jb,k-1} - W \right)^2 \right\}$$

$$= -W \sum_{j_c \in B_c-B_b} \left(2 \frac{K \cdot N_{jc}}{Q} - 2X_{jc,k-1} - W \right)$$

$$+ W \sum_{j_b \in B_b-B_c} \left(2 \frac{K \cdot N_{jb}}{Q} - 2X_{jb,k-1} - W \right)$$

$$= -2W \sum_{j_c \in B_c-B_b} \left(\frac{K \cdot N_{jc}}{Q} - X_{jc,k-1} \right) + 2W \sum_{j_b \in B_b-B_c} \left(\frac{K \cdot N_{jb}}{Q} - X_{jb,k-1} \right)$$

(because $|B_c - B_b| = |B_b - B_c|$ due to the assumption.)

$$= -2W \sum_{j_c \in B_c-B_b} \left(\frac{K \cdot N_{jc}}{Q} - X_{jc,k-1} \right) + 2W \sum_{j_b \in B_b-B_c} \left(\frac{K \cdot N_{jb}}{Q} - X_{jb,k-1} \right)$$

$$+ 2W \sum_{S \in B_c \cap B_b} \left\{ \left(\frac{K \cdot N_s}{Q} - X_{s,k-1} \right) - \left(\frac{K \cdot N_s}{Q} - X_{s,k-1} \right) \right\}$$

$$= 2W \left\{ \sum_{j_b \in B_b-B_c} \left(\frac{K \cdot N_{jb}}{Q} - X_{jb,k-1} \right) + \sum_{S \in B_c \cap B_b} \left(\frac{K \cdot N_s}{Q} - X_{s,k-1} \right) \right\}$$

$$- 2W \left\{ \sum_{j_c \in B_c-B_b} \left(\frac{K \cdot N_{jc}}{Q} - X_{jc,k-1} \right) + \sum_{S \in B_c \cap B_b} \left(\frac{K \cdot N_s}{Q} - X_{s,k-1} \right) \right\}$$

$$= 2W \left\{ \sum_{j_b \in B_b} \left(\frac{K \cdot N_{jb}}{Q} - X_{jb,k-1} \right) - \sum_{J_c \in B_c} \left(\frac{K \cdot N_{jc}}{Q} - X_{jc,k-1} \right) \right\}$$

Thus, the equivalence relationship was proved.

It is difficult to apply the Goal-Chasing Method since the number of different parts used in an automobile is about 20,000. Therefore, the parts are represented only by their respective subassembly, where each subassembly has many outputs. For example, a car brand may have the following production data:

- Planned production quantity = about 500.
  (= number of sequence orders)

- Number of kinds of cars = about 180.
  (therefore, each kind has about three units)
- Number of subassemblies = about 20.

The main subassembly names are as follows:

1. body types	11. wheels
2. engines	12. doors
3. transmissions	13. user's countries
4. grades (series)	14. air conditioners
5. frames	15. seats
6. front axles	16. ,,
7. rear axles	17. ,,
8. colors	18. ,,
9. bumpers	19. ,,
10. steering assemblies	20. ,,

Note that each subassembly must obviously contain many different parts. To the number of subassemblies, difference in loads (assembly hour) of various cars must be added to handle it in the same way as real parts.

Using the above data, a sequence schedule was developed by using Goal-Chasing Method II. Then, the sequence was divided into 16 equal ranges (each range corresponded to about one hour of production time). Using front axles as an example, refer to Fig. A2.5 to see how many units of each kind of front axle were included in each range. Obviously from the figure, it can be seen that the values of the standard deviation (δ) displays a small variation of speed of utilizing each part.

In practice, Toyota "weights" important subassemblies and in some cases, provides some additional constraints such as facility capacities, etc. The classified categories (a_l, a_m, a_s) of assembly time loads are also given some weight to solve the conflict between the line balancing goal and the part smoothing goal.

Appendix 3

EDP System for Support of the Toyota Production System

Through lack of understanding, the Toyota production system is sometimes considered far removed from modern computerized information systems. Moreover, it is felt that Just-in-time production can be realized only by the "pull system" of Kanban. However, before applying Kanban, detailed schedules must be prepared in advance for each production process using monthly planning data. This scheduling is accomplished utilizing a computerized information system.

Toyota production is supported by the electronic data processing (EDP) system. The example in this appendix is based primarily on the supply systems of Kyoho-Seisakusho Co., Ltd. and Aisin-Seiki Co., Ltd. However, since companies of the Toyota group are closely aligned with the Toyota Motor Corp., similar systems are being developed among the various companies.

The EDP system reported herein consists of seven subsystems that may be classified roughly into three categories (Fig. A3.1):

1. *Technology data base* subsystem, which maintains the data base for the planning and actual performance subsystems.
2. *Planning* subsystem, which provides the plant managers with information for the preparation of production arrangements for the next month, such as determination of the number of Kanban and distribution of workers on the assembly line.
3. *Actual performance* subsystem, which supplies the attention directing information to improve the processes by comparing actual performance with planned data.

193

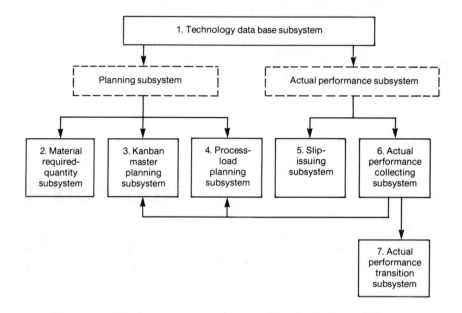

Fig. A3.1 Framework of the information system supporting Kanban.

The subsystems will be examined in detail in the following sections. However, it should be recognized that another computerized planning system (i.e., the heuristic sequencing program) exists for mixed assembly lines at Toyota and its suppliers and is discussed in Appendix 2.

Technology data base subsystem

The technology data base subsystem maintains the basic data for production controls. It includes a parts data base (bill of materials) to compute the various parts quantities required for each finished product and a collection of data reflecting the steps in producing a company's products from the beginning to the final process.

Kyoho-Seisakusho Co., Ltd. utilizes a UNIS data base (UNIVAC Industrial System) with software developed by Japan UNIVAC Co., Ltd. for this subsystem. This UNIS was originally developed for MRP. In this meaning, the Kanban system is compatible with MRP.

Material required quantities subsystem

This subsystem receives a predetermined three months production information tape as input data provided monthly by Toyota to its cooperative parts suppliers. The subsystem then computes the quantity of material required by each process. The outputs of this system are summarized as follows:

- Daily required quantities of each material to be used within the company or by its suppliers.
- Number of pallets to contain each material.
- Production schedule of each finished product to be supplied to each customer company.

In order to accomplish Just-in-time production, daily required materials must be prepared in advance to be available at any necessary point in time. Also, in accordance with Rule No. 3 of the Kanban system: "defective units should never be conveyed to the subsequent process," the defective rate cannot be considered in computing the required material quantities. The Toyota production system consists not only of the Kanban information system, but also the production methods to improve the process when defective units are discovered.

Kanban master planning subsystem

The Kanban master planning subsystem computes the following data based on a daily leveled (average) production quantity:

- Number of each Kanban required for producing a lot.
- Increased or decreased number of each Kanban compared with the previous month.
- Position of a triangle Kanban corresponding to a reorder point, which triggers the timing of production.
- Lot size.

This data will be printed out as a *Kanban master table,* as shown in Fig. A3. 2. The table is delivered to the manager of each process for preparation of the actual number of Kanban. Further, since the daily average production quantity changes basically once a month, the data must be recomputed monthly.

Three different kinds of Kanban master tables are used, depending on the following application:

- *Internally produced parts.* This table is printed out for each part/item at each process. The table is delivered to the Production Control Department for preparation of Kanban and reorganization of each process (i.e., reallocation of workers) in response to demand changes. The formulae used at some suppliers follow:

$$\text{Lot size} = \frac{\text{Monthly production quantity of particular product}}{\text{Monthly setup times for particular product}} \quad (1)$$

Number of Kanban per lot $= \dfrac{\text{Lot size}}{\text{Pallet capacity}}$ (2)

Position of triangular Kanban $= \left[\left[\dfrac{\text{Daily average production quantity}}{\text{Pallet capacity}}\right]\right] + 1$ (3)

Detailed information is available for the above formulae in Appendix 1.

- *Externally produced parts.* This table is printed out for each supplier and each Kanban cycle so that each supplier will know the monthly change in his required production quantities. The formulae used to compute the number of supplier Kanban are different from the equations for internal Kanban because a constant cycle withdrawal system is applied to the supplier Kanban, while a constant quantity withdrawal system is normally applied to internal Kanban. More detailed information and the Kanban-cycle concept appear in Appendix 1.

- *Material usage.* This table is printed out for delivery to the material supplier. For example, if a punch press process is involved, the number of Kanban for a coil lot will be sent to the coil supplier.

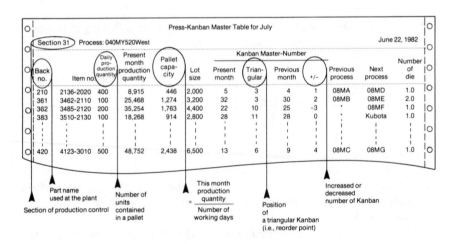

Fig. A3.2 Kanban Master Table.

Process-load planning subsystem

Monthly production quantities fluctuate depending on the predetermined production plan published monthly by Toyota. Thus, each production line must be able to adapt to these monthly changes in production quantity by changing the capacity of each line, that is, by increasing or decreasing the workforce at each line. Such changes can be attained through improvement activities or multi-function workers in a special layout of machines.

196

In order for each process to impact the workforce capacity change, this subsystem computes the following data into a *process-load plan* based on the monthly predetermined production plan:
- Cycle time at each process.
- Processing time or loading time to be spent for a given lot at each process.
- Setup time and the times of setup at each process.

By comparing loading time to the existing capacity at each process, a series of production preparations such as work force planning, machinery layout, and overtime planning can be calculated. The process-load plan reflects data generated for the Kanban master plan and required material quantities. Thus, if the load at a process changes, the work force or number of Kanban changes accordingly. The following formula is used to compute loading time spent for a given production lot:

$$\text{Loading time} = \frac{\text{Order quantity} \times \text{Standard hour}}{\text{Standard quantity} \times \text{Process utilization rate}} + \text{Setup time} \quad (4)$$

The standard quantity and the standard hour are usually predetermined at each process. For example, assume an order quantity (lot size) of 100 units, standard hour equal to one hour to produce ten units of standard quantity, and the setup time of two hours. Then, the loading time for this process is computed as:

$$\frac{100 \times 1}{10} + 2 = 12 \text{ hours}$$

In the case of a punchpress department, "strokes per hour" (SPH) is substituted for "standard quantity times process utilization rate," as noted here:

$$\text{Loading time} = \frac{\text{Order quantity} \div \text{Quantity produced by one pressing}}{\text{SPH}} + \text{Setup time} \quad (5)$$

where, SPH and setup time are computed based on data from the past three months, as collected by the Actual Performance subsystem. Additionally, cycle time will be used to standardize the operations routine and to determine the standard quantity of in-process inventory.

Slip-issuing subsystem

Kanban may be regarded as a kind of money because when a process withdraws a part from the previous process, a withdrawal Kanban must be shown in the partmaking process. However, a Kanban specifies only what type of part is required, from where to where the part must be transferred, and the quantity of parts to be produced until what time. The *transfer price* is not defined by the Kanban, whereas the price and monetary information are necessary between a supplier and a user company. Therefore, in order to deal with accounts payable and accounts receivable in the accounting departments of both companies, some invoices must be issued. Such invoices are also used to confirm and inspect the total quantity of the item supplied by the vendor.

As described in Chapter 3, Toyota applies two different systems to withdraw parts from various suppliers, depending on the physical size of the part. The most prevalent system is the *later-replenishment* system that uses a supplier Kanban. The second system is the *sequenced withdrawal* system based on a sequence schedule for the mixed-parts assembly line (Fig. A3.3). The following are steps involved in the sequenced withdrawal system:

1. Sequence schedule data on *magnetic tape* for transmissions to be produced at the Shiroyama plant of the Aisin Seiki Co., Ltd. is delivered

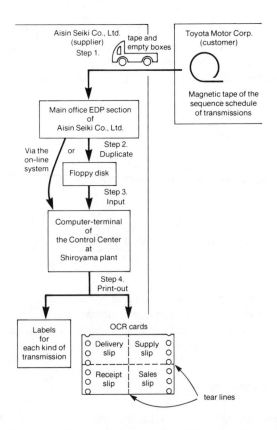

Fig. A3.3 Sequenced withdrawal within the slip-issuing subsystem.

by truck each morning to the EDP section of the Aisin Seiki Co. from Toyota.

2. The EDP section duplicates the magnetic tape on a *magnetic disk* (floppy disk).

3. The magnetic disk is then delivered to the control center at the Shiroyama plant. (Note Fig. 3.4 in Chapter 3.)

4. The data on the disk is input into a computer terminal (called System K) to print out the sequence schedule. At the same time, labels for each type of transmission are printed out, along with a set of *OCR cards* that include such information as a *delivery slip card* and a *receipt slip card.* (Note Fig. 3.4 in Chapter 3.)

In another situation, the contents of the magnetic tape may be transmitted directly from the main office EDP to the computer terminal at the Shiroyama plant via an on-line system at Aisin Seiki.

If the later-replenishment system is applied, the supplier Kanban is bar coded for processing by a computer. At Toyota, all supplier Kanbans are *bar coded* Kanbans, also known as *OCR* Kanbans, as shown in Fig. 2.5 in Chapter 2. In this case, two types of bar coded Kanbans are used to issue vouchers:

1. The Toyota OCR supplier Kanban is processed through a bar code reader at Toyota to print out the OCR cards. These cards are delivered to the supplier along with the supplier Kanban itself. At the supplier, the parts,

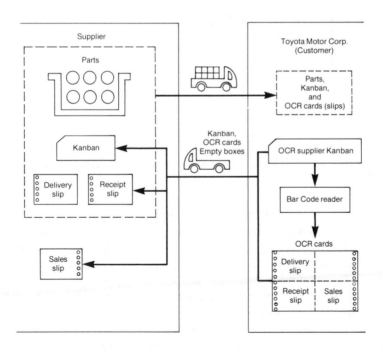

Fig. A3.4   Type I later-replenishment within the slip-issuing subsystem.

Kanban, and cards are loaded together onto the truck and delivered to the Toyota process (Fig. A3.4).

2. The Toyota OCR supplier Kanban is delivered directly to the supplier where it is processed through the supplier's bar code reader. The OCR cards are generated and matched with parts for delivery to the Toyota plant along with the supplier Kanban (Fig. A3.5). At present, this situation is the most prevalent among Toyota suppliers.

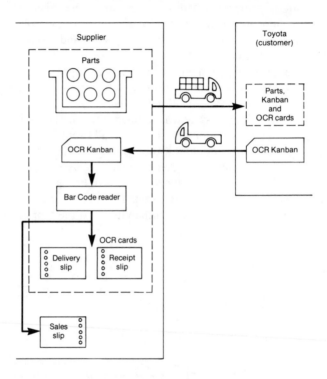

Fig. A3.5   Type II later-replenishment within the slip-issuing subsystem.

There are four types of OCR cards: delivery slip, supply slip, receipt slip, and sales slip. The supplier delivers its parts with the delivery slip and the receipt slip.

At the Toyota receiving location (i.e., Purchasing Department), both the delivery slip and the receipt slip will be sealed (signed). Toyota retains the delivery slip and returns the receipt slip to the supplier. The delivery slip is forwarded to the Toyota Computer Department where it is processed to output accounts payable data. This data, in turn, will be given to the Accounting Department for entry in the creditors ledger, the purchase book, and the accounts payable section of the general ledger.

The sales slip, on the other hand, is kept by the supplier where it is processed through the OCR to output accounts receivable data. The supplier enters this data in his customers' ledger, the sales book, and accounts receivable section of the general ledger. An example of the flow of these vouchers between Toyota and its suppliers appears in Fig. A3.6.

When Aisin Seiki delivers its finished parts to another cooperative company (in this case, Hino Motors, Ltd.), it sends the delivery slip, the receipt slip and the supply slip along with the parts. Hino Motors retains the sealed delivery slip, returns the sealed receipt slip to Aisin Seiki, and sends the sealed supply slip to Toyota. Toyota processes this supply slip through OCR to output accounts payable data. The amount of this accounts payable data will be paid to Aisin Seiki by Toyota. The same amount will be paid later to Toyota by Hino Motors (Fig. A3.7).

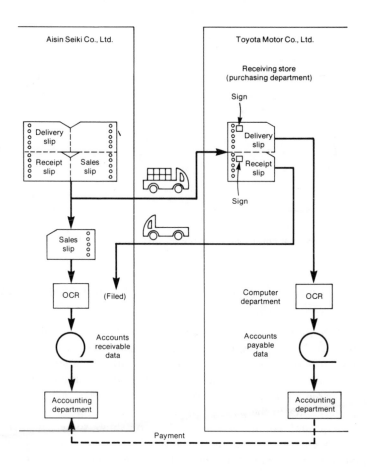

Fig. A3.6 Voucher flow between Toyota and its suppliers.

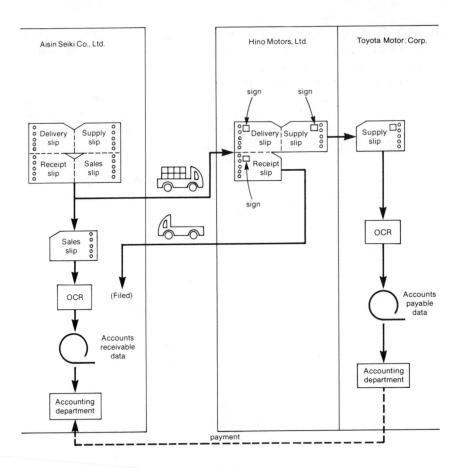

Fig. A3.7 Voucher flow between Toyota, the first supplier and the second supplier.

Actual performance collection and transition subsystems

The *Actual Performance Collection* subsystem collects daily the actual performance data of each process and compiles it as monthly production information. The performance data includes production quantity, processing time, setup time, cycle time, machine idle time, stroke number, etc. Monthly production data is related into the monthly planning cycle. Comparing actual performance data to the planned figures produces variance figures. If these variances are unfavorable (i.e., processing too slow), some remedial action must be taken to minimize the variances. In other words, this subsystem highlights problem areas and helps to evoke improvement activities to optimize Toyota production methods. Additionally, actual performance data, such as stroke number and setup time, are fed back as basic data for computation of the loading or cycle time for the next period.

The *Actual Performance Transition* subsystem transforms the actual performance data into time-series data of the latest three months to show the progress of actual performance. This time-series information emphasizes the technical differences between processes and the capacity-utilization situations within each process, thus enabling promotion of company-wide improvements in engineering techniques.

Appendix 4

Toyota Production System and Kanban System — Materialization of Just-in-Time and Respect-for-Human System

Y. SUGIMORI†, K. KUSUNOKI†, F. CHO† and S. UCHIKAWA†

The Toyota Production System and Kanban System introduced in this paper was developed by the Vice-President of Toyota Motor Company, Mr. Taiichi Ohno, and it was under his guidance that these unique production systems have become deeply rooted in Toyota Motor Company in the past 20 years. There are two major distinctive features in these systems. One of these is the ' just-in-time production ', a specially important factor in an assembly industry such as automotive manufacturing. In this type of production, " only the necessary products, at the necessary time, in necessary quantity " are manufactured, and in addition, the stock on hand is held down to a minimum. Second, the system is the ' respect-for-human ' system where the workers are allowed to display in full their capabilities through active participation in running and improving their own workshops.

Starting point of concept—making the most of Japanese characteristics

The starting point of the concept of the Toyota Production System was in the recognition of Japan's distinguishing features.

The most distinctive feature of Japan is the lack of natural resources, which makes it necessary to import vast amounts of materials including food. Japan is placed under a disadvantageous condition in terms of a cost of raw material when compared to the European and American countries. To

Presented at the 4th International Conference on Production Research (Tokyo) August 1977.
†Production Control Department, Toyota Motor Co., Ltd. 1 Toyota-cho Toyota-shi 471 Japan.
Published by Taylor & Francis Ltd, 10–14 Macklin Street, London WC2B 5NF.

Reprinted with permission from the *International Journal of Production Research*, 1977, Vol. 15, no. 6, p. 553-564, ©1977 Taylor and Francis, Ltd.

overcome this handicap, it is essential for the Japanese industries to put forth their best efforts in order to produce better quality goods having higher added value and at an even lower production cost than those of the other countries. This was the first thing that Toyota recognized.

The second distinctive feature is that Japanese concept of work, such as consciousness and attitude, differed from that held by the European and American workers. The Japanese traits include: (1) group consciousness, sense of equality, desire to improve, and diligence born from a long history of a homogeneous race; (2) high degree of ability resulting from higher education brought by desire to improve; (3) centring their daily living around work.

Such Japanese traits have also been reflected in the enterprises. Customs such as (1) lifetime employment system, (2) labour unions by companies, (3) little discrimination between shop workers and white-collar staff, and (4) chances available to workers for promotion to managerial positions, have been of great service in promoting the feeling of unity between the company and workers. Also, unlike European countries, Japan does not have the problem of foreign workers.

Therefore from the standpoint of labour environment, Japan is much better off than the European and American countries. In order to make full use of the Japanese advantages, it is important that the industries have their workers display their capabilities to the utmost. This was the second thing that Toyota recognized.

Toyota production system and its basic concept

Upon recognition of the matters related above, Toyota is planning and running its production system on the following two basic concepts.

First of all, the thing that corresponds to the first recognition of putting forth all efforts to attain low cost production is " reduction of cost through elimination of waste ". This involves making up a system that will thoroughly eliminate waste by assuming that anything other than the minimum amount of equipment, materials, parts, and workers (working time) which are absolutely essential to production are merely surplus that only raises the cost.

The thing that corresponds to the second recognition of Japanese diligence, high degree of ability, and favoured labour environment is " to make full use of the workers' capabilities ". In short, treat the workers as human beings and with consideration. Build up a system that will allow the workers to display their full capabilities by themselves.

Cost cutting by thorough removal of waste

For materialization of this system, Toyota has attached special importance to ' just-in-time production ' and ' Jidoka '.

Distinguishing features of automotive industry: In order to have an efficient production system in the automotive industry, it is required that the following three distinguishing problems be solved.

(1) The automotive industry is a typical mass production assembly type where each vehicle is assembled from several thousand parts that have undergone numerous processes. Therefore, a trouble in any of the processes will have a large overall effect.

(2) There are very many different models with numerous variations and with large fluctuation in the demand of each variation.

(3) Every few years, the vehicles are completely remodelled and there are also often changes at a part level.

The ordinary production control system in such an industry consists of fulfilling the production schedules by holding work-in-process inventory over all processes as a means of absorbing troubles in the processes and changes in demand. However, such a system in practice often creates excessive unbalance of stock between the processes, which often leads to dead stock. On the other hand, it can easily fall into the condition of having excessive equipment and surplus of workers, which is not conformable to Toyotas' recognition.

Just in time production: In order to avoid such problems as inventory unbalance and surplus equipment and workers, we recognized necessity of schemes adjustable to conform with changes due to troubles and demand fluctuations. For this purpose, we put our efforts in development of a production system which is able to shorten the lead time from the entry of materials to the completion of vehicle.

The just-in-time production is a method whereby the production lead time is greatly shortened by maintaining the conformity to changes by having " all processes produce the necessary parts at the necessary time and have on hand only the minimum stock necessary to hold the processes together " In addition, by checking the degree of inventory quantity and production lead time as policy variables, this production method discloses existence of surplus equipment and workers. This is the starting point to the second characteristic of Toyota Production System, that is, to make full use of the workers' capability.

(*a*) *Withdrawal by subsequent processes*: The first requirement of just-in-time production is to enable all processes to quickly gain accurat knowledge of ' timing and quantity required '.

In the general production system, this requirement is met as follows. The production schedule of the product (automobiles in the case of automotive plant) is projected on the various parts schedules and instructions issued to the various processes. These processes produce the parts in accordance with their schedules, employing the method of " the preceding process supplying the parts to its following process ". However, it can be seen that this kind of method will make it vastly difficult to attain production adaptable to changes.

In order to materialize the first requirement, Toyota adopted a reverse method of " the following process withdrawing the parts from the preceding process " instead of the " the preceding process supplying the parts to the following process ".

The reason for this is as follows: Just-in-time production is production of parts by the various processes in the necessary amounts at necessary timing for assembling a vehicle as a final product of the company. If such is the case, it can be said that only the final assembly line that performs the vehicle assembly is the process that can accurately know the necessary timing and quantity of the parts.

Therefore, the final assembly line goes to the preceding process to obtain the necessary parts at the necessary time for vehicle assembly. The preceding process then produces on the parts withdrawn by the following process. For the production of these parts, the preceding process obtains the necessary parts from the process further preceding it. By connecting up all of the process in chain fashion in this way, it will be possible for the entire company to engage in just-in-time production without the necessity of issuing lengthy production orders to each process.

(*b*) *One piece production and conveyance*: The second requirement of just-in-time production is that all processes approach the condition where each process can produce only one piece, can convey it one at a time, and in addition, have only one piece in stock both between the equipment and the processes.

This means that no process for any reason is allowed to produce extra amount and have surplus stock between the processes. Therefore, each process must approach the condition where it produces and conveys only one piece corresponding to the single unit that is coming off the final assembly line. In short, all the shops are withheld from lot production and lot conveyance.

Toyota has succeeded in reducing the lot size through greatly shortening the setup time, improving production methods including the elimination of in-process inventory within the process resulting from ordering of multi-purpose machining equipment in accordance with the processing requirements for a product line, and improving conveyance resulting from repetitive mixed loading. All of these have been carried out, including large numbers of subcontractors.

(*c*) *Levelling of production*: Provided that all processes perform small lot production and conveyance, if the quantity to be withdrawn by the subsequent process varies considerably, the processes within the company as well as the subcontractors will maintain peak capacity or holding excessive inventory at all times.

Therefore, in order to make a just-in-time production possible, the prerequisite will be to level the production at the final assembly line (the most important line that gives out the production instructions to all processes). A degree of this levelling is determined by top managers.

(1) Final assembly lines of Toyota are mixed product lines. The production per day is averaged by taking the number of vehicles in the monthly production schedule classified by specifications, and dividing by the number of working days.

(2) In regard to the production sequence during each day, the cycle time of each different specification vehicle is calculated, and in order to have all specification vehicles appear at their own cycle time, different specification vehicles are ordered to follow each other.

If the final assembly line levels the production as related above, the production of all processes practising subsequent process withdrawal and one piece production and conveyance are also levelled.

The second significant point in levelled production is to observe the basic rule of just-in-time; to produce only as much as possibly sold, on the one hand adjusting its production level according to the change in market, on the other hand producing as smoothly as possible within a certain range. Even after the monthly production schedule has been decided, Toyota will still make changes among the different specification vehicles on the basis of daily orders, and even when it comes to the total number, if there is necessity to meet the changes in market conditions, Toyota will make revisions in the monthly schedule so as to reduce the shock of market fluctuation as much as possible.

When the production system related above is compared with the generally adopted scheduled production system, the former system can operate with smaller production changes than the latter system. Consequently, it will be possible to do with the less equipment capacity and more stable number of workers. (This is specially important to Japanese companies that have lifetime employment system.)

A production control system which has been developed to practise the above three general rules is Kanban System.

(d) *Elimination of waste from over-producing*: The underlying concept in just-in-time production systems is that thevalue of existence of inventory is disavowed.

In the conventional production control system, existence of inventory is appreciated as a means to absorb troubles and fluctuations in demand and to smooth fluctuations in load of processes.

In contrast to this, Toyota sees the stock on hand as being only a collection of troubles and bad causes. We consider that virtually most of the stock on hand is the result of ' over-producing ' more than the amount required, and is the worst waste that can raise the production cost.

The reason why we consider inventory resulting from over-producing is the worst waste is that it hides the causes of waste that should be remedied such as unbalance between the workers and between the processes, troubles in various processes, workers' idle time, surplus workers, excessive equipment capacity and insufficient preventive maintenance.

Such latency of waste makes it difficult for workers to display their capability and it even becomes obstructive of an ever-lasting evolution of a company.

Jidoka: The term ' Jidoka ' as used at Toyota means ' to make the equipment or operation stop whenever an abnormal or defective condition arises '. In short, its distinctive feature lies in the fact that when an equipment trouble or machining defect happens, the equipment or entire line stops, and any line with workers can be stopped by them.

The reasons for ' Jidoka ' being so important are as follows:

(1) To prevent making too much. If the equipment is made to stop when the required amount is produced, making too much cannot arise. Consequently, the just-in-time production can be accurately carried out.

(2) Control of abnormality becomes easy. It will only be necessary to make improvements by directing attention to the stopped equipment and the worker who did the stopping. This is an important requirement when making up the system of ' full utilization of workers' capabilities ' related next.

Toyota has made countless number of improvements to realize ' Jidoka '.

Full utilization of workers' capabilities

This is Toyota's second basic concept of making the best use of Japan's favoured labour environment and excellent workers. It has built up a system of respect for human, putting emphasis on the points as follows: (1) elimination of waste movements by workers; (2) consideration for workers' safety; and (3) self-display of workers' capabilities by entrusting them with greater responsibility and authority.

Elimination of waste movement by workers: Workers may realize their work worthy only if the labour of diligent workers is exclusively used to raise added value of products.

Then what are the waste movements that lower added value and which we must eliminate? The first of these is workers' movements accompanying the waste of making too much. The movements of material handling operations between the equipment and between the processes due to large inventory are all waste movements. It has become possible for Toyota to effect large reductions of this waste by making up a system that allows thorough just-in-time production.

However, even though the waste of making too much is reduced, it will be of no avail if the waste of worker's waiting time is created as a result. In the just-in-time production, even when there is surplus capacity in the equipment, only as much as the subsequent process has withdrawn is produced. Thus, if the equipment and workers are tied together, workers are subject to idleness. To prevent such waste of waiting time being created, various improvements have been made such as: (1) separating the workers from the equipment by assigning a worker to multiple equipments; (2) concentration of workers' zones at the automatic lines; and (3) making up lines that do not require supervisory operation.

The second waste is to have the workers perform operations that are by nature not suitable for men. Operations involving danger, operations injurious to health, operations requiring hard physical labour, and monotonous repetitive operations have been mechanized, automated and unmanned.

The third waste is workers' movements as a result of troubles of defects. Thorough ' Jidoka ' by Toyota has greatly reduced this kind of waste.

Considerations to workers' safety: Workers of Toyota are diligent and enthusiastic about attaining production. Thus, he may not stop operation if the trouble is not of a serious nature and will take non-standard methods just to keep the line running. If waiting time occurs, he will become impatient and eventually start doing something extra. However, such kinds of unusual operation or extra work are often accompanied by accidents, troubles, or defects.

The ' Jidoka ' and elimination of waiting time now being advanced by Toyota is not only for reducing the production cost, but also effective as a measure for safety.

The results have been reflected in the fact that from an international stand-point the frequency rate of injury at Toyota is low.

Note: Comparison with the frequency rate of injury in American automotive industry shows that against the 1·5 shown in the United States (ILO 1974 statistics), Toyota had 0·8 or about one-half lower.

Self-display of workers' ability: Nowadays, it has become an international interest to respect humanity of workers in production shops.   Toyota firmly believes that making up a system where the capable Japanese workers can actively participate in running and improving their workshops and be able to fully display their capabilities would be foundation of human respect environment of the highest order.

As the first step in this method, all workers at Toyota have a right to stop the line on which they are working.

Even in a long line like the final assembly line, if any abnormality comes up such as the worker finding himself unable to keep up or discovering an incorrect or defective part, he can stop the entire line by pressing the stop button near at hand.   It is not a conveyer that operates men, while it is men that operate a conveyer, which is the first step to respect for human independence.

As the second step, at all shops in Toyota, the workers are informed of the priority order of the parts to be processed and the state of production advancement.   Therefore, the actual authority for decisions of job dispatching and overtime is delegated to the foreman, and this allows each shop to conduct production activities without orders from the control department.

As the third step, Toyota has a system whereby workers can take part in making improvements.   Any employee at Toyota has a right to make an improvement on the waste he has found.

In the just-in-time production, all processes and all shops are kept in the state where they have no surplus so that if trouble is left unattended, the line will immediately stop running and will affect the entire plant.   The necessity for improvement can be easily understood by anyone.

Therefore, Toyota is endeavouring to make up a working place where not only the managers and foremen but also all workers can detect trouble. This is called ' visible control '.

Through visible control, all workers are taking positive steps to improve a lot of waste they have found.   And the authority and responsibility for running and improving the workshop have been delegated to the workers themselves, which is the most distinctive feature of Toyota's respect for human system.

Kanban system

Aim of Kanban System

A production control system for just-in-time production and making full use of workers' capabilities is the Kanban System.   Utilizing Kanban

System, workshops of Toyota have no longer relied upon an electronic computer. It is shown in Fig. 1.

The reasons to have employed Kanban System instead of computerized system are as follows:

(1) Reduction of cost processing information. It calls for huge cost to implement a system that provides production schedule to all the processes and suppliers as well as its alterations and adjustments by real time control.

(2) Rapid and precise aquisition of facts. Using Kanban itself, managers

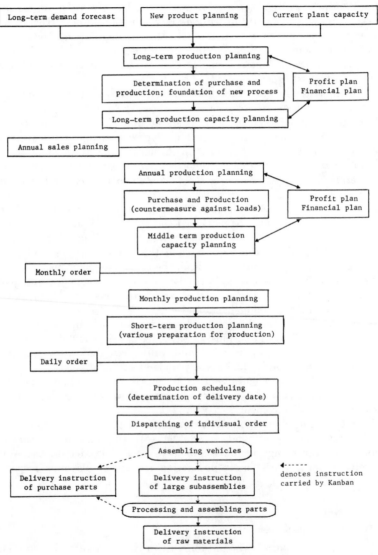

Figure 1. Structure of production planning.

of workshops may perceive such continuously changing facts as production capacity, operating rate, and man power without help of a computer. Hence, data of schedules corresponding to the change are accurate, which urge workshops to found responsibility systems and to promote activities for spontaneous improvements.

(3) Limiting surplus capacity of preceding shops. Since an automotive industry consists of multistage processes, generally the demand for the item (the part) becomes progressively more erratic the further the process point is removed from the point of the original demand for finished goods. Preceding processes become required to have surplus capacity, and it is more liable to have waste of over-producing.

3.2 *Description of Kanban system*

(1) In the Kanban System, a form of order card called Kanban is used. These come in two kinds, one of which is called ' conveyance Kanban ' that is carried when going from one process to the preceding process. The other is called ' production Kanban ' and is used to order production of the portion withdrawn by the subsequent process.

These two kinds of Kanban are always attached to the containers holding parts.

(2) When content of a container begins to be used, conveyance Kanban is removed from the container. A worker takes this-conveyance Kanban and goes to the stock point of the preceding process to pick up this part. He then attaches this conveyance Kanban to the container holding this part.

(3) Then, the ' production Kanban ' attached to the container is removed and becomes a dispatching information for the process. They produce the part to replenish it withdrawn as early as possible.

(4) Thus, the production activities of the final assembly line are connected in a manner like a chain to the preceding processes or to the subcontractors and materialize the just-in-time production of the entire processes.

The flow of parts and Kanban are as shown in Fig. 2.

The equation for calculating the number of Kanban that play the most important part in this system is as follows:

Let,

y = Number of Kanban.

D = Demand per unit time.

T_w = Waiting time of Kanban.

T_p = Processing time.

a = Container capacity (not more than 10% of daily requirement).

α = Policy variable (not over 10%).

Then,

$$y = \frac{D(Tw + Tp)(1 + \alpha)}{a}.$$

Notable points of operations of Kanban System—meaning of the equation computing number of Kanban

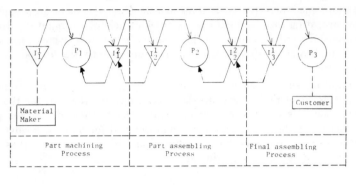

Pi: Operation of process i

I_i^1: Part inventory for process i

I_i^2: Finished good inventory for process i

———▶ : Flow of Kanban

——⇢ : Flow of parts

Figure 2.　Flow of parts and Kanban.

In order to materialize Toyota Production System through Kanban System, we do not accept each factor as a given condition, but we attach importance to modify each by means of positive improvements.

(1) α is a policy variable which is determined according to workshop's capability to manage external interference.

(2) D is determined with a smoothed demand.

(3) Value of y is rather fixed despite variation of D. Therefore, when D increases, it is required to reduce the value of $(Tp + Tw)$, that is, a lead time. At a workshop with insufficient capability of improvement, they cannot avoid overtime for a while. They might even cause line-stops. However, the ultimate objective of Toyota Production System is to visualize such wastes as overtime and line-stop, and to urge each workshop to become capable in improvement. Incapable shops might have to cope with the situation by means of increasing α, that is, number of Kanban for the time being. Hence, the top managers consider the value of α as an indicator of shop capability in improvement.

(4) In the case that demands decreases, the lead time becomes relatively larger. Consequently waste of increasing idleness becomes visible, which is an object of improvement called ' Syojinka '—to decrease the number of workers as demand (production) decreases.

(5) Work-in-process inventory could become much less by conducting an improvement to reduce the value of a, α, and $(Tp + Tw)$.

What Toyota considers as a goal through Kanban System related above is total conveyor line production system connecting all the external and internal processes with invisible conveyor lines. Because, a set of values of α, a, and Tw is 0, 1, and 0, respectively, which means nothing but attributes of a conveyor line. All the parts that constitute a vehicle are processed and

214

assembled on a conveyor line, raising its added value. Finally they come out as a completed vehicle one by one. On occurrence of troubles, the whole line may stop, but it begins to move again immediately. Toyota Production System is a scheme seeking realization of such an ideal conveyor line system, and Kanban is a conveyer connecting all the processes.

Expansion of just-in-time production by reduction of set-up times of pressing dies

In applying the concept of just-in-time production for reduction of lead times and work-in-process inventory, we faced difficulty in press shops practising lot production. After discussing a solution of this difficulty in lot production, we concluded that lead time was proportional to set-up times, using the following illustration.

Let,

T = Operation time a day or 480 minutes.

S = Total set-up time for all products, assuming that S is independent of sequence of products.

t_{mi} = Unit processing time for the ith product.

d_i = Demand for the ith product per day.

x = Lead time for all products (in number of days).

Q_i = Lot size for the ith product.

Then, $T \cdot x = S + \sum_i t_{mi} \cdot d_i \cdot x$.

Hence,

$$x = \frac{S}{T - \sum_i t_{mi} \cdot d_i}.$$

	Toyota	A (U.S.A.)	B (Sweden)	C (W. Germany)
Set-up time (hour)	0·2	6	4	4
Number of set-ups a day	3	1	–	0·5
Lot size	1 day-use †	10 days-use	1 month-use	—
Strokes per hour	500–550	300	–	—

† For less demanded products (below 1000 units per month), as large as 7 days-use.

Table 1. Press plant productivity characteristics (hood and fender).

	Takaoka plant of Toyota	A (U.S.A.)	B (Sweden)	C (W. Germany)
Number of employees	4300	3800	4700	9200
Number of outputs a day	2700	1000	1000	3400
Man-hours for completion of vehicle	1·6	3·8	4·7	2·7

Table 2. Man-hours for completion of a vehicle in automotive assembly plants of major counties.

	Toyota	A (Japan)	B (U.S.A.)	C (U.S.A.)
1960	41	13	7	8
1965	66	13	5	5
1970	63	13	6	6

Table 3.   Turnover ratio of working assets in automotive companies of major countries.

Year	Total number of proposals	Number of proposals per capita	Acceptance
1965	9000	1·0	39%
1970	40000	2·5	70
1973	247000	12·2	76
1976	380000	15·3	83

Table 4.   Transition of number of annual proposals per capita and acceptance rate.

Lead time is proportional to set-up times for a given set of t_{mi} and d_i for all $i = 1, 2, \ldots, n$. And lot size for each product Q_i is;

$$Q_i = d_i \cdot x \quad \text{for all } i = 1, 2 \ldots, n.$$

Improvements in production engineering have been made so as to reduce set-up times since 1971. We have succeeded in reducing set-up time down to 10 min at 800 ton-line pressing hood, fender and others, while it used to take 1 hour. (Under the present condition of western countries, 4 to 6 hours as shown in Table 1.)

The result = the present condition of Toyota

As related above, Toyota has built up a unique production system through its history of more than 20 years. The results are as follows:

(1) Labour productivity is the highest among automotive industries of major countries. (Table 2.)

(2) Turnover rate of working asset is also extremely high. (Table 3.)

(3) Number of proposals and rate of acceptance in a proposal system shows the condition that workers positively participate in improvement (Table 4.)

Le système de production Toyota et le système Kanban présentés dans cet article ont été mis au point par le Vice-Président de la Toyota Motor Company, M. Taiichi Ohno et c'est sous sa direction que ces systèmes de production uniques se sont implantés si profondément au sein de la Toyota Motor Company au cours des 20 dernières années. Ces systèmes comportent deux caractéristiques distinctives principales: l'une d'elles est la 'production au moment opportun', un facteur spécialement important dans une industrie d'assemblage telle que la fabrication de voitures. Dans ce type de production, " seuls les produits nécessaires, au moment nécessaire et en quantités nécessaires ", sont fabriqués. En plus, les stocks sont maintenus au minimum. La seconde est 'le respect de l'être humain'. Dans ce système, on permet aux ouvriers de révéler toutes leurs capabilités par une participation active à l'exploitation et à l'amélioration de leurs propres ateliers.

Das Toyota Produktionssystem und das Kanban System, welche in dieser Arbeit vorgestellt werden, wurden vom Vize-Präsidenten der Toyota Motor Company, Herrn Taiichi Ohno, entwickelt; und unter seiner Leitung wurden diese einmaligen Produktionssystem in den letzten 20 Jahren zu einem fest verankerten Bestandteil der Toyota Motor Company. Diese Systeme haben vor allem zwei hervorstechende Merkmale. Eines davon ist die ' gerade-zur-rechten-Zeit '-Produktion, ein besonders wichtiger Faktor in der Montageindustrie, wie z.B. der Kraftfahrzeugindustrie. Bei dieser Art der Produktion werden "nur die notwendigen Produkte, zur notwendigen Zeit, in der notwendigen Menge " hergestellt, und die Vorräte werden auf ein Minimum Beschränkt. Zweitens handelt es sich bei dem System um ein ' Respektierung des Menschen '-System, in denen den Arbeitern die Möglich keit gegeben wird, ihre Fähigkeiten voll zu entfalten, indem sie sich aktiv an der Organisation und der Verbesserung ihrer Werkstätten beteiligen.

References

JAPAN INDUSTRIAL MANAGEMENT ASSOCIATION, 1975, *Handbook of Industrial Engineering* (in Japanese), (Tokyo: Maruzen).
MURAMATSU, R., 1977, *Production Planning and Production Control* (in Japanese), (Tokyo: Kigyo-Shindan-Tsushin-Gakuin); 1976, *Production Control* (in Japanese), (Tokyo: Asakura-Shoten).
TOYOTA MOTOR CO., LTD., 1973, *Toyota Production System* (in Japanese), (unpublished).

Appendix 5

Design and Analysis of Pull System, A method of Multi-Stage Production Control

OSAMU KIMURA† and HIROSUKE TERADA†

We classify production control systems for a multistage production process into two species, namely Push, or Pull, Systems.

The former is a conventional method in which inventoried parts at each stage are forecast, considering the total flow time to the completion of the process at the final stage. Production and inventory control is based on the forecast value.

The latter is a proposed system in this paper in which a certain amount of inventory is held at each stage and whose replenishment is ordered by the succeeding process at the rate it has been consumed.

We formulate the Pull System and give a model simulation of fluctuation in production and inventory through the whole process in terms of system parameters like lot size, lead time, etc.

Introduction

Conventional production order system and its problems

In general, a multi-stage manufacturing process calls for prospective production on account of the longer flow time than the allowance for delivery lag. We may classify production control systems of such a series of processes into two species as follows.

(1) The Push Systems: The systems forecast the demand of inventoried parts or material in-process at each stage, considering the flow time up to the final

Reprinted with permission from the *International Journal of Production Research,* 1981, Vol. 19, no. 3, p. 241-253, ©1981 Taylor and Francis, Ltd.

stage. Based on this forecast value, they control the whole multistage by justifying inventory of final products and parts in each process. We call this Push type production order system, or Push System in brief.

(2) The Pull Systems: There is certain amount of inventory at each stage. A succeeding process orders and withdraws parts from the storage of the preceding process, only at the rate and at the time it has consumed the items. We call this Pull type production order system, or Pull System in brief.

Most of the conventional production control systems belong to the former species. The larger a system becomes, the more the following problems are inherent.

(a) When drastic changes in demand or snags in production happen, it is virtually impossible to renew the production plan for each process. Therefore it is likely that such difficulties cause excess inventory or even dead stock.

(b) It is practically impossible for production control staff to scrutinize all the situations related to production rate and inventory level. Hence, a production plan must have excess safety stock.

(c) Improvement with regard to lot size and timing of processing could not progress, because it is too cumbersome to compute optimal production plans in detail.

The 'Pull System' has been devised as a measure to solve such problems. We may achieve improvement, provided that it is possible in a simple and dependable manner to replenish the item, at the rate that the succeeding shop has consumed.

Aims of the Pull System

In multi-stage production processes including outside suppliers:

(1) To prevent transmission of amplified fluctuations of demand or production volume of a succeeeding process to the preceding process.

(2) To minimize the fluctuation of in-process inventory so as to simplify inventory control.

(3) To raise the level of the shop control through decentralization: to give shop supervisors or foremen a role of production control as well as inventory control.

Objectives of this research

The objective of this research is to prove that the Pull System actually satisfies the aims noted above. We especially consider the influence of fluctuation of demand or production volume in a succeedding process on production and inventory fluctuation in the preceding process in terms of the characteristics of the relevant system parameters such as the ordering unit and the lead time from ordering to delivery.

Outline of the Pull System

Methodology of the Pull System

As defined before, the Pull System is:

(1) To hold the inventory at a certain level at each stage.

(2) A succeeding process orders from the preceding process what has been consumed, in order to replenish the materials.

In order to practise this system, the procedures are followed:

(a) To establish a standard re-order point and standard lot size.

(b) To know the inventory level and back order all the time.

(c) To give a continuous check upon the level and replenishment orders for the items below re-order point.

The system must satisfy all the requirements mentioned above. It is, however, quite difficult to design a system to meet all the above conditions in a complex multi-stage production process, because the cost and performance to achieve condition (2) conflict.

In Toyota Motor Co., Ltd., we have approached this problem by means of Kanban, a sort of tag.

Kanban

The Kanban carries the information given below.

(1) Part name, part number

(2) Quantity designated usually equals a container capacity. The re-order point and ordering quantity are equal to the container size multiplied by an integer.

(3) Preceding process: manufacturing shop, assembly line or storage location.

(4) Succeeding process; (as above.)

Other information such as the type of packing and the number of identical Kanban issued are also specified as a reference. A typical format of a Kanban is shown in Fig. 1.

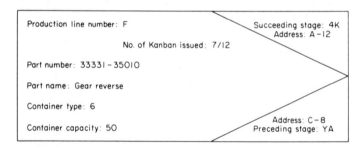

Figure 1. Kanban layout.

Procedure of handling

(1) In-process Kanban

The parts processed at a certain stage are put in a container. A Kanban is attached or hung on the container and then stored at the location designated by the Kanban (see Fig. 2 ①).

When a succeeding process withdraws this part or material, a worker lifts off the Kanban and puts it into a Kanban box (see Fig. 2 ②). Kanbans are collected from the box at regular intervals and hung on hooks on a schedule board. The

221

sequence of various Kanbans on the board shows workers the dispatching order of jobs in the process (Fig. 2 ③).

A worker produces various items, in accordance with the sequence of the various Kanbans on the board, as indicated by the Kanban, at the rate which is

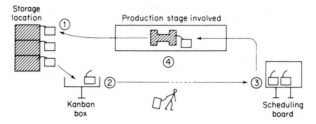

Figure 2.   Recurrent procedure of in-process Kanban.

set in advance. The Kanban itself moves in the process with the first unit of the batch (Fig 2 ④).

The procedure ① through ④ is repeated and the production is continued effectively.

We should keep in mind here that it is probable in procedure ②, that if the succeeding process never withdraws material from the preceding process, then the Kanban is neither collected from the Kanban box nor is it hung on a hook of the schedule board. Consequently, the item is never processed at this shop.

(2) Inter-process Kanban

As procedure to handle an inter-process Kanban is operated just the same as that of an in-process Kanban, considering transportation as an operation similar to manufacturing (Fig. 3).

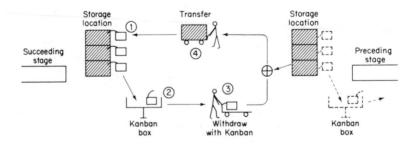

Figure 3.   Recurrent procedure of inter-process Kanban.

We should keep in mind that it is also the rule that withdrawals are equal to what the Kanban indicates and nothing will be withdrawn unless a Kanban is in the box.

In Fig. 3 broken lines imply an in-process Kanban and its movement in the preceding shop. When material or parts are withdrawn from storage, an in-process Kanban on the container is exchanged with an inter-process Kanban. The in-process Kanban removed will be transferred to an in-process Kanban box.

As we have illustrated above, the rate (quantity) of production of the succeeding process is transmitted to the preceding process through in-process Kanbans and inter-process Kanbans. The total of the Kanbans in such a multistage production process maintain complete production through all of the stages.

Production plan for adjusting facilities, work-force and raw material.
We give a detailed production plan to the final stage only since we employ the Pull System. The detailed production plan is a daily schedule, and not a long range production plan to adjust facilities, work-force and raw material which require longer lead times for provision. We release such a plan to each stage far in advance, considering the necessary lead times.

System formulation
We formulate the Pull System to clarify the system characteristics, and illustrate it as follows. We consider here the system simply as a multistage series process with a single item.

Notation
t period
O_t^n production (transportation) order quantity for the nth stage in the tth period.
P_t^n production quantity for the nth stage in the tth period.
I_t^n finished goods inventory at the nth stage in the end of tth period.
M^n order unit (number of units indicated by a Kanban).
Z_t^n remainder of division of I by M^n.
C^n production capacity of the nth stage.
L_1^n a flow time between the moment when a Kanban is removed from a container and the moment when production (or transportation) begins.
L_2^n a flow time between the moment when production begins and the moment when the operation is completed.
D_t demand of final product in the tth period.
$\hat{D}_{t,t+L}$ demand forecast at the end of tth period for the $(t+L)$th period.

Flow chart of information and materials
Information and materials' flow of the Pull System are illustrated in Fig. 4.

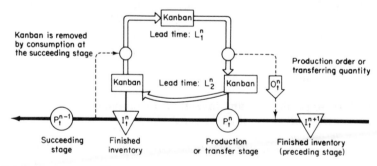

Figure 4.   Flow chart of pull system.

Note ←: Flow of materials
⇒: Flow of Kanban
⇢: Flow of ordering information via Kanban

Basic equation of the system

In the Pull System, a Kanban is removed from a container when the first piece of the content has been used. Therefore, in every inventory station, one container holds a content which is partially used, from which the Kanban has been already removed. The other containers are filled with the full content, with Kanban attached. Let Z_t^n be the number of the content partially used, written as

$$Z_t^n = \text{Mod}\,(I_t^n,\ M^n)$$

where the symbol $\text{Mod}\,(A,\ B)$ signifies remainder of A/B. The number of Kanban removed from containers at the nth inventory is determined by the production quantity P_t^{n-1} of the succeeding stage. But the portion of P_t^{n-1}, which corresponds to Z_{t-1}^n at most, could be covered by the material of the container from which the Kanban is already removed.

Therefore

$$\left.\begin{array}{ll} X = P_t^{n-1} - Z_{t-1}^n & (P_t^{n-1} \geqslant Z_{t-1}^n) \\ \quad\text{or} & \\ X = 0 & (P_t^{n-1} < Z_{t-1}^n) \end{array}\right\} \tag{1}$$

are the amount of material which is indicated by the number of Kanban removed in this period. Then the number of the Kanban removed in the tth period is

$$\left[\frac{X}{M^n}\right]_+ = \left[\frac{\max\,(0,\ P_t^{n-1} - Z_{t-1}^n)}{M^n}\right]_+$$

The symbol $[A]_+$ signifies the Gaussian symbol raising A to a unit. After the period L_1^n, those Kanban which have been removed are added to the orders to the nth production stage. So the production order O_t^n is

$$O_t^n = \left[\frac{\max\,(0,\ P_{t-L_1^n}^{n-1} - Z_{t-L_1^n - 1}^n)}{M^n}\right]_+ M^n + O_{t-1}^n - P_{t-1}^n \tag{2}$$

where $O_{t-1}^n - P_{t-1}^n$ is the backorder at the end of the preceding period. Production quantity is

$$P_t^n = \min\,(O_t^n,\ C^n,\ I_{t-1}^{n+1} + P_{t-L_2^n}^{n+1}) \tag{3}$$

where $I_{t-1}^{n+1} + P_{t-L_2^n}^{n+1}$ signifies the restrictions of inventory worked at the preceding stage.

The nth inventory level is given by

$$I_t^n = I_t^{n-1} + P_{t-L_2^n}^n - P_t^{n-1} \tag{4}$$

Equation (2)–(4) above are the basic equation of the Pull System.

The analysis of production and inventory fluctuations

With a relatively small unit ordering quantity

Production fluctuations

When unit ordering quantity M^n is relatively small compared with production quantity P_t^n, we may let

$$\left[\frac{\max\,(0,\ P_{t-L_1^n}^{n-1} - Z_{t-L_1^n - 1}^n)}{M^n}\right]_+ M^n \fallingdotseq P_{t-L_1^n}^{n-1}$$

then from (2)

$$O_t^n \fallingdotseq P_{t-L_1^n}^{n-1} + O_{t-1}^n - P_{t-1}^n \tag{5}$$

When there are no restrictions for production capacity C^n and the inventory of the preceding stage I_t^{n+1}, (3) would then be written as

$$P_t^n = O_t^n \tag{6}$$

from (5) and (6)

$$P_t^n = P_{t-L_1^n}^{n-1} \tag{7}$$

$$= P_{t-(L_1^n+L_1^{n-1})}^{n-2}$$

$$\vdots$$

$$P_{t-(L_1^n+L_2^{n-1}+\ldots+L_1^2)}^1 \tag{8}$$

As the result in the Pull System, when the unit ordering quantity is relatively small compared with the production quantity the production fluctuation in the succeeding stages is transmitted to the preceding stages in a form which is identical with that of the original pattern. The timelag between them equals the summation of flow time between the moment when a Kanban gets removed from a container and the moment when production begins.

Especially, when the production series of the final stage $\{P^1\}$ are mutually independent, the variance of $\{P_1^n\}$ is

$$V(P^n) = V(P^{n-1}) = \cdots = V(P^1) \tag{9}$$

Under the definition of amplification ratio;

$$\text{Amp}(P^n) = \frac{V(P^n)}{V(P^1)}$$

from (9)

$$\text{Amp}(P^n) = \text{Amp}(P^{n+1}) = \cdots = 1 \tag{10}$$

Inventory fluctuation
From (7)

$$P_{t-L_2^n}^n = P_{t-(L_1^n+L_2^n)}^{n-1}$$

Hence from (4)

$$I_t^n = I_{t-1}^n + P_{t-(L_1^n+L_2^n)}^{n-1} - P_t^{n-1}$$

By solving this equation, we obtain

$$I_t^n = A - \sum_{R=t-(L_1^n+L_2^n)+1}^{t} P_R^{n-1} \tag{11}$$

where

$$A = I_0^n + \sum^{R \leqslant 0} P_R^{n-1}$$

is the initial condition.

When $\{P_t^1\}$ are mutually independent, we get from (1)

$$V(I^n) = (L_1^n + L_2^n)V(P^{n-1}) \tag{12}$$

Substituting (9) into (12), we obtain

$$V(I^n) = (L_1^n + L_2^n)V(P^1) \tag{13}$$

Let

$$\mathrm{Amp}(I^n) = \frac{V(I^n)}{V(P^1)}$$

then from (13)

$$\mathrm{Amp}(I^n) = \frac{V(I^n)}{V(P^1)}$$

$$\mathrm{Amp}(I^n) = L_1^n + L_2^n \tag{14}$$

$L_1^n + L_2^n$ means that the flow time between the moment when a Kanban is removed from a container and the moment when production of the stage is completed.

Hence, in the Pull System, when the fluctuation of $\{P^1\}$ is mutually independent, the inventory fluctuation at each stage is amplified in comparison with the fluctuation of final stage $\{P^1\}$. The degree of amplification becomes larger in proportion to the flow time between the moment when a Kanban is removed from a container and the moment when production of the stage is completed. However, the amplification does not increase by going farther up the stream of production.

So far, we have assumed that there are no restrictions in the production capacity and inventory level. If there are these restrictions, the upper values of series $\{P_t^n\}$ are constrained under the level of C^n or $I_t^{n+1} + P_{t-L_2^n+1}^{n+1}$ (see eqn. 3), so the fluctuations become smaller in this case than in the case of no restrictions. But with the smaller fluctuations, there will be an increase of back orders and production delay. In any case, these are different management problems from the objectives of our research.

With a relatively large unit ordering quantity

In the case where the unit ordering quantity M^n in nth stage is relatively large as compared with production quantity P_{t-1}^n, eqn. (2) giving the production quantity O_t^n cannot be regarded as an approximation to eqn. (5). Therefore it is difficult to, analyse theoretically. Thus, here we try an analysis by the simulation method as follows.

Notation

O_t^n order quantity of transportation from the nth stage to the $(n-1)$th stage in the tth period.

R_t^n quantity of transportation from the nth stage to the $(n-1)$th stage in the tth period.

B_t^n inventory quantity carried from the $(n+1)$th stage, awaiting processing in the nth stage at the end of the tth period.

$L_{P_1}^n$ the same meaning of L_1^n previously defined.

226

$L_{P_2}^n$ the same meaning of L_2^n previously defined.

$L_{H_1}^n$ a flow time between the moment when a Kanban is removed from a container and the moment when transportation begins.

$L_{H_2}^n$ a flow time between the moment when transportation begins and the moment when the operation is completed.

S^0 safety stock of the final product.

The other symbols except above defined refer to the previous definitions.

Simulation model

(1) General figure of model; illustrated as Fig. 5.
This is the single item multi-stage process which consists of n producing stages and n transporting stages from each stage to the succeeding stage.

(2) Demand of final product D_t; normal distribution of average $\bar{D}$, variance σ_D^2, both of which are already known.

(3) Timing of production and transportation; production and transportation start at the beginning of each period.

(4) System equation
Inventory quantity of the final stage

$$B_t^0 = B_{t-1}^0 + R_{t-L_{H_2}^1}^1 - D_t \tag{15}$$

Shipment of product

$$R_t^1 = I_{t-1}^1 \tag{16}$$

Inventory quantity before shipment

$$I_t^1 = P_{t-L_{P_2}^1}^1 \tag{17}$$

Production ordering quantity in the first stage.
(We adopt the Push System only for the final stage.)

$$O_t^1 = \hat{D}_{t-1.t+L} + \hat{D}_{t-1.t+L-1} - P_{t-1}^1 - B_{t-1}^0 + S^0 \tag{18}$$

where $L = L_{P_2}^1 + L_{H_2}^1$
The equations of production, transportation and inventory from the second stage are found by the method mentioned above.

Value of input data and parameter

(1) t $1, 2, 3, \cdots, 100$
(2) D_t $\bar{D} = 100 \quad \dfrac{\sigma_D}{\bar{D}} = 0 \cdot 1$

(3) $\hat{D}$ $\bar{D}$
(4) n 5
(5) I_0^n, C^n very large numbers
(6) $L_{P_1}^n = L_{P_2}^n = L_{H_1}^n = L_{H_2}^n = 0 \quad (n = 1, 2, \cdots 5)$

Experimental results

Under the conditions mentioned above, the experiment with order unit M^n changing, resulted as Figs. 6 and 7.

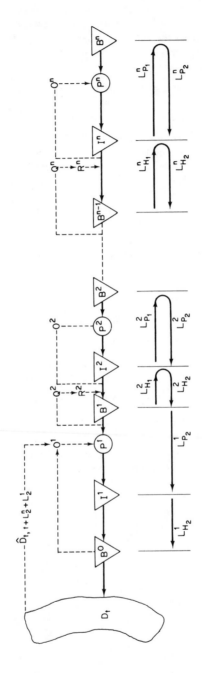

Figure 5. Conceptual chart of simulation model.

228

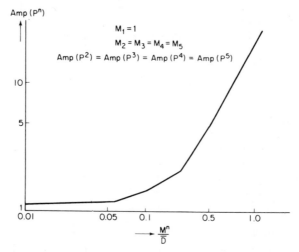

Figure 6.   Influence of ordering unit M^n on production fluctuation.

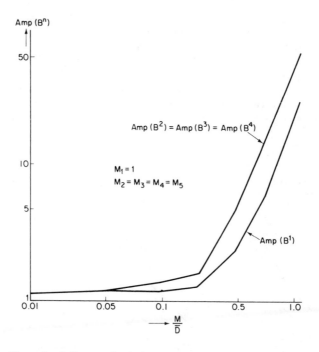

Figure 7.   Influence of ordering unit M^n on inventory fluctuation.

In the case of the Pull System, production and inventory fluctuations become larger as unit order quantity becomes larger compared with producing quantity level although the fluctuation is not magnified going to farther preceding stages.

Comparison with the Push System

In order to compare between Push and Pull Systems about the influence on production fluctuation of succeeding stages on those of the preceding stages, the experimental result of the Push System (which has been found by Mr. Y. Tanaka and T. Tabe in Waseda University) and the result of the Pull System in this research are illustrated as Figs. 8 and 9.

The value of input data and parameters are the same except $L_{P_1}^n = 0$, $L_{P_2}^n = 1$. $L_{H_1}^n = 1$, $L_{H_2}^n = 0$ and the unit order quantity M in the case of the Push System is always '1'. The detail of the Push System Model is shown in Muramatsu *et al*.

As these figures show, in the case of the Push System, the fluctuation is more amplified in the farther preceding stage. This is a consequence of errors in forecasting. Therefore, it is necessary to keep the control parameter at the proper level in the case of the Push System. On the other hand, in the case of Pull System, the amplification ratio becomes larger as the order unit becomes large. Thus, it will be necessary to attempt to minimize the ordering unit.

Conclusions

(1) In the case of the Pull System, the size of the order unit has much importance. In cases where the size is small compared with the production quantity level, production fluctuation will not be amplified in the preceding stage. Amplification will be brought about when the size is rather large although, in this case also, the amplification is not further magnified in farther preceding stages.

(2) In the case of the Push System, amplifications of production and inventory fluctuations occur under the influence of errors in forecasting. As far as amplification is concerned, the choice between the Push and Pull Systems is determined by the degree of errors in forecasts.

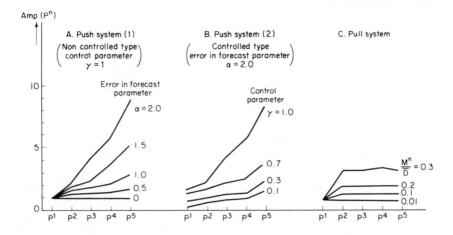

Figure 8.   Amplification rate of production fluctuation.

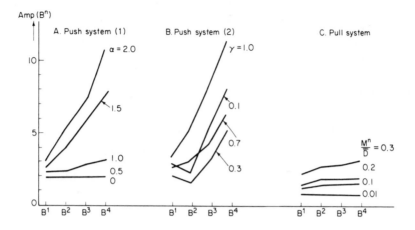

Figure 9. Amplification rate of inventory fluctuation.

(3) The other factor in the system parameters of the Pull System, which affect the amplification ratio is the 'Lead-Time' from the moment when a Kanban is removed from a container to the moment when production of the stage is completed. The longer is the lead-time, the larger becomes the amplification ratio.

Acknowledgment

We would like to express our sincere gratitude to Dr. Rintaro Muramatsu in Waseda University for his considerable instruction and advice.

Nous classons les systèmes de contrôle de production pour des procédés de fabrication en plusieurs étapes en deux groupes, à savoir le système Push et le système Pull.

Le système est une méthode conventionnelle dans laquelle des prévisions des pièces inventoriées sont faites à chaque stade en considérant le temps d'écoulement total jusqu'à l'achèvement du processus au stade final. Le contrôle de la production et de l'inventaire est effectué sur la base des valeurs prévues.

Dans le système Push proposé dans cet article, une certaine quantité de pièces en inventaire est maintenue à chaque stade et son réapprovisionnement est commandé par le processus suivant, à la cadence à laquelle elles auront été consomées.

Nous formulons le système Pull et donnons les résultats d'une simulation sur modèle de fluctuations de la production et de l'inventaire pour tout le processus en termes de paramètres systémiques tels que taille des lots, délais d'approvisionnement, etc . . .

Produktionskontrollsysteme für Mehrstufen-Produktion zerfallen in zwei Kategorien, 'Drucksysteme' und 'Zugsysteme'.

Im ersteren Fall handelt es sich um das herkömmliche Verfahren, wonach der Teilebestand in jedem Stadium vorausgesagt wird, unter Berücksichtigung der Gesamtablaufszeit bis zum Abschluß des Verfahrens im letzten Stadium.

Das zweite System wird in diesem Artikel vorgeschlagen. In diesem System wird in jedem Einzelstadium ein gewisser Lagerbestand gehalten, der vom derauffolgenden Produktionsvorgang aus in dem Ausmaß ergänzt wird, in welchem er verbraucht wird.

Wir haben das 'Zugsystem' formuliert und Simulationsmodelle der Produktions- und Bestandschwankungen über den gesamten Fertigungsprozeß im Sinne von Systemparametern wie z.B. Losgröße, Vorbereitungs- und Anlaufzeit usw. aufgestellt.

References

KUSUNOKI, K., and SUGIMORI, Y., Fourth International Conference on Production Research, Five Paper Sessions.

MAGEE, J. F., Production planning and inventory control.

MURAMATSU, R., TANAKA, Y., and TABE, T., Analysis of production order and inventory fluctuations. Fifth International Conference on Production Research, Free Paper Sessions.

Bibliography and References

English written literature

AIAG and APICS. *Proceedings of the Production and Inventory Control Conference, Fall 1981.* Sponsored by Detroit chapter of APICS and Automotive Industry Action Group.

Aisin Seiki Co., Ltd. "Outline of Shiroyama Plant." Pamphlet, September 1981.

——————. "Outline of Shinkawa Plant." Pamphlet, September 1981.

American Machinist. "Kanbans are Discovered." February 1981, p.222.

American Machinist. "Japan's Twenty-Firm Joint FMS Plan." February 1981, pp.98-100.

American Production and Inventory Control Society. Pittsburgh Chapter, Proceedings from "Productivity: The Japanese Formula." October 1980.

Ashburn, A. "Toyota's 'Famous Ohno System'." *American Machinist,* July 1977, pp.120-123.

Bodek, N., and Scanlan, J. *Quality Control Circles: A Practical Guide.* Productivity, Inc. 1981.

Bodek, N., ed. "Kanban — The Coming Revolution?" *Productivity* 1(7): December 1980, pp.1-2.

Bodek, N., ed. *Productivity: Three Practical Approaches.* Proceedings of the Productivity Seminar held by Productivity, Inc. February 23, 1981, Chicago.

Bunke, H.C. "A Japanese Pilgrimage." *Business Horizons* 24(3): 1981, pp.2-9.

Butt, D. "Just-in-Time in Lincoln, Nebraska: Why and How." In Bodek [1981].

Byron, C. "How Japan Does It." *Time,* March 30, 1981, pp.54-60.

Cho, F. and Makise, K. "Toyota's Kanban, The Ultimate in Efficiency and Effectiveness." American Production and Inventory Control Society, 1980.

Cole, R.E. *Work, Mobility, and Participation: A Comparative Study of American and Japanese Industry.* University of California Press, 1979.

Cook, J. "A Tiger by the Tail." *Forbes,* April 13, 1981, pp.119-128.

Drucker, P.F. "What We Can Learn From Japanese Management." *Harvard Business Review,* March-April 1971.

_____. "Behind Japan's Success." *Harvard Business Review,* January-February 1981.

Ellis, H.B. "U.S. Production, Japanese Style: Kawasaki Motorcycle Plant in Nebraska." *The Christian Science Monitor,* March 6, 1981, p.1.

Feigenbaum, A.V. *Total Quality Control.* New York: McGraw-Hill, 1961.

Fortune. "How the Japanese Manage in the U.S." June 15, 1981, pp.97-103.

Fujimoto, K. "Serving the Big Manufacturers: How to Cope with Short Lead Time and Changing Delivery Schedules." American Production and Inventory Control Society, 1980.

Hall, R.W. and Vollman, T.W. "Planning Your Material Requirement." *Harvard Business Review,* September-October 1978.

Hall, R.W. *Driving the Productivity Machine: Production Planning and Control in Japan.* American Production and Inventory Control Society, 1981.

_____. "The Toyota Kanban System." Article presented at The Japan-United States Business Conference, October 4-7, 1981.

Harsch, J. "U.S. Executives Eager To Import Ringi, Ukezara." *The Christian Science Monitor,* March 6, 1981, p. 1.

Japan Management Association. *Proceedings of the International Conference on Productivity and Quality Improvement — Study of Actual Cases.* Tokyo: October 1980.

Kimura, O. and Terada, H. "Design and Analysis of Pull System — A Method of Multi-Stage Production Control." *International Journal of Production Research* 19(3): 1981, pp.241-253.

Kobayashi, S. "The Creative Organization: A Japanese Experiment." In *Organizational Behavior: A Book of Readings,* 4th ed., edited by K. Davis. New York: McGraw-Hill, 1974.

Konz, S. "Quality Circles: Japanese Success Story." *Industrial Engineering,* October 1979, pp.24-27.

Kraft, J. "Japan's Sick of Being Punished for Excellence." *Chicago Sun-Times,* May 6, 1981.

Lawrence, P.R. and Lorsch, J.W. *Organization and Environment: Managing Differentiation and Integration.* Harvard University Press, 1967.

Mammone, J.L. "A Practical Approach to Productivity Measurement." *NAA Management Accounting,* July 1980, pp.40-44.

Monden, Y. "What Makes the Toyota Production System Really Tick?" *Industrial Engineering,* January 1981, pp.36-46.

——————. "Adaptable Kanban System Helps Toyota Maintain Just-in-Time Production." *Industrial Engineering,* May 1981, pp.28-46.

——————. "Smoothed Production Lets Toyota Adapt to Demand Changes and Reduce Inventory." *Industrial Engineering,* August 1981, pp.41-51.

——————. "How Toyota Shortened Supply Lot Production Time, Waiting Time and Conveyance Time." *Industrial Engineering,* September 1981, pp.22-30.

Mori, M. and Harmon, R.L. "Combining the Best of the West with the Best of the East — MRP and KANBAN Working in Harmony." American Production and Inventory Control Society, 1980.

Muramatsu, R. and Miyazaki, H. "A New Approach to Production Systems through Developing Human Factors in Japan." *International Journal of Production Research* 14(2): 1976, pp.311-326.

Muramatsu, R., Miyazaki, H., and Tanaka, Y. "An Approach to the Design of Production Systems Giving a High Quality of Working Life and Production Efficiency." *International Journal of Production Research* 18(2): 1980, pp.131-141.

——————. "Example of Increasing Productivity and Product Quality through Satisfying the Worker's Desires and Developing the Worker's Motivation." *AIIE 1981 Spring Annual Conference Proceedings,* Industrial Engineering and Management Press, pp.652-660.

Nakane, J. "The Waseda University Report—From SEIBAN to KANBAN/MRP." American Production and Inventory Control Society, 1980.

Nellemann, D. "Productivity—The Japanese Formula." In Bodek [1981].

Nicholson, T. "GM Takes on the Japanese." *Newsweek,* May 11, 1981.

Okamura, K. and Yamashita, H. "A Heuristic Algorithm for the Assembly Line Model-Mix Sequencing Problem to Minimize the Risk of Stopping the Conveyor." *International Journal of Production Research* 17(3): 1979, pp.233-247.

Patchin, R. "Quality Control Circles." In Bodek [1981].

Riggs, J.L. and Seo, K.K. "Wa: Personal Factor of Japanese Productivity." *Industrial Engineering,* April 1979, pp.32-35.

Runcie, J.F. "By Days I Make the Cars." *Harvard Business Review,* May-June 1980.

Shingo, S. *Study of 'Toyota' Production System from Industrial Engineering Viewpoint.* Japan Management Association, 1981.

Smith, L.F. "Japanese Productivity—The Three-Pronged Attack." American Production and Inventory Control Society, 1980.

Stewart, W. "Productivity Measurement." In Bodek [1981].

Sugimori, Y.; Kusunoki, K.; Cho, F.; and Uchikawa, S. "Toyota Production System and Kanban System, Materialization of Just-in-Time and Respect-for-Humanity System." *International Journal of Production Research* 15(6): 1977, pp.553-564.

Toyota Motor Co., Ltd. *Outline of Toyota,* 1981a.

——————. *Toyota Motor Co., Ltd. Annual Report 1981,* 1981b.

Toyota Motor Sales, U.S.A., Inc. "Toyota, The Quality Story." In *1981 Cressida By Toyota* pamphlet, 1980.

U.S. Department of Commerce, Bureau of International Commerce. *Japan: The Government-Business Relationship, A Guide for the American Businessman,* 1972.

Vogel, E.F. *Japan as Number One: Lessons for America.* Harvard University Press, 1979.

Waterbury, R. "How Does Just-in-Time Work in Lincoln, Nebraska?" *Assembly Engineering,* April 1981a, pp.52-56.

——————. "Kanban Cuts Waste, Saves $ with Minimum Effort." *Assembly Engineering,* April 1981b, pp.52-56.

Yamada, T., Kitajima, S. and Imaeda, K. "Development of a New Production Management System for the Co-elevation of Humanity and Productivity." *International Journal of Production Research* 18(4): 1980, pp.427-439.

Yamazaki, K. "Engineers as Managers." *Tradepia International,* Winter 1980, pp.20-21.

Yoshimura, M. "Efficient Operation with Few People is Key Factor in High Productivity." *The Japan Economic Journal,* February 10, 1981.

Yoshino, M.Y. *Japan's Managerial System.* MIT Press, 1968.

Japanese written literature

Akao, Y. "Functional Management and Departmental Management." *Hinshitsukanri* 31(5): 1980, pp.14-18.

Aoki, S. "Functional Management as Top Management—Concepts at Toyota Motor Co., Ltd. and Its Actual Execution." (1), (2), (3) *Hinshitsukanri* 32(2): 1981, pp.92-98; 32(3): 1981, pp.66-71; 32(4): 1981, pp.65-69.

————————. *Toyota, Its True Nature.* Seki Bun Sha, 1978.

Arita, S. "A Consideration of the Effect of Smoothed Production on the Reduction of Work-in-Process Inventory." *Kojokanri* 24(13): 1978, pp.109-115.

Bingham, H.E., Wayman, R.W. and Brock, M.R. "Quality Controls in Japan and Western Countries: A Comparison." *Hinshitsukanri* 32(10): 1981, pp.8-13.

Endo, K. "Toyota System—Image and True Nature." *Kojokanri* 24(13): 1978, pp.141-145.

Freund, R.A. "International Implications of Japanese Quality Control." *Hinshitsukanri* 32(10): 1981, pp.21-26.

Fujii, F. "Company-Wide IE and PM Activities of Yasugi Denki Co. Which Achieved the Cost-Reduction Goal of 15%." *IE,* May 1982, pp.31-42.

Fujimoto, K. "Toward Eliminating the Attaching and Adjusting Mistakes in Punchpress Operations and the Work-in-Process Inventory." *Kojokanri* 24(7): 1978, pp.25-31.

————————. "Increase of the Workshop Morale by a Unique Points-Evaluating System and Various Contests." *IE,* April 1980, pp.72-77.

————————. "Ideas of Variable Kanban System." (1), (2), (3), (4), (5) *IE,* January 1982, pp.18-26; February 1982, pp.26-32; March 1982, pp.40-47; April 1982, pp.66-68; May 1982, pp.44-48.

Fujita, A. "Merits and Faults of Toyota Production System." *Kojokanri* 24(13): 1978, pp.120-124.

Fukushima, S. "Toyota's Parts-Integration from Product-Planning Stage." *IE,* March 1978, pp.58-63.

Furukawa, Y. "System Theory of Quality Control." *Operations Research,* August 1981, pp.443-450.

Harazaki, I. "Multi-Functioned Worker Role in Many Varieties, Short-Run Production." *Kojokanri* 27(2): 1981, pp.86-87.

Hasegawa, M., Tanaka, T., and Sugie, K. "In-Process Quality Control for Each Job Position Realized Zero Delivery Claim at Akashi Kikai Co. Ltd." *Kojokanri* 27(1): 1981, pp.15-24.

Hashimoto, F. "Assignments to Realize the Unmanned Plant from Software Viewpoints." *Kojokanri* 27(4): 1981, pp.26-36.

Hatano, T. "Vendor's On-Line Delivery System Correspond to the Line-balanced Production." *IE,* January 1982, pp.30-34.

Hattori, M. "Production System Adaptable to Changes—An Example of Nippon-Denso's Mixed-Model High-Speed Automatic Assembly Line." *IE,* January 1981, pp.22-27.

Hitomi, K. "A Consideration of the Toyota Production System." *Kojokanri* 26(13): 1978, pp.116-119.

——————. "GT System for Many Varieties, Short-Run Production." *Kojokanri* 25(8): 1979, pp.111-119.

Iijima, A. "Implementation of Company-Wide Quality Control at Toyota Auto Body Co., Ltd." *Hinshitsukanri* 32(1): 1981, pp.20-26.

Ikari, Y. *Comparative Study, Japan's Automotive Industry—Production Technology of Nine Advanced Companies.* Nippon Noritsu Kyokai, 1981.

Ikeda, M. *Informal History of Toyota—Sakichi, Risaburo, Kiichiro, Ishida, and Kamiya.* Sancho Co., Ltd. 1980.

Ishibashi, Y. "Flexible Manufacturing for Adapting to Environmental Changes." *IE,* April 1980, pp.18-19.

Ishikawa, K. *Japan's Quality Control.* Nikka Giren, 1981.

Ishikawa, K. and Isogai, S. "Introduction and Promotion of TQC: Functional Management." *Hinshitsukanri* 32(11): 1981, pp.88-96.

Ishitsubo, T. "Reduction of the Die-Change Time for the Washer Outside-Frame." *Kojokanri* 24(7): 1978, pp.40-44.

Itami, H. *Beyond Japanese Management.* Toyokeizai Sinpo Sha, 1982.

Ito, T. "Complete Change in Thinking Lets Arai Seisakusho, Ltd. Promote Production Smoothing." *Kojokanri* 25(8): 1979, pp.157-163.

Iwai, M. "How the No. 1 Improvement Proposers Are Making Their Ideas." *President,* December 1981, pp.146-155.

Kanpo. Questions by Ms. Michiko Tanaka to the Ministers of State. *Proceedings of the House of Representatives,* No. 4, October 7, 1977, pp.62-66.

Kato, J. "Introduction of Robotics to the Manaufacturing Floor—Japanese Industrial Relations Will Not Break." *Nippon Keizai Shinbun,* May 3, 1982.

Kato, T. "Revolutional Management of Punchpress Process—From the Introduction of Kanban System to the Scheduling by Microcomputer." (1-14) *Press Gijutsu,* 19(1-2): 1981; 19(4-13): 1981; 20(1-3): 1982.

——————————. "New Production Management for the Punchpress Process." (3) *IE,* December 1981, pp.77-80.

Kawaguchi, H. "Visual Control at Toyoda Gosei's Cutting Operation Process." *Kojokanri* 26(13): 1980, pp.26-33.

Kawashima, Y. (Colloq.) "Overseas Strategy of Honda, A Pioneer Company Which Extended to America." *Kojokanri,* 26(7): 1980, pp.40-47.

Kikuchi, H. "Recent Problems Concerning the Subcontract Transactions." *Kosei-Torihiki,* November 1978, pp.11-18.

Kisaka, M. "DATS System for Production Control at Daihatsu Diesel Co., Ltd." *Kojokanri* 25(8): 1979, pp.164-173.

Knowles, R. "Quality Circles in England." *Hinshitsukanri* 32(10): 1981, pp.27-31.

Kobayashi, I. "Remarkable Reduction in Time and Workforce by Applying the Single-Setup at Machining and Pressing Operations." *Kojokanri* 24(7): 1978, pp.45-52.

——————————. "Flexible Manufacturing System Using VCS by Mitsu-bishi Heavy Industries, Ltd." *Kojokanri* 25(8): 1979, pp.130-148.

Kojima, A. "Productivity Arguments in the United States." (1), (2) *Nippon Keizai Shinbun,* June 10-11, 1980.

Kojokanri, "Standard Operations and Process Improvements at Toyoda Gosei Co., Ltd." 24(13): 1978a, pp.70-82.

——————————. "Improvements of Production Processes at Jeco Co., Ltd. to Synchronize the Logistics Flow." 24(13): 1978b, pp.53-69.

——————————. "Multi-Process Holdings at the Casting Processes of Aisin Seiki Co., Ltd." 24(13): 1978c, pp.83-88.

——————————. "A Case of the Auto-Parts Maker Who Realized Small Lot, Short-Cycle Delivery Via MRP." 26(12): 1980, pp.61-67.

——————————. "Production Revolution at Reviving Toyo Kogyo Co., Ltd." 27(6): 1981a, pp.17-37.

——————————. "Practices of the Small Lot, Mixed-Model Production System—Seven Cases." 27(7): 1981b, pp.17-64.

Konno, K. "Small Group Activities of Honda's Overseas Plants Are Developing under Trial and Error." *IE,* February 1982, pp.18-23.

Kotani, S. "On the Sequencing Problem of the Mixed Model Line." *Japan Operations Research Society Spring Conference Proceedings.* 1982, pp.149-150.

Koura, K. "Quality and Economy." *Operations Research,* August 1981, pp.437-442.

Kozu, S. and Fujibayashi, A. "MRP-Based Production Control System of Tomy Kogyo Co., Ltd." *Kojokanri* 25(8): 1979, pp.182-190.

Kubo, N. "Production Control at Yammer Diesel Co., Ltd. Synchronizes with the Master Schedule." *Kojokanri* 25(8): 1979, pp.149-156.

Kudo, H. "Industrial Robotics, Double-Edged Sword—Labor Management Policy Must Be Considered Now." *Nippon Keizai Shinbun,* March 1, 1982, p.8.

Kumagai, T. "Characteristics of Toyota Production System." *Kojokanri* 24(13): 1978, pp.152-157.

Kuroda, H. "Single Setup at the Plastic Processing Helps Achieve Line Balancing." *Kojokanri* 24(7): 1978, pp.32-39.

Kuroyanagi, M. "Visual Control of Aisan Kogyo's Machining Line." *Kojokanri* 26(13): 1980, pp.15-25.

Kusaba, et. al. "Report of the 11th Overseas Quality Control Observation Team." (2) *Hinshitsukanri* 32(10): 1981, pp.58-64.

Maeda, S. "FMS without Failure—A Case of Tokyo Shibaura Electric Co., Ltd." *Nippon Keizai Shinbun,* August 9, 1982.

Makido, T. "Recent Tendency of Cost Management Practices in Japan." *Kigyo Kaikei,* March 1979, pp.126-132.

Matsumae, H. "Toyota Production System and VE." *Kojokanri* 24(13): 1978, pp.149-152.

Matsuura, M. *Secret of Toyota's Sales Power.* Sangyo Noritsu Tanki Daigaku Publishing Division, 1979.

Matsuura, T., Ojima, T., and Ohmori, K. "Single-Setup at Punch Press and Resin-Molding Lines." *Kojokanri* 24(7): 1978, pp.53-58.

Minazu, K. "What We Learn from the Toyota Production System." *Kojokanri* 24(13): 1978, pp.89-101.

_____. "Eight Articles of Basic Know-How for Introducing the Toyota Production System." *Kojokanri* 25(8): 1979, pp.202-220.

Mizushima, T. and Keibu, J. "Plant-Wide Small Group Activities Can Reduce Twenty Percent of the Workforce." *Kojokanri* 26(7): 1980, pp.18-21.

Monden, Y. "Integrated System of Cost Management." *Sangyo Keiri,* December 1978, pp.21-26.

Mori, K. "The Negative and the Positive of Toyota Production System for My Standpoint." *Kojokanri* 24(13): 1978, pp.145-148.

Mori, M. and Yui, N. "Comparison of Production Systems of Japan–U.S. Auto Makers—Productivity Improvement Strategy and System of U.S. Automobile Industry." *Kojokanri* 28(8): 1982, pp.17-65.

Mori, M. "Theory and Practice of MRP." *Kojokanri* 25(8): 1979, pp.80-95.

Morita, T. "TQC and Toyota Production System Applied Together to the Production Control of Akashi Kikai Co., Ltd." *Kojokanri* 25(8): 1979, pp.174-181.

_____. "Technology Strategy of Nissan Motor Co., Ltd. to Win Out the Worldwide Small Car War." *Kojokanri* 26(1): 1980, pp.62-67.

_____. "Unmanned Machining Process and FCCS (Kanban System) Increased Productivity at Toshiba's Yanagimachi Plant." *Kojokanri* 26(11): 1980, pp.47-59.

Muramatsu, R. "Basic Concepts and Structure of Toyota Production System." *Kojokanri* 24(13): 1978, pp.162-165.

_____. *Foundation of Production Control, A New Edition.* Kunimoto Shobo, 1979.

Nakai, S. "Toyota's Unique Vitality and Practicing Ability Developed Its Own System." *Kojokanri* 24(13): 1978, pp.158-161.

Nakamori, K. "Cost Management at the Design Department." (1), (2) *IE,* November 1981, pp.65-70; December 1981, pp.58-64.

Nakane, M. "Mixed-Model Production System at the Body Assembling Line." *Kojokanri* 27(7): 1981, pp.59-64.

Nakata, I. "Complete Master of the Basic Concepts of Toyota System." *Kojokanri* 24(13): 1978, pp.128-130.

Niigaki, K. "The Ideas at the Workshop Floor Challenged to Make the Line of Single-Piece Production and Conveyance." *IE,* June 1980, pp.66-72.

Nikkan Kogyo Shinbun Sha, *Kojokanri* editorial division, ed. *Honda's Small Group Activities.* Nikkan Shobo, 1980.

Nikkan Kogyo Shinbun Sha. *Business Group for Support of Toyota.* 1980.

Nikko Research Center, ed. *Toyota in the 1980's—Its Growth Strategy Investigated by Analysts.* Nippon Keizai Shinbun Sha, 1979.

Nippon Electric Co., Ltd., Production Equipment Office. "Challenging Shop Toward Multi-Functioned Workers." *IE,* May 1981, pp.6-9.

Nippon Keizai Shinbun, "Office Rationalization by Applying Kanban." November 7, 1981.

_____. "Employee Stock Ownership Plan, Conducted by U.S. Labor Unions." February 5, 1982a.

_____. "Experimentation of Life-Time Employment System— Tentative Agreement Between Ford and UAW." February 15, 1982b.

_____. (Editorial) "Agreement of Labor Contract Revision between Ford and UAW." February 17, 1982c.

_____. "'Teach Me the Kanban System'—Request by U.S. Bendix Company to Jidosha Kiki Co., Ltd." March 2, 1982d.

_____. "Shock by the Alliance of Giant Automotive Companies." (1), (2) March 9 and 10, 1982e.

_____. "What a Surging Crowd to the Unmanned Factory!" March 27, 1982f.

_____. "U.S. Auto Industry—Detroit Wagers to Get Out of the Bottom Condition." April 10, 1982g.

_____. "Canada Wants to Learn from Japan—Polishing up the Strength of Resource Holding, April 12, 1982h.

_____. "Cooperative Movement in U.S. Industrial Relations is for Real?" June 7, 1982i.

_____. (News Colloq.) Mr. Toyoda, President of Toyota Motor Corporation, "Acceleration to the Effective Management of New Toyota." July 5, 1982j.

_____. "U.S. Reconsiders Japanese-Style Management." (1), (2) July 22 and 23, 1982k.

_____. "CAD/CAM System of Toyota—Body Development Process." August 5, 1982l.

_____. "Toward the Birth of the Future Typed FMS: Flexible Manufacturing Complex." August 4, 1982m.

Nippon Keizai Shinbun Sha, ed. *1982 Mechatronics Show: A Guide Book.*

Nippon Noritsu Kyokai, ed. *Toyota's Shop-Floor Management—How to Promote Kanban System,* 1978.

Noboru, Y. "Cost Accounting and Cost Management at Daihatsu Motor Co., Ltd." Pamphlet, 1982.

Noboru, Y. and Monden, Y. "Total Cost Management in Japanese Auto Industry." *Kigyo Kaikei,* February 1983, pp.104-112.

Ogawa, T., Tamechika, N. and Muramatsu, T. "Expectation and Demand to the Designing Department and Systematization of Designing Management." *IE,* January 1981, pp.26-30.

Ohno, T. "Companies Gap Will Be Determined by the Productivity Gap When the Quantity Decreases." *IE,* March 1978a, pp.4-9.

_____. *Toyota Production System—Beyond Management of Large Scale Production.* Diamond Publishing Co., Ltd., 1978b.

Okazaki, K. "Business Analysis of Automobile Makers in Australia— Management Problems in GM, Ford, Mitsubishi (Chrysler), Toyota, and Nissan." (1), (2) *Sangyo Keiri,* August 1981, pp.66-75; September 1981, pp.78-83.

Okumura, M. "Toyota's Energy Conservation Prevailing throughout the Shop Floor." *IE,* September 1979, pp.18-24.

Pino, A.P. "Perspectives of Company-Wide QC in Mexico." *Hinshitsukanri,* 32(10): 1981, pp.32-37.

Saito, S. *Secret of Toyota Kanban System.* Kou Shobo, 1978.

Sakakibara, K. "Organizational Structure and Technology." *Business Review* 27(1): pp.26-37.

Sandholm, L. "Can Japanese QC Circles Be of Any Use for Western Quality Problems?" *Hinshitsukanri* 32(10): 1981, pp.14-19.

Sasaoka, K. and Yoshiya, R. "What Production Control Ought to Be in the Manufacturing Industry." (1), (2) *Nippon Keizai Shinbun,* April 3 and 21, 1982.

Sawabe, M. "Automatic Inspection System and Flexible Manufacturing System." *Kojokanri* 25(8): 1979, pp.50-57.

Seki, M. "MRP System in IBM and CMIS, *Kojokanri* 25(8): 1979, pp.191-200.

Sekine, K. "Steps Toward Single-Setup: Procedures and Practices for Reducing the Setup Time in Half." *Kojokanri* 24(7): 1978, pp.59-64.

——————. "Toyota Kanban System, The Practical Manual." *Kojokanri* 24(13): 1978, pp.2-52.

——————. *Practical Toyota Kanban System—How to Make a Profit by Eliminating Waste.* Nikkan Shobo, 1981.

Shibata, Y. and Hasegawa, N. "Software Package for Support of Kanban, New Production Control System at Kyoho Seisaku Co., Ltd." *Kojokanri* 27(4): 1981, pp.17-25.

Shimada, H. "U.S. Industry is Enthusiastic about Its Restoration Efforts for Improving the Quality of Labor." *Nippon Keizai Shinbun,* October 26, 1981.

Shimokawa, K. *U.S. Automobile Civilization and Japan.* Bunshin Do, 1981.

Shingo, S., et al. "Single-Setup Will Change the Business Constitution." *Kojokanri* 24(7): 1978b, pp.20-24.

Shingo, S. "Revolution of Setup Time Development to the Single-Setup." *Kojokanri* 24(7): 1978b, pp.20-24.

——————. *Study of Toyota Production System from Industrial Engineering Viewpoint—Development to the Non-Stock Production,* Nikkan Kogyo Shinbun Sha, 1980.

Shioka, K. "Toyota Production System and Work Design." *Kojokanri* 24(13): 1978, pp.124-127.

Shishido, T. and Nikko Research Center, ed. *Japanese Companies in USA— Investigation in the Possibility of Japanese-Style Management.* Toyokeizai Shinpo Sha, 1980.

Shomura, O. "Contemporary Auto Workers and Their Job Discontent—An Examination of the International Comparative Study by William H. Form." *Rokkodai Ronshu* 28(2): 1981, pp.90-106.

Shukan Toyokeizai. "Toyota Kanban System Greets the New Stage" in *The Toyota in 1990*. (extra issue) July 1, 1982, pp.21-25.

Suzuki, Y. "Multi-Functioned Worker and Job-Rotation Can Make Flexible Workshop." *IE*, May 1980, pp.22-28.

Tagiri, I. "'The Vitalities' are Making Lively Activities around Mr. H.—A Case of Toyota's QC Circle." *Kojokanri* 27(13): 1981, pp.139-144.

Takahashi, M., Kondo, J., and Tsuihiji, T. "Fuji Heavy Industries, Ltd.—The Present Condition and Purpose of the Automation at Its Body Welding Plant." *Kojokanri* 27(4): 1981, pp.37-45.

Takahashi, M. and Kondo, J. "MicroComputer Aided Lamprey Type, Model Discriminating System for Supporting the Flexibility of Mixed-Model Production." *IE*, February 1981, pp.28-30.

Takahashi, T. "Automation of the Conveyance and Storage in the Flexible Manufacturing System." *Kojokanri* 25(8): 1979, pp.42-49.

Takano, I. *Complete Information of the Toyota Group*. Nippon Jitsugyo Publishing Co., 1978.

Takezawa, N. "Quality Assurance in the Manufacturing Engineering Department." *Hinshitsukanri* 31(8): 1980, pp.34-39.

Tanaka, H. "Employment Hold-down without Long-term Consideration Is Risky." *Nippon Keizai Shinbun*, November 6, 1977.

——————. *Employment Conventions in Japan and U.S.*, Nippon Seisansei Honbu (Japan Productivity Center), 1978.

Tanaka, M. "Cost Planning in the Process of Determining the Technology Conditions of the Product." *Genka Keisan*, December 1981, pp.3-32.

Tohno, H. "Toyota System Lets Today's Production Follow Yesterday's Sales." *Kojokanri* 24(13): 1978, pp.134-136.

Tokyo Shibaura Electric Co., Ltd., ed. *Promotion of the Management by Objective*. Aoba Shuppan, 1977.

Tonouch Kogyo PCS Group, "Computer-Aided Dispatching for the Mixed Body-Models at an Assembly Painting Maker." *Kojokanri* 26(12): 1980, pp.68-72.

Toyota Motor Co., Ltd., Suggestion Committee Office, ed. *Manual of Suggestion System*, 1964.

Toyota Motor Co., Ltd., QC Promoting Office. "Promotion of Quality Control at Toyota Motor Co., Ltd." *Hinshitsukanri*, 17(1): 1966, pp.14-17.

Toyota Motor Co., Ltd. *Toyota Production System for Cost Reduction.* (unpublished) 1st ed. 1973, 2nd ed. 1975.

――――――――. *Financial Statements 1980.* Printing Bureau of the Ministry of Finance, 1980.

――――――――. *Outline of Business* (Business Report), August 1981.

Toyota Motor Sales Co., Ltd. *Financial Statements 1980,* Printing Bureau of the Ministry of Finance, 1980.

Tsumura, T. "New Development of Industrial Engineering Closely Connected with Management." *Kojokanri* 24(13): 1978, pp.136-140.

Uno, K. "Japanese Technology Potentials Close in Upon the United States." *Nippon Keizai Shinbun,* December 5, 1981.

Volle, J. "Product Quality in France—Concerning the Influence by Japan." *Hinshitsukanri,* 32(10): 1981, pp.39-46.

Wada, R. "Machining Automation in the Flexible Manufacturing System." *Kojokanri* 25(8): 1979, pp.29-41.

Washida, A. "A Comment on the Toyota Manufacturing Methods." *Kojokanri* 24(13): 1978, pp.131-134.

Yamada, M. "The Course Toward a Business Elite by Developing the Career." *Diamond Harvard Business,* November-December 1979, pp.111-117.

――――――――. "Management System of Japanese Companies in U.S." *Diamond Harvard Business,* May-June 1980, pp.113-119.

Yamada, T. and Fujita, M. "Practice of the Process Improvements at Tokai Rika Co., Ltd." *Kojokanri* 25(8): 1979, pp.120-129.

Yamada, Y. "Points of Community and Difference between MRP and Toyota Production System." *Kojokanri* 25(8): 1979, pp.96-110.

Yoshida, O. "Challenge to the Zero Defective Units by Completely Controlling the Abnormalities." *Kojokanri* 26(8): 1980, pp.58-150.

Yoshida, S. "Overseas Operations and the Quality Assurance at the Shop Floor." *Kojokanri* 26(8): 1980, pp.24-30.

Yoshikawa, A. and Minato, A. "Total Optimization by Integrating the Design and Manufacturing Technologies." *IE,* April 1980, pp.20-22.

Yoshimura, M., Miyamoto, T. and Hori, E. "Optimal Sequencing Algorithm for the Assembly Line of the Medium Variety-Medium Quantity Models" in Japan Operations Research Society, ed. *Proceedings of Abstracts of 1982 Spring Research Conference,* pp. 147-148.

Yoshimura, T. "The Single-Setup and the Process Improvements for Line Balancing." *IE,* April 1980, pp.27-28.

Yoshiya, R. and Nakane, J. *MRP System—New Production Control in the Computer Age.* Nikkan Kogyo Shinbun Sha, 1977.

_____. "Toyota Production System viewed from the Standpoint of the MRP System Researchers." *Kojokanri* 24(13): 1978, pp.102-108.

Yoshiya, R. "Management Revolution by Means of MRP." *Diamond Harvard Business,* March-April 1979, pp.85-90.

Translation of the names of major Japanese journals appearing in this bibliography:

Kojokanri	= Factory Management
IE	= Industrial Engineering
Hinshitsukanri	= Quality Control
Nippon Keizai Shinbun	= Japan Economic Journal

About the author

Yasuhiro Monden is a professor of accounting at the University of Tsukuba, in Sakura, Ibaraki, Japan. He has authored numerous books and articles, and has translated German and English books into Japanese. During his stay in the U.S. as a visiting associate professor at the School of Management, State University of New York at Buffalo in 1980-81, Professor Monden lectured on the T /ota production system at ten professional conferences and seminars. His series of articles on the system in *Industrial Engineering* (1981) prompted his latest book, *Toyota Production System.*

He resides in Tsukuba, Japan with his wife and three children.